America's
Labor Leaders

America's Labor Leaders

Philip L. Quaglieri
University of Massachusetts/Boston

Lexington Books
D.C. Heath and Company/Lexington, Massachusetts/Toronto

HD
8073
A1
A47
1989

Photograph credits

Mr. Chavin— © Karsh, Ottawa
Mr. Chavez—Victor Aleman, LePaz, California
Mr. Gannon—Affiliated Graphics, a division of Fontana Lithograph, Inc., Brentwood, Maryland
Mr. Griffith—Clark's Photo Art, Greeley, Colorado
Ms. Miller— © Ed Snider, Still Photography, Video Productions, New York
Mr. Norton—Standard Studios, New York
Mr. O'Neal—Tucker
Mr. Porter—Mike Campbell
Mr. Rogers—Affiliated Graphics, a division of Fontana Lithograph, Inc., Brentwood, Maryland

Library of Congress Cataloging-in-Publication Data

America's labor leaders.

   Bibliography: p.
   Includes index.
   1. Trade-unions—United States—Officials and employees—Biography.
   2. Trade-unions—United States—History. I. Quaglieri, Philip L.
HD8073.A1A47   1989   331.88'092'2 [B]   87–46240
ISBN 0–669–17425–4 (alk. paper)
ISBN 0–669–17427–0 (pbk. : alk. paper)

Published simultaneously in Canada
Printed in the United States of America
Casebound International Standard Book Number: 0–669–17425–4
Paperbound International Standard Book Number: 0–669–17427–0
Library of Congress Catalog Card Number 87–46240

The paper used in this publication meets the minimum requirements of American National Standard for Information Sciences—Permanence of Paper for Printed Library Materials, ANSI Z39.48–1984. ∞™

88 89 90 91 92 8 7 6 5 4 3 2 1

Contents

Preface

THIS book began as an academic study, but along the way, it became a hobby. I am indebted to all the leaders who shared with me their time and patience, their histories and ambitions, and their observations and insights. If there are any misunderstandings, omissions, or errors within these pages, they are my responsibility.

I would also like to thank Mr. William Hamilton, a former editor with D.C. Heath & Company, who also believed in the need for "telling" the stories of America's labor leaders and encouraged the development of this book. To the staff of various labor unions who answered my questions and provided me with background material, my gratitude.

Finally, to Emily, Katharine, and Maureen—you have made my life so rich.

1. Introduction

Ask any American to tell you about their country's political leaders, and you'll probably get a long recitation of names and biographical details. The same is true for major league athletes and America's business leaders. Many Americans can, for example, name some of the "captains" of U.S. industry, people like Lee Iacocca, Ted Turner, Donald Trump, or T. Boone Pickens. And while they might not know the names of the chief executives of say, IBM, Exxon, GE, GM, or AT&T, Americans will quickly rattle off a list of superlatives—such as "intelligent," "ambitious," "hard working," "respectable," and "honest"—to describe those leaders' traits and behaviors.

What do Americans have to say about America's labor leaders? If you ask someone to name the chief executive of any of the 200-plus labor organizations in the United States, and who together represent nearly 16 million working people, the typical answer is none at all—silence and a long blank stare. And if you ask people to describe the characteristics of labor's leaders, the epithets of derogation flow in words like "crooked," "on the take," "sleazy," "foul mouthed," "rough edged," and "labor boss," "racketeer," "embezzler," "rip-off artist." Yet, if asked to substantiate their image of labor's leaders, most people are at a complete loss or offer the name of a single individual, Jimmy Hoffa.[1]

True, there are labor leaders who have abused the authority and responsibility of their positions, and some are "loud-mouthed, cigar-chomping tough guys," but the same can be said for as many of America's business leaders. The corruption stigma that haunts the ranks of labor's leaders, is not substantiated by the facts: unions are less of a bonding risk than businesses, financial institutions, the civil government.[2]

The image most Americans have of labor leadership can only be described as a stereotype, and like most stereotypes, this one does not fit the vast majority of persons to which it is attributed. The purpose of *America's Labor Leaders* is to provide first hand information, so that you can make an informed judgment about the validity of the stereotype surrounding labor leaders, and by extension, their organizations. What is offered here goes beyond what Americans are used to hearing about labor from the evening news. *America's Labor Leaders* is not just a thirty-second TV spot about a labor strike, the AFL-CIO's endorsement of a presidential candidate, or a union's demands from some organization. It is about the life and times of labor leaders and the inherently rich mix of people, events, and issues affecting the United States industrial relations system.

America's Labor Leaders is also about working class America. Since it is largely the working class who comprise labor unions, and it is they whom labor leaders ultimately serve, this book provides a unique perspective on the frustrations, needs, and ambitions of many of America's working people.

Who really are America's labor leaders? What are their backgrounds, and how did they get to where they are now? What does their work involve? What are their ideological beliefs, their achievements, and their failures as leaders? What strategies do they use in dealing with employers? What is the agenda of their unions? Finally, what are their views regarding the future of the labor movement in America?

The answers to these and other questions are provided in *America's Labor Leaders* by way of interviews with twenty-nine top labor leaders. As a group, these leaders represent employees in organizations as varied as machine shops, hospitals, newspapers, shipping concerns, theatres, and farms. Some of these organizations are relatively small, like the 9,000-member United Farm Workers. Others, including the 1-million-member United Food and Commercial International Union and the 600,000-member United Brotherhood of Carpenters and Joiners of America, are among the largest unions in the United States. The combined membership of the unions represented in *America's Labor Leaders* totals approximately eight million members, or about one-half of all of organized labor in America. As you can tell from these figures (see also appendix A), unions are very large organizations, really too large for us not to be better informed about them and their leaders.

The preparation of *America's Labor Leaders* began in the spring of 1986, when I sent "fill-in-the-blank" type surveys to senior officers of U.S. unions.[3] These surveys were designed to gather information about the backgrounds, careers, and responsibilities of the current leadership, something that had not been done in nearly a generation.[4] Since surveys about such matters rarely tell the "full" story, I decided to conduct follow-up interviews with the respondents in order to provide some breadth to the survey findings. What I heard in those interviews was so rich in biography, Americana, politics, money matters, the struggle between idealism and practicality—all the things a good novel might be made of—that I decided the interviews themselves would make for the most telling portrait of labor's leaders. I began interviewing other leaders. Some were individuals whose names were offered to me during those initial interviews as persons whom I "should speak to";

others were approached because they represented either the more influential unions, or a particular point of view or set of values.

For each interview I prepared a list of "who," "what," "why," type questions focusing on the interviewee, the union, and labor-related issues. In doing the interviews, which lasted about one and one-half to two hours each, I learned very early on to expect more than just ordinary responses to my questions. While I did get answers to most of my questions, I was always treated (as Studs Terkel was in his interviews with working people[5]) to something more valuable—a conversation.

America's Labor Leaders is an unusual type of labor-management relations text. While other texts about labor are designed to teach the principles of organizing, bargaining, and contract administration, the unique feature of this text is that it puts personality and immediacy into the study of labor relations. Chapters 3 through 31 provide an opportunity for you to hear directly from some of the leaders of organized labor. These chapters are edited only so as to preserve the natural flow of discourse, but without disrupting the integrity of the person's comments or speaking style. I have provided subject headings throughout the conversations to serve as bridges within the interviews and to identify specific topics and issues relevant to the field of labor-management relations. These headings include the following:

My Work/Getting Started focuses on the day-to-day activities of the leaders; their careers, leadership style, and ideological beliefs; the exercise of authority; their motivations for pursuing a labor career; and their experiences with notable figures and events in labor history.

The Members/Spirit of Unionism relates the leaders' perceptions regarding the issues of concern to their members and the members' level of involvement and commitment to the union.

Management/The Hostile Environment provides the leaders views as to how businesses and government have undermined the effectiveness of unions, and the strategies of unions in dealing with these challenges. A recurring theme here is the role of the Reagan administration in activating antilabor sentiment throughout the country and its effects on the present and future status of the labor movement. Some leaders believe that President Reagan's firing of the striking members of the Professional Air Traffic Controllers Organization (PATCO) in 1981 heralded a new era of "union bashing."

Organizing describes the strategies of the leaders in dealing with the increasingly difficult task of bringing new workers into the labor movement. In this section the leaders discuss (1) the reasons for the ambivalence of many unorganized workers; (2) the exportation of jobs, plant closings, and the effect of right-to-work laws[6] on organizing; (3) union avoidance tactics of management; and (4) the failure of labor unions to adapt the focus and techniques of their organizing drives to the issues that concern a diverse workforce.

Collective Bargaining relates the strategies and issues involved in establishing a working relationship (contract) with an employer. Included here are discussions of: two-tier wage systems[7]; givebacks and concessions; the de-skilling of America; health and safety; productivity improvement plans/ quality of work life (QWL) programs[8]; strikes; and the technological changes that are displacing the jobs of union members. You will be treated in this section (and others) to some fascinating insights as to how jobs, the work force, and industries have changed over the course of a leader's union career, and how some, but not all, of their unions have successfully adapted to these generational dynamics.

Other issues identified in headings include such matters as the public's image of organized labor, women in union leadership positions, the problems facing specific unions, and the future of unionism in America.

In the end, the goal throughout the development of *America's Labor Leaders* is to present, as much as possible through words on a page, the reality of a leader's personal qualities, institutional role, and concerns.[9] The following section, discussing biographical and work-related characteristics of the leaders included in this text, and chapter 2, dealing with the structure and government of labor unions, provide general background information that will help to put later chapters in perspective.

America's Labor Leaders: A Collective Portrait

Given the stereotype of labor's leadership, it's a bit ironic to find them among the honorees and members of our society's leading political and educational institutions. Some of those I interviewed have been elected or appointed to political office or received honorary degrees from colleges and universities; some sit on the boards of charitable organizations, businesses, and universities. They are members of service and fraternal clubs, chambers of commerce, and veterans organizations. In brief, they are as much a part of the American community as any other group of citizens.

Early Backgrounds

In most cases, the early socioeconomic milieu of a labor leader is prototypic American working class, circa 1920–1940. Their fathers were wage earners, and their mothers, homemakers. While a few grew up in two-income households, the vast majority of families got along on relatively low incomes. Typical of the jobs held by a leader's father were boiler tender, postman, day laborer, factory worker, or blacksmith. If their mother worked she was a secretary, retail clerk, charlady, or teacher.

Education

The level of formal education achieved by labor leaders ranges from the ninth grade to completed graduate degrees. Among those included in this volume are two who hold law degrees, two others with masters' degrees, fourteen with baccalaureate degrees or some college-level education, and eleven who completed their studies at the secondary school level. While they are better educated than earlier generations of labor leaders, the scholastic accomplishments of contemporary leaders, at least in the formal sense, pale in comparison to those of business executives, who typically have earned at least a baccalaureate degree.[10]

Career Beginnings

Most leaders began their working lives among the rank and file of the industry in which they now hold leadership positions. A few had considered pursuing a management career, and some even had the opportunity, but they were either never really interested enough, or had pangs of conscience over the possible conflict of interest between their social democratic ideals, and the demands associated with having to be a "boss."

Most leaders will tell you that there were no great awe-inspiring events that led them to choose a career in labor and that in fact they seem to have "fallen" into their labor careers. The experience of Marshall Hicks of the Utility Workers Union of America is typical. He relates that when he told his coworkers they should get involved in the local, they turned to him and said, "What about you?" At the same time, many leaders grew up in union households, with fathers, uncles, and cousins who were members or active as leaders in their unions. Shannon Wall's father, for instance, was a pioneering member of the Teamsters, Chuck Perlik's father was the driving force behind the creation of the first Meat Salesman's Union in the nation, and Bill Bywater's father was a shop steward. Given the types of jobs held by the leaders as young adults and the fact that many of their families were "union people," the factors that led them to become involved in union affairs may not be as coincidental as they often claim.

Career Paths

Although there are several ways to reach the top positions in a labor organization, most of today's leaders did it the old fashioned way: by working their way up from the very bottom of labor's officialdom. Typically, their first position in labor was either in a local, where they served as a council member, vice-president, or secretary-treasurer, positions which offered nothing or very little in the way of remuneration (dues might be waived), or as a union organizer employed by the national union.[11] Their careers followed a steady path upwards through a combination of appointed, but mostly elective office positions. (Federal law requires that all executive officers of unions be periodically elected to office by either a direct vote of the membership or by member-elected delegates. See below for some highlights of the law.)

While you will hear from many leaders that they have not lost an election over the course of their union careers, which by the way extends over

---

Major Federal Provisions for the Election of Officers of Labor Organizations

The Labor-Management Reporting Disclosure Act of 1959 (the Act) requires unions to conduct periodic elections of officers and prescribes minimum standards to insure that such elections will be fairly conducted. Some highlights of the Act are:

Frequency of Elections:
The Act requires that all national labor organizations elect their officers not less often than every five years, and officers of local labor organizations not less often than every three years.

Reasonable Qualifications of Candidates for Office:
Ordinarily the following types of requirements may be considered reasonable: period of prior membership, continuity of good standing, meeting attendance requirements, and employment in the trade of the union.

Section 504(a) of the Act bars individuals convicted of certain crimes from holding office in labor organizations. These include robbery, bribery, extortion, embezzlement, grand larceny, burglary, arson, violation of narcotics laws, murder, rape, assault with intent to kill, assault which inflicts grievous body injury, or any felony, or conspiracy, involving abuse or misuse of a position or employment in a labor organization or an employee benefit plan to seek or obtain an illegal gain at the expense of the members of the union or the beneficiaries of the employee benefit plan.

Source: Adapted from *Election of Officers of Labor Organizations* Washington, D.C.: Office of Labor-Management Standards, U.S. Department of Labor, 1986.

the entire course of their working lives (see table 1–1), they'll also tell you that this accomplishment is not as impressive as it sounds. Union elections are typically pro forma events, and outcomes are never really in doubt. In most, there is usually only one slate of "real" candidates, and that slate is the incumbent administration's slate. Lower echelon leaders must either wait their turn for advancement via the attrition process (death, resignation, retirement, or advancement of higher-level office holders), or try to unseat a presumably better organized and more visible incumbent. In most cases, the former path is followed, with the result that most leaders advance through a kind of "dead man's shoes" process. Despite this bureaucratic pattern, careerist feelings run strong, especially among secretary-treasurers, who in many unions are the "heirs" to the presidency.

Much has been made of the fact that union officers, once elected to the presidency of their unions, remain in office for considerable lengths of time. For example, John L. Lewis was president of the Mine Workers for 40 years; William Hutcheson of the Carpenters for 42 years; Joe Curran of the Maritime Union for 36 years; and Sidney Hillman of the Amalgamated Clothing Workers of America for 32 years. As one might expect, these are really exceptional cases, and very few presidents today expect, or even desire, to experience that sort of tenure in office. Further, a close examination of the relationship between chronological age and tenure in office reveals no great disparities between union leaders and corporate executives.[12] Among the presidents included in *America's Labor Leaders,* those who assumed office at a relatively young age are Albert Shanker of The American Federation of Teachers at forty-six, John Sweeney of the Service Employees International Union at age fifty, and William Wynn of the United Food and Commercial Workers International Union at forty-eight.[13]

Management Style

The management styles of the labor leaders I have met run the gamut from participatory to autocratic. Although a few take their electoral mandates as

Table 1–1
Career Patterns of Leaders Included in *America's Labor Leaders*[a]

Present age	59
Age first joined a union	22
Age starting first union position	29
Age starting present position	50

[a]Data are expressed in mean numbers of years. Retirees are included.

an ultimatum for them to run their union, most rely on a consensual decision-making style as a matter of standard practice. Participative management for them basically reflects the essence of unionism—that is, a democratic people-involved institution. Regardless of style, though, a leader will regularly make use of a very well-developed network of personal contacts to verify information or as a sounding board for ideas, strategies, and decisions. Generally these networks serve as an extra pair of eyes and hands.

A typical work day for a leader is ten to twelve hours long, with an agenda characteristically marked by variety, complexity, and fragmentation.[14] Some of the day will be devoted to planning negotiation strategies, or taking part in negotiations, reviewing contracts and arbitration cases and performing regular administrative chores. The leader may be involved in charting organizing strategies or corporate campaigns (a union tactic that enlists a company's directors, consumers, lenders and shareholders as well as the general public to pressure a company into yielding to a union's demands), reviewing staff and field reports, testifying before a congressional committee, or working on the latest emergency to hit the union and its membership. There are meetings and phone calls with other union officers, employers, lawyers, financial advisors, the press, lobbyists, staff, and visits by members, their families, and retirees. Some meetings can run several hours, others, a few minutes; some require immediate decisions, while some are for information purposes only. Sometimes the leader's presence and input at a meeting are essential; at other times they are useful in lending a measure of moral support or expertise to those actually performing a task.

A good "chunk" of a day will also involve handling a great amount of paperwork—bills, memos, and reports—and correspondence both to and from the membership. In fact, most leaders readily admit their members are "none too shy" about phoning or writing the leadership to express opinions or ask for advice and help. Finally, at the end of a typical day, more work will be routinely brought home, where there will be more phone calls from members, field reps, or perhaps a local just completing a late night meeting and wanting to "touch base." (See appendix B for an example of the constitutional duties of the executive officers of a union.)

Paradoxically, one of the more difficult managerial tasks for a labor leader is negotiating a collective bargaining agreement with their staff's union. The change of place at the negotiating table is pure role reversal and particularly onerous for those leaders whose memberships have lost benefits or taken wage cuts in recent years. While they will express solidarity with the goals of their staffs' unions, most leaders admit to being pretty tough "managers" at the bargaining table.

Not surprisingly, labor leaders are really not that excited by the administrative routine required of their position, or by being "housed-up" in headquarters. They are "doers" who have made their mark while serving in the field, where they feel more comfortable. As a rule, a leader will get out among the members, as often as possible, either by touring plants or work sites or by walking picket lines, or by attending regional conferences, workshops, or the monthly meeting of a local. They use these visits to explain the national union's agenda, or to get the membership fired up on a political action initiative, or explain what's going on in collective bargaining negotiations or the industry. As might be expected, all these visits and activities have political undertones. They provide visibility for the leaders, which, by the way, they relish.

The salaries of labor leaders are lower than most people would suspect (see table 1–2). In fact their salaries are in no way comparable to those received by senior officers of major business organizations. The highest-paid union president received slightly more than a third of a million dollars in salary and expenses in 1986, while the highest paid corporate executive, Lee Iacocca, received over $20 million. The twenty-fifth highest paid, Roberto Goizueta of Coca-Cola, received more than $3 million.[15] While the work and responsibilities of the two groups may not be exactly comparable, the differences in salaries are really quite striking. In fact, even if one were to compare the salaries of top labor leaders with those of business managers of lesser rank, the differences are still impressive. Arch Patton, a noted authority on the compensation of business executives, has stated that not only

Table 1–2
The Range of Compensation of Labor Union Presidents (1986)

Name	Union	Total Compensation[a]
1. Henry A. Duffy	Air Line Pilots	346,195
2. William H. Wynn	Food/Commercial Workers	288,118
3. Edward T. Hanley	Hotel/Restaurant Employees	222,334
4. Thomas W. Gleason	Longshoremen	220,492
5. Gerald W. McEntee	AFSCME	167,576
6. Lane Kirkland	AFL-CIO	161,772
7. Marvin J. Boede	Plumbers	151,754
8. John J. Barry	IBEW	150,013
9. Albert Shanker	Teachers	138,315
10. William W. Winpisinger	Machinists	136,236
11. Owen F. Bieber	Auto Workers	133,396
12. John J. Sweeney	Service Employees	126,877
13. Lynn R. Williams	Steelworkers	115,569
14. Moe Biller	Postal Workers	107,623
15. Cesar E. Chavez	Farm Workers	5,140

Source: The unions' 1986 labor-organization annual reports filed with The U.S. Department of Labor.
[a]Includes salary and all expenses.

have the salaries of most of the 100 largest industrial corporation's chief executives exceeded the $1 million mark, but those of many of their immediate subordinates have also topped the million-dollar mark.[16]

2. The History, Organization, and Consequences of Unions

LABOR unions are organizations of working people who have agreed as one to improve the conditions of employment for all who belong. The following sections provide some highlights on the history, organization, and consequences of these organizations.

Historical Highlights

• Unions first appeared in the United States as early as the 1790s when groups of craftsmen, such as cordwainers (shoemakers) in Philadelphia, carpenters in Boston, and printers in New York City, established organizations to control wage levels in their cities, and set professional standards for their members.[1]

• While the labor movement is nearly as old as the United States, national unions of working people generally began to emerge in the latter half of the nineteenth century, a time of great industrialization in the United States, rapid development of national markets, and the establishment of nationwide monopolies. One of the more interesting attempts to form a national union was the Noble Order of the Knights of Labor. Founded in 1869, the "Knights" sought to improve the status of all working men (business managers included), skilled and unskilled, regardless of race, national origin, or gender. In fact, only "economic parasites," such as gamblers, politicians, lawyers, and bankers, were excluded from its ranks. Despite a large membership (700,000 members in 1886) and early successes, the Knights as an organization all but disappeared by 1895 as a result, in part, of its leadership's egalitarian orientation and the disenchantment among some members with the "one big union" concept.

• A casual reading of the life and times of unions in twentieth-century America reveals a history that has followed a "bumpy road." Unions have expanded or contracted along with the national economy and with technological developments that have eliminated jobs of union members or created new ones.

• A significant force in the shaping of the labor movement in the United States has been the direction of the courts, legislative bodies (see table 2–1 for summaries of the provisions of the principal labor laws) and the National Labor Relations Board (NLRB).[2] For instance, in 1908, the Supreme Court ruled that the Sherman Act made "every contract, combination, or conspiracy in restraint of trade illegal." This decision in turn was used by the courts for over twenty years as a basis for issuing injunctions, most often at the request of employers, to prevent employees from organizing unions, or unions from striking an employer.

A more favorable climate for unions and collective bargaining came with

Table 2–1
Principal Labor Laws

Law	Major Thrust	Coverage
Railway Labor Act (1926)	Gave employees the right to organize and bargain collectively	Railroads, airlines
Norris-LaGuardia Act (1932)	Prohibited federal courts from enjoining strikes and from enforcing yellow dog contracts	Private sector employment
Wagner Act (1935)	Established the right to organize and engage in other concerted activities; declared certain employer actions to be unfair labor practices; established procedures for employees to elect a union; regulated collective bargaining; established the National Labor Relations Board (NLRB)	Private-sector employment: business, nonprofit hospitals and nursing homes, private colleges and universities, performing arts
Taft-Hartley Act (1947)	Established the right to refrain from the activities protected in the Wagner Act; declared certain union actions to be unfair labor practices; provided for passage of state right-to-work laws; established the Federal Mediation and Conciliation Service (FMCS)	Same as Wagner Act
Landrum-Griffin Act (1959)	Established standards for union treatment of union members; regulated internal union affairs	Same as Wagner Act and Taft-Hartley Act
Title VII, Civil Rights Act (1964)	Prohibits discrimination on the basis of race, color, religion, sex, or national origin, in all employment practices and in union membership	Private and public sector employment
Title VII, Civil Service Reform Act (1978)	Established the right to collective bargaining; required arbitration of impasses and grievances; prohibited strikes and other disruptions	Federal employment

Source: Adapted from V. G. Scarpello and J. Ledvinka, *Personnel/Human Resource Management* (Boston: PWS-Kent Publishing Co., 1988), p. 583. © by PWS-Kent Publishing Co. Reprinted by permission of PWS-Kent Publishing Company, a division of Wadsworth, Inc.

the enactment of the Norris-LaGuardia Act of 1932, which effectively restricted the role of the courts in settling labor-management disputes and with the New Deal labor legislation of Franklin D. Roosevelt. The latter, including the National Industrial Recovery Act of 1933 (declared unconstitutional by the Supreme Court in 1935), and the National Labor Relations Act, known also as the NLRA or Wagner Act, played an important role in the unionization of millions of Americans during the 1930s. The NLRA, for example, guaranteed that:

> Employees shall have the right to self-organization, to form, join, or assist labor organizations, to bargain collectively through representatives of their own choosing, and to engage in concerted activities for the purposes of collective bargaining or other mutual aid or protection. [NLRA, Section 7][3]

However, since many of those who joined organized labor during this time period possessed little or no skill, their arrival into the ranks of labor caused an ongoing conflict within the American Federation of Labor (AFL), the premier labor federation at that time, to escalate.
• The AFL was founded in 1886 by representatives of several skilled worker unions. Under the leadership of Samuel Gompers, the AFL was fervently committed to the principles of business unionism (sometimes referred to as unionism of "bread and butter issues"), trade union autonomy, exclusive jurisdiction (that is, only one national union would represent individuals performing related types of work) and the organization of skilled rather than unskilled or semiskilled workers.[4]
But in the early 1930s a small group of union presidents, including David Dubinsky of the International Ladies' Garment Workers' Union (ILGWU), Sidney Hillman of the Amalgamated Clothing Workers, and John L. Lewis of the United Mine Workers, whose unions were affiliated with the AFL, began to promote the cause of unionization of workers employed in mass production industries such as auto, steel, rubber, and textile. And after much debate and some very "hot" confrontations (see "AFL vs. CIO: Round I," page 14) between the two sides on the industrial unionism question, these three individuals, along with several other presidents of AFL-affiliated unions, established in 1935 the Committee for Industrial Organization. By 1936, the split between the sides became official, when the federation's executive board expelled the "renegade" unions, and the committee became the Congress of Industrial Organization (CIO).
Over the next twenty years, both AFL and CIO unions were adding thousands of working people to their membership rolls, due in good measure to a wartime expansion of U.S. industries, and the fact that each was organizing workers in the other's jurisdictions. For instance, CIO unions recog-

AFL vs. CIO: Round I

The cue for the launching of the CIO was appropriately dramatic—physical combat between two men who personified the differences between craft and industrial unionism.

At the 1935 convention of the AFL, during a discussion of industrial unionism in the rubber industry, "Big Bill" Hutcheson, president of the Carpenters Union and a staunch defender of the craft union position, raised a point of order to object that the industrial union issue had already been settled in favor of the craft unions.

John L. Lewis, president of the United Mine Workers and leader of the industrial-union forces within the AFL, snorted scornfully, "This thing of raising points of order all the time on minor delegates is rather small potatoes."

"I was raised on small potatoes, that's why I'm so small," shot back Hutcheson, one of the tallest and heaviest men in the convention." . . .

"Well, then, it's about time you were mashed," Lewis said, striking Hutcheson, and the two tangled and fell to the floor.

Excerpt, page 24, from *The Unions: Structure, Development, and Management* by Marten Estey, copyright © 1976 by Harcourt Brace Jovanovich, Inc., reprinted by permission of the publisher.

nized craft unions, and not to be outdone, AFL unions like the Carpenters and Machinists began organizing outside of their crafts and among industrial workers. The result was that by the early 1940s there was little difference in the organizing efforts of the AFL and CIO. Yet, it was not until 1955 when the two federations would merge and officially become the American Federation of Labor and the Congress of Industrial Organization (AFL-CIO). At that time, George Meany, president of the AFL was elected as the AFL-CIO's first president. Meany held that position until 1980, when, at the age of eighty-five, he retired because of ill health.[5]

Finally, although the merger created a federation of nearly 16 million workers, it has been argued that the merger itself had little effect on the economic power of organized labor. Unions retained their autonomy and "lived or died" based to a great extent on the events influencing their specific industries. However, the merger did lessen the amount of "raiding" of other unions' jurisdictions in seeking new members, and it did have a positive effect on labor's political influence.[6]

AFL vs. CIO: Round 2

The unhappy by-product of these developments was the spread of jurisdictional quarrels between competing unions. The A.F. of L. carpenters fought the C.I.O. woodworkers, the C.I.O. automobile workers fought the A.F. of L. machinists, and A.F. of L. and C.I.O. longshoremen, textile workers, electrical workers, packing house workers and retail clerks battled indiscriminately. The heavens rang with charges of union raiding, scabbing, and mutual betrayal. The bitterness of these family squabbles often exceeded that of labor-capital disputes. The recriminatory attacks of the two organizations upon one another, and sometimes union battles within either the A.F. of L. or C.I.O., were on occasion more violent than labor attacks upon industry. Strikes broke out again and again for no other cause than a quarrel over jurisdiction, to the great loss of the workers immediately concerned and to the immense harm of all organized labor.

Source: Foster Rhea Dulles, *Labor in America: A History* (Arlington Heights, Illinois: Harlan Davidson, Inc., 1949 [First edition]), p. 310. © by Harlan Davidson, Inc. Reproduced by permission.

The Organization of Unions

• Some unions represent individuals sharing a distinct skill, or who are employed in a single industry, such as the Associated Actors and Artistes of America (entertainment industry), or the International Union of Journeymen Horse Shoers of the United States and Canada. Others, such as the International Brotherhood of Teamsters, Chauffers, Warehousemen and Helpers of America (the Teamsters), the United Automobile, Aerospace and Agricultural Implement Workers of America (the Autoworkers), the United Brotherhood of Carpenters and Joiners of America, and the United Steelworkers of America, accept as members all workers, regardless of skill or industry. The Teamsters, for example, not only represent truckers,[7] but also teachers and nurses. And the Steelworkers' constitution states that membership is open to: "all working men and working women in the United States, Canada, insular areas adjacent thereto and the Western Hemisphere" (Article III, Section 1, August 28, 1986).

• Although we often use the word "union" in a generic sense, there are at least four different levels or units of organization to which it can be applied: the local (sometimes called a lodge, or chapter); the intermediate (including district, council, region, or joint board); the national or international union[8] (see appendix A); and the federation of unions.

The Local

The local (for example, United Paperworkers International Union, Local 189) is the level where individuals and the labor movement come together. The local is what a person joins when becoming a union member. An initiation fee may be charged amounting to several dollars or several hundred dollars; the latter is typical in those unions representing professional or high-salaried employees. Generally though, the typical union member will be required to pay as monthly dues to his or her local an amount equivalent to about two hours pay per month, or about $18–$25 for the average industrial worker.

As of 1988 there were approximately 46,000 union locals in the United States. Some of these represent employees in a single large plant, others serve those employed in smaller plants, or all workers in a sparsely populated geographic area. Locals range in size from a dozen or so members to the giant 64,000-member local 32B-32J of The Service Employees International Union, which represents building service employees in New York City. The size of the average local is estimated to be about 300 to 400 members.

Intermediate Level

Above the local level in the hierarchy of unions are the intermediate and national levels. Where the latter represents the parent organization of a union, the intermediate level typically represents a region of the parent union. It will assist those locals in collective bargaining or political action, or provide research support, and other services to the members.

National Level

The primary responsibility for the health of a union lies with the national level. The national may either directly engage employers in negotiations on behalf of its member locals or provide technical expertise and resources in support of those locals which bargain directly with employers. Other activities of the national include the following:

- Organizing nonunion workers
- Participating in community affairs
- Providing educational courses, information, and research support to its members on subjects such as negotiations, health and safety, wages, benefits, pensions and labor laws

- Representing members in grievance hearings and arbitration cases
- Directing corporate campaigns
- Proposing to its members, for their approval, a merger with another union
- Establishing policy for the union
- Providing for the effective coordination of its consistent locals

To carry out its service function, the national ordinarily collects from its locals, usually monthly, a portion of the dues paid to the local by the members. This share of the dues, referred to as "per caps" (actually, per capita assessment or taxes), represents on average about ⅓–½ of an individual's dues payment to the local. The national level (or a local) might also assess the members a special payment (or special assessment) to build up its strike fund, or support some other labor related initiative (see page 18 for more information about dues, fees, and assessments).

The Federation

At the top of the hierarchy of unions is the federation level. The best known of these is the American Federation of Labor and Congress of Industrial Organization (AFL-CIO). The AFL-CIO is not a trade union per se. It does not accept individuals as members. Rather, it is an affiliation of ninety-seven national unions for which it acts as a service organization, or a kind of "United Nations" of unions. In that role, it has no direct authority over the administration, policy, or finances of its affiliated members, but must depend on their acceptance of its activities, which include the following:

- Lobbying Congress and other levels of government in support of labor-related issues
- Sponsoring political action initiatives in support of "labor's friends"
- Settling jurisdictional disputes between affiliates
- Coordinating bargaining activity of its affiliates[9]
- Supporting organizing efforts
- Providing education and research support on issues related to the workplace
- Acting as a representative of American labor to other labor federations and organizations throughout the world
- Providing financial, manpower, and moral support to its members or to nonunion employees in the United States who wish to form a union.

Rights of Unions Regarding Dues, Initiation Fees, and Assessments

The Labor Management Reporting and Disclosure Act of 1959 stipulates that in local unions, dues and fees may be raised and assessments imposed only by:

A majority vote by secret ballot of the members in good standing at a special or regular meeting, after reasonable notice of the proposal has been given; or

A majority vote of the members in good standing in a secret ballot membership referendum.

In unions other than local unions and federations of national or international unions, dues and fees may be raised and assessments imposed only by:

A majority vote of the delegates voting at a regular convention, or at a special convention for which the affiliated local unions have received 30 days' advance notice. Delegates may cast weighted votes in accordance with the number of members they represent, if the constitution and bylaws of their union so provide;

A majority vote of the members in good standing voting in a secret ballot membership referendum; or

A majority vote of the members of the organization's executive board if this authority has been expressly given to the board by the union's constitution and bylaws. This action, however, is effective only until the next regular convention.

Source: U.S. Department of Labor. *Rights and Responsibilities,* Office of Labor-Management Standards, 1986.

The AFL-CIO has also recently instituted a union privilege benefit program, which makes available to the members of its affiliates a low-interest credit card, travel and legal services, and low-cost term life insurance plans.

In all, the AFL-CIO enhances the economic and political clout of its member affiliates to a degree that many, alone, could not afford. In return for that support, an affiliated union agrees to abide by the ethical codes of conduct covering union democracy; refrain from discriminatory behavior on the basis of race, color, creed, or gender; and support the administration of the AFL-CIO and its activities through "per caps."

Beyond the mission it pursues on behalf of its affiliates, the AFL-CIO has supported a variety of initiatives aimed at improving the status of working people in other countries. For example, it has called upon the United States government to deny preferential trade status to South Korea, Chile,

Taiwan, Romania, and Nicaragua, countries the federation considers to have a "lamentable record of worker rights violations."[10] The AFL-CIO has also supported democratic trade unions in other countries such as Poland's Solidarnosc, Nicaragua's CUS, and the black trade unions in South Africa (see appendix C for a schedule of the AFL-CIO's contributions).

The supreme authority of the AFL-CIO is its biennial convention, where delegates from the affiliated unions discuss and vote on policies or programs, elect officers, and resolve jurisdictional problems. The real authority of the AFL-CIO rests with its two elected officers (currently Lane Kirkland, president, and Thomas R. Donahue, secretary-treasurer), and an executive council comprised of thirty-four vice-presidents (see fig. 2–1).[11] Parenthetically, thirteen of the leaders you will hear from in this book are vice-presidents of the AFL-CIO.

Union Membership

• Being a union member is similar to being a member of any organization. One can either be actively involved and participate in meetings and perhaps stand for office or remain an inactive, nominal member. While most union members follow the latter course, their lack of involvement should not be construed as an indication of lack of interest or disenchantment with unionism. For example, union leaders have long lamented the poor turnout at the monthly meetings of a local, but rarely the lack of involvement of their members in discussions and votes about dues increases, contract proposals or ratification votes, strikes, or participation in solidarity events—issues that touch the pockets and hearts of the members.

• Becoming a union member, in most instances, is not a very exciting event. In fact, for the roughly one million workers who join existing unions each year, membership is nothing more than a condition of employment,[12] no different than abiding by an employer's rules to show up at 8 A.M. for work, or taking lunch at a prescribed hour. Really, the only noticeable changes that come with being a union member are that (1) union dues will probably be deducted from one's payroll checks, and (2) a union representative (often called a steward) will invite the new member to attend the local's meetings and will explain the rules governing the workplace, the status of the collective bargaining agreement between the union and employer, and the role of the union in representing the members. Clearly, becoming a union member in this fashion does not engender a great deal of commitment to a union, nor to the ideals of trade unionism.

However, if a person becomes a union member via the organizing drive that establishes the union's status in the workplace, that can be a very exciting event. In this instance, some workers will "stand up," and in the face of a management that may not be pleased with union organizing efforts,

Figure 2–1. Structure of the AFL-CIO

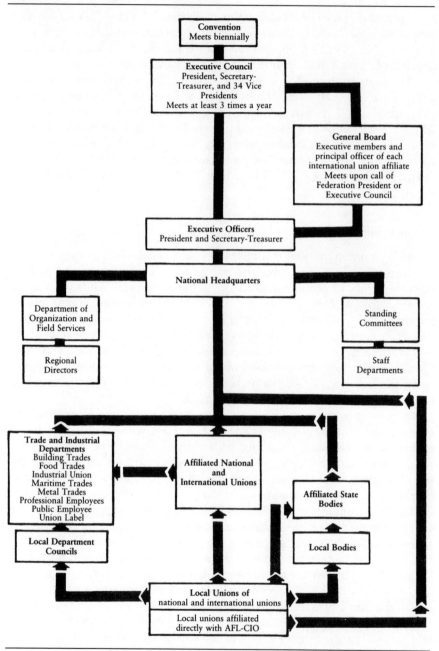

Source: Courtney D. Gifford, *Directory of U.S. Labor Organizations 1984–1985* (Washington, D.C.: Bureau of National Affairs, 1985). Reprinted by permission of the publisher.

publicly express their commitment to the goals of the new union by serving on the union organizing committee or in other leadership positions.

Generally, employees obtain union representation through a certification election procedure administered by the NLRB.[13] The procedure begins with a union's campaign to get as many employees as possible to sign authorization cards. A signature on an authorization card indicates an employee's desire for that particular union's representation. If a minimum of 30 percent of the employees sign cards, the NLRB considers that there is interest among a sufficient number of employees for unionization, and the Board will then schedule a certification election. If the union wins the election by a simple majority of those voting, the union is certified by the Board as the exclusive bargaining agent for those employees. The NLRB will also certify a union even if the union fails to win a majority when an employer commits certain unfair labor relations practices. Although the behavior of a union and management during an authorization card and pre-election campaign is governed by labor law, campaigns are often highly contentious affairs where the law is not always obeyed.[14]

• Union membership over the last three decades has declined in absolute numbers and as a percentage of the workforce. The AFL-CIO reports that since 1954 the proportion of workers who are eligible to join a union and who in fact belong to a union has fallen from close to 45 percent to under 28 percent; and as a percentage of the entire workforce, the decline in union membership has been from 35 percent to under 19 percent (see appendix D for the membership trends of AFL-CIO affiliated unions).[15]

Reasons for the decline in union membership include:

1. The decline or demise of basic industries that once served as the backbone of organized labor

2. An increase in employment opportunities in the difficult-to-organize southern and western geographic areas of the country

3. More sophisticated and frequent use of antilabor tactics by management

4. The image of labor unions as corrupt organizations

5. The belief on the part of unorganized workers that unions stifle individual initiative and increase the risk of strikes and the likelihood of their company's going out of business.[16]

6. The slow response of organized labor in unionizing the rapidly increasing numbers of workers in the service sector of the U.S. economy as well as white collar and professional employees.

To deal with these serious challenges facing organized labor, the AFL-CIO's Committee on the Evolution of Work has proposed a number of new initiatives aimed at increasing labor's strategic power.[17] One recommendation of the committee is to establish a new category of union membership—associate membership—to provide services to those workers who are outside of organized labor. Associates might be provided employment related services such as job training information and health and medical benefits, services that they might not receive from their employers.

In addition, the committee has recommended that labor unions must attend to the changing needs of workers and make greater use of the media to educate the public regarding the accomplishments of unions, and to publicize any interference with the right of workers to organize a union. The AFL-CIO has acted upon the latter recommendation by approving the expenditure of $13 million to initiate a media campaign aimed at presenting the labor "story." The committee also recommended that labor unions begin to coordinate their organizing activities in a given industry or company. One such effort that is currently under way involves the organizing of employees of Blue Cross and Blue Shield by nine major international unions.

The Consequences of Unions

• What do unions do? The answer to this question for many people, both inside and outside of unions, is that unions seek to improve wages and benefits of their members and engage in strikes. That is true, but the answer needs some clarification. First, there are about seventy work related issues that either a union or an employer can raise during collective bargaining negotiations and which the other side must legally bargain in good faith. These are known as *mandatory items* (see table 2–2) and are generally a matter of wages, hours, and other terms and conditions of employment. An employer or a union can also raise what are known as *voluntary or permissive issues* during negotiations (such as a requirement for a performance bond or benefits for retired workers). With the other side's consent, these issues become a part of negotiations. If consent is not given, it is an unfair labor practice to force the issue to impasse.[18]

While unions do engage in strikes or work stoppages (management does as well), it should be kept in mind that the overwhelming majority of labor-management agreements negotiated in the United States are routinely settled, a fact that is rarely mentioned in the press. Strikes are simply uncommon phenomena. In fact, it has been estimated that strikes account for far less (one-tenth) of the time lost in the workplace than that resulting from industrial accidents.[19]

• Further, regarding the effects of union wages on inflation and the productivity of union workers, the results of a study by Freeman and Medoff indicate that 1. union wage gains were not a major inflationary factor in the 1970s; and 2. productivity is generally greater in many unionized organi-

Table 2–2
Mandatory Bargaining Issues

Wages	Work loads
Overtime pay	Change of employee status to independent
Hours	contractors
Discharge	Price of meals provided by company
Arbitration	Group insurance (health, accident, life)
Holidays (paid)	Promotions
Vacations (paid)	Seniority
Sick leave	Layoffs
Duration of agreement	Transfers
Grievance procedure	Work assignments
Layoff plan	No-strike clause
Reinstatement of economic strikers	Cancellation of seniority upon relocation of
Change of payment from hourly base to	plant
salary base	Discounts on company products
Union security and dues checkoff	Shift differentials
Work rules	Contract clause providing for supervisors
Merit wage increase	keeping seniority in unit
Work schedule	Procedures for income tax withholding
Lunch periods	Severance pay
Rest periods	Nondiscriminatory hiring hall
Pension plan	Plant rules
Retirement age	Motor carrier-union agreement providing
Bonus payments	that carriers use own equipment before
Safety	leasing outside equipment
Prohibition against supervisor doing unit	Agency shop
work	Employer's insistence on clause giving
Superseniority for union stewards	arbitrator right to enforce award
Partial plant closing	Management rights clause
Hunting on employer forest reserve where	Bargaining over "bar list"
previously granted	Truck rentals—minimum rental to be paid
Plant closedown and relocation	by carriers to employee-owned vehicles
Change in operations resulting in	Musician price lists
reclassifying workers from incentive to	Arrangement for negotiation
straight time, or cut work force, or	Change in insurance carrier and benefits
installation of cost-saving machine	Profit sharing plan
Plant closing	Company houses
Job-posting procedures	Subcontracting
Plant reopening	Discriminatory racial policies
Employee physical examination	Production ceiling imposed by union
Piece rates	Most-favored-nation clause
Stock-purchase plan	

*Source:*Reed C. Richardson, *Collective Bargaining by Objectives: A Positive Approach,* 2/E, © 1985, 116–117. Reprinted by permission of Prentice-Hall, Inc., Englewood Cliffs, NJ.

zations than nonunion organizations ". . . due in part to the lower rate of turnover under unionism, improved managerial performance in response to the union challenge, and generally cooperative labor-management relations at the plant level (p. 22)."[20]

• Beyond their role as workplace representatives for their members, unions have also contributed to the welfare of all Americans. Organized labor demanded equal universal education as far back as the early 1800s and aggressively lobbied Congress to bring about the passage of, among others, the Social Security Act and the Occupational Safety and Health Act. It strongly supported the enactment of Medicare in 1965; and promoted over the years a variety of employee benefits, including pensions for retirees, paid vacations and lunch periods, unemployment benefits, thrift plans, health and other insurance coverage. And it is now being proposed that the system of industrial jurisprudence (that is, a grievance procedure based on principals of just cause and adjudication), which unions long ago achieved for their members, should be made a standard policy in all work settings.[21]

3. Without Dialogue There Can Be No Cooperation

Morton Bahr

We have the privilege of representing working men and women, and by extension, their families, and the American community. And therein lies our great responsibility.

Morton Bahr is the third president of the Communications Workers of America (CWA), the world's largest communications union. *Business Week* described Mr. Bahr as ". . . in some respects a throwback to the charismatic and pugnacious labor captains of 50 years ago," and "As the head for 16 years of the CWA's northeast region [District 1] . . . he had an old-style, bare knuckled approach to labor relations. But he also developed a more modern, cooperative stance."[1]

Prior to his election as president in 1985, Mr. Bahr served as a CWA organizer, director, assistant to the vice-president, and vice-president. Among his many community and political activities, Mr. Bahr is a member of the board of governors of the United Way of America and was a delegate to the Democratic National Convention in 1976, 1980, and 1984.

Born in Brooklyn, New York in 1926, Mr. Bahr holds a bachelor of science degree in labor studies from Empire State College.

The Communications Workers of America traces its origins to the formation of the National Federation of Telephone Workers in 1938. In the early years, the major employer of CWA members was AT&T, and although the company recognized the union, it refused to bargain with it on an industry-wide basis, claiming that its associated telephone companies were autonomous units. It was not until 1974 that national bargaining with AT&T was achieved. Since the breakup of AT&T, the CWA has fought various regional "Baby Bells" over their attempts to circumvent labor contracts and has also vigorously pursued the organization of workers at other telecommunications companies. Today, the CWA represents more than 650,000 communications workers in approximately 900 locals throughout the United States.

* * *

THERE are tens of thousands of minimum wage workers in this country who are voiceless and powerless, and they need the labor movement desperately. Let me give you an illustration. In 1973, 150 black women who were cafeteria workers at the Stephen F. Austin University in Nacogdoches, Texas filed a discrimination suit against the university, and three years later they won a $16 million judgment. Of that amount, not a nickel had been paid up to 1987.

However, about three or four years ago one of our local unions in Texas began to organize at the university, and when it looked like we would be successful, the university contracted out the cafeteria services to ARA Services, which is a notoriously antiunion firm. After going through countless numbers of unfair labor practice charges, we won the election in October of 1986.

Now I went there a few months later to participate in a rally in support of the effort to get a decent contract, but that trip turned out to be an experience I shall never forget. I have been exposed to the degradation of city poverty, I've been in the Harlems and the Bedford-Stuyvesants [communities in New York City] and in those apartments, in those basements, but I've never been exposed to rural poverty such as exists in east Texas. Shacks with two rooms, it was deplorable.

I visited some of the cafeteria workers who lived under those conditions on the evening that I arrived in Nacogdoches, and one woman said to me, "Do I look like an animal? Do I walk on all fours? I'm a human being, I think I deserve to be treated with some dignity." None of those I visited said anything about earning a nickel more, all they talked about was being treated like a person.

Now, the next day we had our rally in the center of the campus with about 3,000 people in attendance. There were at least fourteen different unions represented. Members of the American Federation of State, County, and Municipal Employees (AFSCME) came on a bus from El Paso, Texas, which is 850 miles away, and some of our own people from Austin paid $20 a piece to rent four buses so they could participate in the march and rally. Well, when I got up to speak, someone whispered to me that the president of the university had just come out with a number of administrators. I couldn't see them but I knew they were within earshot.

In my comments, I shared with the crowd my emotions of the night before, and I told them about the lawsuit, and the fact that I had instructed our attorneys to do whatever they could to expedite the settlement. Then I told them we would demand in negotiations that supervisors will not use abusive or profane language when speaking to employees. At that point I directed my comments to the president of the university. I said, "What is it that is being taught at this college? How can you treat the workers who serve you every day any different from the way you want your children to be treated? What kind of future leaders of America will be turned out from this school?"

Well, obviously, it was a very emotional day, but we were able to do some things for those people. For example, we negotiated a good contract, and it included a stipulation about supervisor's language. We were also able to get the state's attorney general to move on getting the settlement's monies loosened up, and seeing that $2 million worth of interest was added to it. But this was not just an isolated incident. As I said, there are thousands of workers who are being abused in America, and if we as a people have any compassion or decency at all, we have to act on their behalf.

The Image of Labor

Labor has had a problem with its image for many, many years. While we tend to blame the media for not giving us a fair shake, I think it's more complicated than that. Really, you have to look at what is newsworthy. The fact that 99 ½ percent of all contracts are resolved without a strike is not newsworthy. And the same is true for a peaceful picket line, and the fact that most everyone in labor is an honest and law abiding citizen. Sure, we have our share of bad apples, just as there are on Wall Street with the Ivan Boesky's [a financier convicted of violating U.S. Securities and Exchange Commission regulations in 1987], or the presidents of banks who embezzle funds. But unfortunately, we tend to make the news when a bad apple is found out.

Ironically though, what's lost in all this about labor's image is our support for the recent amendment to the Landrum-Griffin Act. That amendment requires the automatic removal from office of any union officer who is convicted of certain felonies and misdemeanors. There's no similar penalty for employers who are convicted of a felony, or for that matter anything like being disbarred or prohibited from pursuing their careers. But we supported the amendment anyway because we think we are different from corporate management and ought to be held to a higher standard. We have the privilege of representing working men and women, and by extension, their families, and the American community. And therein lies our great responsibility.

But labor ought to work more on getting its correct image out to the public because the public really doesn't know us. For example, I spoke recently to some 300 undergraduates of the Wharton School, at the University of Pennsylvania, and it appeared to me that those students were like "blotters," when it came to hearing about something they had not been exposed to.

Now I don't kid myself that I could have signed up all 300 as new union members, but I did give them a good deal to think about. For instance, the first question that was asked of me implied that the idea of a union was out of step with America's ideal of individualism. I responded by saying that was President Reagan's view of America, but that I felt otherwise. America is not just a group of individuals, because all through our history we have cared for one another, and that when one part of the community hurts, everybody hurts. That's why Americans contribute hundreds of millions of dollars to the United Way, or give blood to the Red Cross, or participate in countless numbers of other activities such as the scouts. Alone, we cannot impact the quality of our own lives, much less our families or communities. And so I tried to get that message across to those students, that sure, while we're individualists, and we may have the ability to rise above others, we're all in this thing together, and that the nation as a whole is indeed a family.

Another student wanted to know about the differences between a unionized and a nonunionized facility. So I used as an example the operations in Silicon Valley, California. Remember, every community in the country fights to get a Silicon Valley for themselves because there are no smokestacks, only clean industry. But what do we see happening in these areas now? We see the drinking water being polluted, a higher rate of miscarriages, and a higher rate of some types of cancers.

So I said, "I don't want anyone in this room to think that I'm indicting any corporate owner, that they would deliberately cause death or harm to their employees," but in a unionized plant, once a month, there's a union safety representative, who, along with a company safety representative, makes an inspection of the facility. If there are new types of substances that are going to be used, we make sure that our members know what it is that they're working with, and what is it that they're breathing.

One student suggested that was all taken care of by OSHA [Occupational Health and Safety Administration]. To that I said, "Great. Imagine you are in a nonunion place, and you find something that will cause bad publicity for your employer, or which might result in a multi-million dollar fine. Are you the one ready to stand up and be the complainant?" Again, it's unfortunate, but a lot of young people grow up alienated from unions. They only know about unions from what they read in the newspaper.

The New Generation of Workers

We're trying all kinds of new ways to make unions more relevant to the new generation of workers. With AT&T, for example, we have negotiated for greater employee participation and input on how jobs are to be done. Our contract with AT&T provides for the company and union to select a new work location in a pilot program and for the workers to design it from scratch, including the logistics and the ergonomics.

Let me give you an example where one of these programs has occurred and resulted in a gain for the company, as well as our members. We represent telephone operators in Grand Rapids, Michigan, and they've come up with all sorts of things that created a better and more efficient work atmosphere. And because there were efficiencies derived, they've been getting a few hundred dollars bonus every three months through the gain sharing program which they also designed.

Some of the things they did though, I had to ask myself, why weren't they done twenty years ago? Look, because of technology and the way it's laid out, a telephone operator's job is very demanding. Unlike the Scandinavian experience where a job is harnessed to the employee's brain, in America, employees are appendages to machines. So what the operators in Grand Rapids did was to modify the office so that it has several standing positions from which they could also work. This gives the employee an opportunity to move around and get away from the tedium of just sitting.

And because Grand Rapids has rough winters, the operators negotiated a flex-plan work schedule whereby they could come in up to a half hour late, and then decide at the end of the day whether they wanted to be docked a half hour, or stay the additional time and not be docked. These things taken individually might sound *de minimus,* or perhaps even childish, but when you listen to the operators as I have, and you hear them say, "This is our room, we designed it this way, we run it, nobody tells us how to run it, and if we see people beating up on the half-hour flex-plan or abusing any other things, we'll take care of it ourselves," you know they are feeling good about themselves.

Now these sorts of quality of work life programs are only possible where you have a strong union and a good steward system. Where you don't, the company will take over the program and turn it into a productivity vehicle.

Labor-Management Cooperation

Although we and AT&T have a healthy adversarial relationship and will always have our differences at the bargaining table, we've learned that there's also room for cooperation. Let me explain how you can have both. We have negotiated something that no other union has with any of their employers. That's a recognition by AT&T management of the CWA's institutional status. This means that we get recognition for new work groups without an election if we have a majority of the employees signed up on authorization cards. In fact, a couple of months ago we organized 380 white collar salary workers at the Norcross, Georgia, factory based on a card check. No union in America has that. Sure, other unions and managements have neutrality clauses when it comes to a union's organizing campaign, but not a recognition clause.

And we have also developed with AT&T something that came out of the '86 contract in the auto industry. It's a nonprofit corporation that's jointly owned and managed by us, and whose purpose is to train workers for new jobs or careers, and to help them in career development. The corporation's name is the Alliance for Employee Growth & Development and it has done some pretty marvelous things.

For example, when AT&T told us in October 1986 that it was shutting down the overseas operators center in Springfield, Massachusetts, the alliance went in and worked with our local union to help the 186 women, many of whom were single heads of households, find jobs. By the time the facility closed, we had achieved an 81 percent job placement rate within AT&T or in the community for those employees. The remaining 19 percent either took early retirement or got involved in something else. These are things labor and management can do when both want to do it.

Although the alliance's purpose is essentially aimed at providing opportunities for workers to continue with their education, its board of trustees, which is made up of equal numbers of CWA and AT&T members, decided recently to tackle a really extraordinary task.

That task involves serving as the catalyst in seeking federal and state monies, as well as some from other companies, to train youngsters in New York and New Jersey in basic reading and writing skills. What got this started was the fact that in the first seven months of last year, New York Telephone interviewed 90,000 applicants to fill 2,000 entry level jobs. The economic cost for those 88,000 people who didn't get a position is apparent, but there was an even bigger cost. That was in the human cost of all those people who didn't have the reading and writing comprehension to perform the job.

Getting Started

After I left the U.S. Merchant Marine in 1946, I went to work for Mackay Radio & Telegraph Company as an ordinary worker. Nine months later I was on strike. And although I didn't pay much attention to it at the time, somewhere midway in the strike, our union, the American Communications Association, was decertified because its officers had refused to sign the non-communist affidavit that was required at the time.[2] In fact, it was one of the unions ultimately kicked out of the CIO in 1949 because of its communist ties.

After the strike ended—which we lost by the way—the union told us to report back to work on the shift we struck. I was on the midnight shift, so at midnight, April 1, I was in the first group that was put through the indignity of lining up at work, and being told by management, "Don't call us, we'll call you." I suppose that was a turning point for me, because up to then, I was a member just like everyone else. But that situation made me a union person.

Several years later, while I was working at ITT, the CWA won the election to represent us, and although I wasn't even a candidate, I was nominated to be president of our local. One other person was nominated, but he declined, and so I got the job. In 1957, I was asked if I wanted to work for the union with the assignment of organizing New York Telephone. I took the job and once we won the election in 1961 and brought in 24,000 new members, my career really took off, like I was a ninety-day wonder. In 1963, I became assistant to the vice-president of the district and in 1969 vice-president in my own right. But there's no question, circumstances and accidents of chance have a lot to do with moving up in unions.

But I tell you that I'm very surprised at where my career has taken me. I don't think you start out saying "I'm going to be a labor leader," or certainly, the president of the largest communications union in the world. In fact, I was happy being someone's assistant because it reminded me of the feeling I had as an officer in the U.S. Merchant Marine. There, you didn't have to use initiative, you lived pretty well, other than the time when they're shooting torpedoes at you, and you could kind of get into a comfortable rut. As an assistant there is always someone else to whom the buck passes. However, after my predecessor in New York came down to Washington, and I took over the region, I found that I liked the number one spot and never really thought about being anywhere else but in that job.

Leadership

I think leadership is a number of things. It means a willingness to take some risks and a willingness in bilateral relations to share information. We keep talking about the need for greater cooperation between labor and management, but without dialogue there can be no understanding, no cooperation, just greater . . . [conflict]. But as Tom Donahue [secretary-treasurer of the

AFL-CIO] has said, "We're ready to cooperate—our problem is finding the management to do it."

Leadership also involves taking a good hard look at yourself, and making hard decisions about what needs to be done for the future. Look, for forty years the IBEW and CWA were mortal enemies in jurisdictional disputes, and granted, a lot of it was our own fault because we were the dominant union in the old Bell system, and we wanted to set the pattern. But what happened? The world around us changed in 1986, and AT&T, using the tactics of the marketplace, used the split between the two unions to get a cheaper contract. When it happened, I made a vow it would never happen again. And two weeks ago we signed an agreement, AT&T, CWA, and IBEW to bargain at the same table. A first.

And where a number of us like SEIU [Service Employees International Union] and AFSCME have been spending millions of dollars competing with one another over the right to represent public employees, we have decided to work together in those states where there are no collective bargaining laws for public employees. We'll get those laws changed to permit collective bargaining, and then we'll decide who gets what.

The Role of President

My role as president of a union is very different from that of a president of a generation ago. Do you know how different? Last November [1986] I had to go to Osaka, Japan, to meet with the chairman of Sanyo to discuss bringing 2,500 jobs to the United States. That's how different my role is. If we don't respond now to the internationalization of markets, they'll leave us behind.

IBM

In my inaugural address as president, I devoted two or three minutes, out of about forty minutes, to IBM. It's almost laughable, if it weren't so serious, that what I said in those few minutes was all that was considered newsworthy. I said in view of IBM's purchase of ROLM Electric, which is a manufacturing outfit, and their interest in MCI, that they now are head-to-head competitors with our major employer, AT&T. I said that if we want to maintain the conditions and benefits that we had built up over forty years in our industry, it was incumbent on us to organize IBM.

What happened? Those comments made their way into the *London Financial Times*, the *Japan Times*—in short order, I got press all over the world.

Well, a couple of important things did come of all of it though. Suddenly, that very secure company went into panic. In fact, we got hold of an internal IBM document out of their headquarters in New York that had been sent to all of their stations around the world. That document gave a day and night telephone number for their people to report any organizing activity among the employees, or any organizing activity at any company in the vicinity of an IBM facility.

One other thing that came out of my comments was a conference in London in January, 1986, of all unions interested in IBM. There were people from twenty-six countries, and at least three international trade secretariats [ITS's] were represented. We were astonished. In the seventy-five-year history of ITSs, this was the first time there had ever been a meeting of more than one.

I used to be astonished at the lockstep procedures of the old Bell system, but from what I've learned about IBM, they make AT&T look like a junior military. A couple of observations about IBM. Performance appraisals are life and death situations. Don't ever file a worker's compensation claim against IBM because you will be out. IBM doesn't lay off workers, they just transfer you frequently, and by several hundred miles at a time, until you give up. And don't take advantage too often of the open-door policy of the president of the company or the head of the division, because the manager who controls your destiny doesn't take well to going over his head.

I'm not saying it is a bad company, but it's not what it's cracked up to be. And so, there are a number of things which make IBM interesting from our perspective. But it's not going to be an easy project—we never said it would be. In fact, I'm trying to get two or three other unions involved because we just can't handle it all.

4. In Pursuit of Human Dignity

John J. Barry

Free enterprise doesn't mean you can just do what you please without any kind of consideration for the people that you're dealing with.

John J. Barry became president of the International Brotherhood of Electrical Workers (IBEW) in August 1986. Prior to his election, he had served as an IBEW international vice-president (1976–1986) and international representative (1968–1976). He was also the business manager of Local Union 43 (1967–1968), in Syracuse, New York, where he got his start as an apprentice electrician.

While unions of electrical workers existed in the United States during the mid-1800s, the National Brotherhood of Electrical Workers, the forerunner of today's IBEW, was established in 1883. Today the IBEW represents approximately 900,000 craft and industrial workers employed in the construction, utility, manufacturing, telecommunications, broadcasting, and railway industries. The IBEW, which is the largest electrical workers union in the world, has nearly 1,500 locals throughout the United States and Canada and negotiates several thousand contracts for its members.

* * *

THE image of labor leaders is a "live with" kind of thing. Unfortunately, students coming out of high school are not even taught that the labor movement contributed significantly to the elimination of child labor, supported the development of a public education system, Social Security, unemployment insurance, and a multitude of other things. A well-rounded student should not be someone who's just hearing one side, or no side, of the trade union movement.

But the negative image of labor is here to stay, there's no question about it. Trade unions have a built-in condition of being unpopular because we're trying to get something from someone who doesn't want to give it. So whenever we use our last resort tactic, a strike, a community only sees that you're disrupting their normal way of life with your selfish demands and all this kind of stuff. What they don't realize though, or appreciate, is what it's like to be subjected to some of the things that union members are put to. The irony is that a lot of inroads and improvements we make positively affect other than our own members. But few people recognize our contributions, and that's what really upsets me.

You know, a lot of these doomsayers are predicting the demise of the trade union movement. It's just not going to happen. The trade [union] movement is as progressive as ever, and it's doing an excellent job of representing its people. What you have to keep in mind is something that the chief rabbi said to one of our employers one time. He said, "The first thing that happened in Germany was they got rid of the church, and the second thing was they got rid of the unions." Now, there isn't going to be any time in our lifetime, yours and mine, that there won't be active trade unions in this country. What came out of the thirties? There was no middle class left in this country, it was rich and poor. And it was the labor movement that got Congress to pass the antitrust laws, the Wagner Act, things of that nature that brought back a middle class to this country. Those protections all came about because of the trade union movement, and we're doing the same things today.

Getting Started

I was from a union family. My father was a union electrician and I developed an interest in union matters because of his activities. I became an apprentice, a journeyman, a foreman, and ran for the executive board of my local. After I served on the board, I then became business manager. I was also a representative in the brotherhood, which is a nonelected post, for ten years. Then I was a vice-president, which was an elected post, and in this job, I had my first election last September in Toronto, Ontario, and I won that.

I will be a candidate for president in 1990. There's no one snapping at my heels now, but recall one of Aristotle's famous quotes—"Man by his very nature is politically oriented." So naturally, I expect that somebody wants to be president just like I wanted it. I mean, that's only human nature. But as I always say, you better be ready to win if you run against me.

Making It to the Top

To be a successful trade unionist, you have to spend a lot of time at it. There's no changing that, nor the fact that you will be rubbing shoulders, competing, with others for union slots. There's varying degrees of that, depending on the union you're with, but it is just like how you might get ahead in corporate setups. There really is no easy path, except if you're somebody's son or something like that, then you might have a break. But if you like working with people, you'll never find a better place to work than in a union.

In general, if you are going to make a run for the top, your track record has to be impressive, and you'd probably have a better chance if you come from one of the vice-presidential districts, covering states with a large IBEW membership. I guess, too, there would be some cutoff points actuarially. Generally speaking, if you arrive at say a representative slot when you're in your late fifties or early sixties, that's about as far as you're going. And if the immediate vice-president that you work for is say, fifty, you know you're not going any further. Which is not to say you're being relegated to some secondary slot, but your horizon will be limited.

You can spot the young people though who have a chance at making it to the top. Number one, they're good on paper, they can prove they've been active. Before we hire anyone for a staff job, we get as much input and feedback as we can about them. We talk to the people who were their mentors, working associates, and look at their record from when they served as a local official. Did he organize effectively? Did he process grievances on a timely basis? Was he popular? By popular I mean was he appealing to people? Or, did he act like a big shot or a dictator? We don't need any of those.

Frankly, if anyone tells you that they, a single person, runs a union they're full of shit. That person would not be speaking through an intelligent brain, because the very essence of trade unionism is togetherness. That's what we have preached since our founding. Together we can do everything, individually we can't do much. So for anyone to say "I, I, I," they're in the wrong business.

As well, if anyone were to say he could guarantee so many votes on an issue, that would be absolutely wrong. We can't speak for people's voting. We can ask them, but we cannot guarantee a block of votes. The brotherhood for example is a very sophisticated group. Our people work in telephone, manufacturing, utilities, and construction industries and we also have some government employees, CATV, and some others. Because of the type of work our members perform, they have to be intelligent people, and you're not going to be able to tell them how to vote.

I suppose that working for a union is pretty much like every other job in terms of putting in a lot of hours. The big difference though is that you're in the people business. Solely and entirely, you're dealing with people, with all their warts. You can't just have the nice side of people. You have to accept the fact that all of us have our days in the sun, and in the shade, we have ecstatic days, and depressing days. I just happen to like people, so I try to help them any way I can to make their lives a bit easier, no matter how they come.

Lost Jobs

Of course, our work on behalf of the membership has changed considerably since I started working with the brotherhood. We now spend an inordinate amount of time protecting what we gained in the past, instead of going on to new ventures like new ways to get our people some semblance of security in the job market.

That's our number one concern. When a person has only one thing to offer, his services, he shouldn't be subjected to a company which shuts right down and moves to Mexico. There ought to be some constraints on that company. Free enterprise doesn't mean you can just do what you please without any kind of consideration for the people whom you're dealing with.

Free enterprise is probably not the right word anyway for what we have in this country, it's private enterprise. There's no such thing as free enterprise, everything you do has some statutory regulations covering it. There are laws governing interstate commerce, postal laws, all kinds of rules governing our daily activities. When you drive to work, you've got to observe the speed limits, you've got to stay on the right side of the street, and you can't park in certain areas. The same thing should govern our industrial way of life. Yet, we don't have a national industrial policy. We've had a national agriculture policy since the days of Franklin Roosevelt, but what's more important to a country that wants to be self-sustaining, and wants to be able to defend itself in case of an emergency? Is it right to be dependent on other areas of the globe for what we need?

I don't want protectionist legislation, I want fair trade. That means if Japan says we can't go in there and sell anything to them because they're going to put up some barriers, they shouldn't have a consideration by us to do what they want here. It sounds so simple, straightforward, but the hitch that's holding it up is probably the fact that this country, regrettably, operates by crisis. We have to almost go right down to our knees before we get on board as to what should be done.

Case in point—the energy crisis and oil embargo of 1973. What happened? We had gas lines, we had cutbacks, and we knew that this was coming. The forecasters and the economic advisers were telling us it was going to come. We got through it, but since then we haven't done a damn thing about our energy situation. In fact, we've gone right back to the same type of operation we had. Wouldn't you think, for goodness sake, that they would have done a better job stockpiling oil? Or, they would make some alternate arrangements to be energy self-sustaining? No, we're still debating whether to build nuclear generating stations because Jane Fonda says they're not the right thing to do.

So without a national industrial policy we have to contend with employers, who, rather than staying and working in this country, are moving their operations overseas to these dollar-a-day wage kind of countries. That's disastrous for this country. What jobs are going to be available for us if the economy continues to go offshore? If you want a real vigorous economy that maintains the standard of living that we have now with a viable middle class, you've got to have decent jobs, it's plain and simple.

It's just not our destiny to become a fifth-rate, low standard of living type of nation. So what we want to do is have these other countries emulate us. We've gone to these countries through our involvement with the ILO [International Labor Organization], and helped those people organize so they can get a decent standard of living. Why should they have to be paid off in the dark and get low wages, no fringes, and just cast aside like an old shoe? It's not fair, they're human beings like our people are.

I don't think it's fair to blame the lack of a national policy entirely on the present [Reagan] administration, but a great deal of blame can be cast in their direction. They have seen fit to completely disengage themselves from any involvement in trying to establish one, or even try to set up a fair trade program or deal with all these offshore runaway companies.

What can be more devastating to a community than a corporation that closes its doors and says, "Good by, we're leaving"? Isn't that kind of sad, really? Shouldn't there be some kind of restrictions, or some way of lessening the impact on that community? Shouldn't those people who are left behind be retrained? Who's responsible for that? The government isn't doing anything about it, and yet what does the constitution say, "They shall provide for the common good." I'm not a socialist, but there are certain things incumbent upon the government to provide safeguards against, and this government hasn't done anything.

The Members

Our members are naturally concerned about the fact that we are in a global economy, and that whatever happens in other parts of the world has a direct bearing on their livelihoods. I know there is a lot of churning among them over job displacement and job shortages. They get disenchanted with us and ask, "What do I pay all those dues for? I got laid off and you haven't done anything for me." What they don't realize is that if their dues run $200 a year, granted, a lot of money, it still wouldn't buy them membership in a YMCA. And they do get an awful lot of services for their dues, including a representative who goes to grievance proceedings on their behalf.

But you can still only really count on 10 percent of the membership to be actively involved in union affairs. We just have too many diversions now compared to, say, when trade unions were first getting a full head of steam. What was there to do in the thirties? The biggest thing I can think of was to go to a football or baseball game, and most didn't have enough money to do that. There was no TV. There was certainly no bowling to speak of. And there were no fast food shops. It was just a completely different way of life at that particular time. But one of the places you could go and vent your venom, and all your dissatisfactions, was at a union meeting.

So as a result of the elevation of the standard of living, the members now can do other things, everything is in their easy reach. You can take an airplane and be anyplace you want in a couple of hours for the most part. There's a myriad of changes that have taken place making it much more difficult to get people to go to union meetings, and it's particularly difficult when everything is going well for the union, or at their place of employment. If the member feels they have a good shop steward, business manager, and a good set of officers, they figure that's insurance for them. "They're doing the job, that's why I voted for them, and if they need me, they'll call me."

But any organization of our size will have members that just go along with the crowd, and others who are assertive and intelligent and want to be part of what's going on. And whenever you have nearly a million members, you also find someone off the deep end on something. But for the most part, our members are looking for the normal things in life, good wages and some job security.

My Work

The thing that excites me the most about working in the labor movement is being able to do something that will benefit a good number of people. If you can deliver a contract that has improvements, and enhance a person's ability to raise a family and provide a decent education, that's very satisfying for me. Or, helping someone with a grievance, and maybe winning a battle for them with a company, that's terrific. One of the most appealing things to me though is organizing. I think we have a message to bring to people who are unorganized. We can help them obtain a higher degree of security and a better way of life as far as jobs, pay, fringe benefits, things like that.

Employers however are also telling the unorganized that they can have it all, good wages, security, fringes, without a union. They've been pretty successful too with the help of those antiunion consultants and with right-to-work laws. However, anyone with any degree of intelligence knows that one person against an employer is a pretty uneven contest. So, what we try to do is to combat their initiatives with personal contacts. Our organizing staff is constantly making overtures to people to come in and see what's going on. To see if they can't be part of the mainstream of the trade union movement, and better their lives through joint ventures as opposed to individual efforts.

Organizing is really the one way to preserve an organization like this. We've been trying to organize clerical people in the utility industry, and people in these new Japanese funded companies in Tennessee, and other places. And we've been successful to a degree in those places. We're also trying to organize in the service industries, and in manufacturing where we service machinery, and construction where we do a lot of service work and maintenance. As well, we've had a great degree of success in our organizing efforts with minorities and with females. We have a fine working relationship with these groups because of our own example. We have a number of minorities on our staff, and they're able to get the message across to those groups. This is actually a very fair-minded organization.

So we have to do an effective job in organizing, and as well on the other issues facing us, like the health problems among our utility members that result from working with computer terminals, and employers' desire for two-tier wage systems.

I believe those two-tier systems are just self-defeating in most instances and predict that most of them will fall by the wayside. They just create more disharmony than anything else. Imagine yourself getting the top rate for a particular job, and then someone doing the same identical work as you is getting a couple of dollars per hour less. It's got to have a very debilitating effect on the operation, because you always have one person who's disenchanted with his job, and just figures he's getting the short end of the stick. Management can hold wages in far different ways than that. They could, for example, change the progression rate in a job's salary scale.

My aim with this organization is to bring it to the acme of its ninety-seven year history. I'm looking forward to celebrating our centennial in three years time, and hopefully be able to say at that time we've gotten in excess of a million members, that we improved our continued service to people in addressing their grievances, and gave greater assistance to our affiliate local unions in negotiating good solid contracts. We also want to have a higher level of cooperation with our employers. We want to be able to get together with them and see what we can do to promote the industry from which we all derive benefits.

Looking Forward

I don't know what people will say about me once I leave office. I'm a realist. I know that time has a tendency to, shall we say, make people kind of forget. I'll let history treat my activities in the proper fashion. I do know that retiring will be tough because the work has become such a big part of my life. But just like we're born to die, retirement will come. There's nothing you can do about it.

5. Sharing the Wealth

William H. Bywater

When I was a kid I was already a socialist in my thinking, not that I belonged to any party, but I just believed in a general theory that it isn't right for anyone to be poor, or not have enough food to give a child the requirements they really need.

William H. Bywater became president of the International Union of Electronic, Electrical, Salaried, Machine and Furniture Workers (IUE) in 1982. Prior to his election as president, he served as international secretary-treasurer (1980–1982) and was president of IUE District 3 (New York-New Jersey) from 1969 to 1980.

Mr. Bywater began his union career in 1941 in Local 425, New York City, where he held various local union offices, including the presidency. He became first chairman of the IUE-Sperry Rand Conference Board, leading all of IUE's Sperry locals in major contract negotiations with the corporation. He also served as District 3 executive secretary and as a troubleshooter for the international union, assisting locals throughout the IUE in crisis bargaining situations.

Since 1983, the IUE president has chaired the Coordinated Bargaining Committee (CBC) Steering Committee, which coordinates thirteen unions' negotiations with GE and Westinghouse. In 1985, the IUE and other CBC unions achieved a thirty-five-year goal of an agency shop[1] at those corporations.

Mr. Bywater often testifies before Congress on the need for the curbing of cheap labor imports, for labor law reform, and for plant closing legislation.

The IUE was founded in 1949 and during its first convention, it already had members on strike. In fact, throughout its history, the IUE has faced countless situations of tough bargaining, strikes, and picket lines. For example, during the 1950s and 1960s the union confronted at GE, the practice of Boulwareism (named after GE vice-president Lemuel Boulware), a management strategy that offered a "final" settlement to a union at the outset of collective bargaining negotiations. The IUE was also involved in a 156-day nationwide strike against Westinghouse in 1955–1956, and in 1969–1970 it spearheaded a thirteen-union walkout against GE.

Today, the IUE represents approximately 200,000 workers in the electrical manufacturing industry. Members are employed by such firms as GE, RCA, Sperry, and White Westinghouse. It also represents furniture workers, having recently effected a merger with the 24,000-member United Furniture Workers of America. The IUE has for many years protested American free trade policies and has vigorously pursued the protection of workers' rights. In fact, the following statement from the officers' report of the IUE's first convention seems to best sum up the union's philosophy:

> The IUE-CIO will concentrate all its strength and all its energy in doing an honest-to-God militant Trade Union down-to-earth job in improving pay, security and welfare conditions of the men and women who work in this industry, and fighting shoulder to shoulder with the other great Unions in the CIO, to build a stronger, healthier, happier America.[2]

* * *

I BELIEVE in what I'm doing. I believe that the most important thing for anyone who wants to advance any cause is to believe in it. If you go into it because you think it's like a business, you're not going to have the same fervor or desire to put across your point as you would when you believe in something. I believe in it, I believe in all that . . .

But in the labor movement there are unionists, and there are business unions. And I don't care for the business unions because I don't think they really believe in what labor is all about. It's just a job to them, it's a way of making a living and that's about it. There's no feeling of what the labor movement means to them. To me, the labor movement means an uplifting of people, and not just the organized people, but even the unorganized because many companies try to keep unions out by keeping up with whatever the labor movement does. So really it's an instrument for lifting up all of society in the United States. We can't solve all the problems, we don't have the strength that say, the NAM [National Association of Manufacturers] has, or others who have money. We have the strength of public opinion, and I think that works.

And unions over the years have in my opinion raised the standard of living. I give credit to those labor leaders who were active during the years when it was a real hardship for them, and their families, to go through the constant harassment and blacklisting that lots of them went through at the hands of companies. I haven't been asked to make those kind of sacrifices, so I don't compare myself to them. If I'd lived in their day I would hope that I could've been like they were. I think I would have. But it depends on the circumstances you're put under. People can feel that they'll come out good under pressure and may not. The only time you know really is when you're tested.

See, this is not only my job, it's my hobby. I love it, it's my life. I hate vacations. When my son went into the service, they put him in Hawaii, and my wife and I went to see him. It was the only time we ever went outside the continental states. While we were there I called my office every single day; and on Saturdays and Sundays, I'd call one of the union guys to talk about various problems. So with me, if I work ten hours, twelve hours, that's nothing. I don't count the time. The only pressure that I have that takes me away from the office is my wife. She deserves a vacation, and I'm not really fair to her in many respects because there's always some crisis, negotiations or something else, that I have to attend to. When we've made plans, we have often had to amend those plans. That's not really fair to her and I don't really correct it totally. I try to in some degree.

And if you're really dedicated to the labor movement, you're not really looking to make money. I'm making money because I'm the president of the union. But if you're in the labor movement, you're not really thinking in terms of making money, you're there because of what you believe in. That's the advantage the communists always had in the labor movement, because they believed in what they were doing, and you could get them to work for practically nothing because of their beliefs.

Yet, there's a selfishness in this country that's very unhealthy, and it's going to get worse before it gets better. It's a kind of "I've got mine, Jack, screw you" [attitude]. It doesn't have to be that way. You know, for one day they cheered the Statue of Liberty and all the fireworks went off, and then it's all forgotten about, liberty and all that sort of thing. Another day, everybody holds hands across the nation, and that's the end of it, they've done their share, that's it. "I held hands, I looked at the Statue of Liberty" and that's it. They got it out of the way, then it's "I'm going to the movies, I can enjoy myself, I can do this, that, and the other thing."

This whole attitude is very different from when I was growing up in Queens [New York City] during the Depression. When my mother was sick one time and had to go to the hospital, to a free hospital, the woman next door fed me. She was poor too, but she fed me. When she got sick later on, my mother took care of her daughter. When someone would catch a batch of fish, they would knock on your door and give you a flounder, you know. Or if somebody went out for a bushel of apples, since they couldn't eat them all, they'd come and give you some.

It was just a different feeling then. There was a feeling among families who were all in the same predicament, that we ought to help each other. You don't have that today. Maybe in some small towns, but you don't have it to the extent that I've seen it anyway. So when I was a kid I was already a socialist in my thinking, not that I belonged to any party, but I just believed in a general theory that it isn't right for anyone to be poor, or not have enough food to give a child the requirements they really need. I felt that I'd like to have something to do in my life to raise the standard of living of people.

Those who were brought up in the thirties knew what to struggle was all about. They had it in their gut, and they believed in unions. You don't have that much any more. When I stood up on a bench in Ford Instrument and told everybody to stop working, everybody did. Everybody, the whole damned assembly floor. There must have been 800 people in that one area and they all just stopped and all listened to me. There was discipline, they believed in the union. The union meant something to them. It was an important thing to them, you see?

You don't teach that kind of spirit people felt back then. Now kids go into a plant, the company gets hold of them and tells them they got this benefit, that benefit, so forth. They think the company gave it to them, and that's what the company tells them. But it was the union that got it. I had to beat the hell out of the company to get those benefits for our people. Then if you go to an unorganized plant and they have a lot of good benefits, what people don't understand is that they get them because the company wants to keep the union out, that's why they're giving those benefits! The union doesn't get credit for that. We get beat over the head instead—"bunch of crooks." Anything happens, some corrupt union does something, all you hear is "bunch of crooks, yeah that's the way they are . . ." That's what we get in the press, and it's unfortunate.

Getting Started

After I left high school I couldn't find a job anywhere. Every place I went they'd ask what experience did I have. What experience does a kid have? And that was during the Depression. It was bad in 1939. Really bad. So I would take whatever job—any damn thing—a dollar here, a dollar there, you know you never did make much in those days. Finally I got a job cleaning machines at Remington-Rand, just doing dirty work. But I got lucky one day after I'd been there a couple of months. Two people were out. It was a small shop and they didn't have extras, they just had whatever they needed. So they put me on the drill press first, then they put me on the bench lathe . . . in a matter of three, four months I was an apprentice tool and die maker. I was learning the trade.

While I was there I started talking about organizing a union. But when I talked about it to the older fellows, even though they liked me, they got afraid for what I might do. At the time I didn't realize what they were concerned about—I was a young kid and a bit of a smartaleck, and thought, "Hell, what's the matter? Are you afraid of the foreman?" and that sort of thing. But I realized later on though that they had families, and couldn't afford to lose their jobs because they were messing around with a union.

Well, I quit there, and about a year later took a job with Sperry Division, which is Ford Instrument. They didn't work you like they did at Remington-Rand. Remington-Rand was a sweatshop, you worked very hard. When I got into Ford Instrument, which was a defense plant, the foreman asked me, "Can you read a blueprint?" I said, "Yeah, of course I can read a blueprint." He said, "All right, see those motors? I want you to assemble those motors." So I assembled all the motors that he had on all the shelves, it was about seven shelves of motors. I came back to him and asked him for the next job and he said, "Take the next motor." I told him that I did all of them but he couldn't believe it. The windup, which I didn't realize at the time was, "What's the matter with you, kid, you trying to work yourself out of a job?"

So to avoid that I got in the habit of reading in the men's room. And occasionally I'd hear some argument going on, and I'd get into it. And before you knew it, I was having lots of arguments and lectures with people in the men's room. The old Germans that worked in the plant liked me, they were old-time German Socialists, and one day they put my name up as a nominee for steward. I guess they did it because the incumbent steward was very cozy with the foreman, and I had answered the foreman back—I wasn't afraid of him. I was just a young kid.

So anyway they voted me in, even though it was against the union's constitution because I had only been there something like five months, and you needed six months to be a steward. And both the chief steward and the president tried to convince the others that I shouldn't get the position because of the rule, and all this crap. Well I'll never forget the one German guy, who, when the president asked him "Why'd you elect this kid?", he said, "Because Bywater is too damn dumb to be afraid of the boss." And that was the start of my career.

Old and New

I'm a left-winger, but certainly not a wild-eyed one. I think I'm basically the same person I was when I was in my early twenties. I don't think I've changed that much. I still have the same principles and philosophy that I had when I was a kid. I would probably say one thing that has changed in me is the way I'd handle different situations. When I was in the shop for example, I'd think nothing of telling a foreman who tried moving a bench, which was out of his classification, "I'll knock you on your ass if you touch that again." And I would do it, he knew I would do it. I was really very super militant.

That's the way I was—you're young, you're crazy like that. When I stood up on the bench at Ford Instrument and told everyone to stop working, I mean that was a stupid thing for me to do. It worked, but it was stupid. I wouldn't do that now, I'd file a grievance or create a slowdown in some way where you couldn't actually point a finger and say, "Hey, he stopped the plant from working." I'd do it in a more subtle way. I am more of a diplomat now than I was as a kid.

And while I've never really been in favor of concessions, I'm not one of those who's going to say, "We never make concessions." I think that's bullshit. If you want to save a plant, you may have to make concessions. When I look at the labor movement, I don't look at it as one contract and that's it. For example, we had a strike up in Grand Rapids, Michigan, with a company that really was out to break the union. Prior to the strike, they had hired these people that they called "knuckles." They were a real antilabor group who where there to beat the hell out of the strikers—that's about what it amounted to. And that did happen. They beat up some of our guys. And so our guys got together and beat the shit out of them, O.K.? So when they learned that we have tough guys, the knuckles stopped fighting. I can import guys if I have to, no problem. I know where some tough guys are, in some plants, who could do anything.

So anyway the strike went on for almost a year. I think it was about the eleventh month the company notified the union that they were going to replace everyone permanently. In order to try to get the plant moving, they brought in about 400 scabs. These people are hungry. Not that they want to break a union, but they're hungry so they go for the job, right? So our people called them scabs and everything else, but they went in there and they did the job. But they didn't do the job very well, and the company realized that, and so they asked that our people come back.

But they said that if they're not back by the end of the year, they were going to replace all of them permanently, which they could do. We won some unfair labor practice charges against the company, and they posted the fact that they were guilty, as the NLRB required, but that's all they had to do. It didn't mean anything. It didn't mean a damn thing.

Finally I went in there to talk to the membership. The company was going to fire fifty people. I told the president of the district, "Tell that company that's one thing I will not go along with at all. If that's their position, that they're going to be fired, I want you to know that that strike will continue on 'til doomsday. On the other hand, if they suspend people, I'll go along with a suspension provided that they'll be able to get back to work."

So he went in there and talked to the employers, but they wouldn't budge beyond a one-year suspension for fifteen of our people. So what I did was put the fifteen people on our payroll; the IUE paid them out of the strike fund and used them organizationally for that year. We got better than what we went out for, but not as good as what we wanted.

I told some of the young people there, "Don't look at it as one contract. If you look at this one contract, we're taking a beating. You're only in your twenties—just think, you'll be around for maybe ten more contracts, so you'll have a chance to improve it." I told them that "The company is now able to take a strike, but that wasn't always going to be the case, and then you'll get back a lot of things they took away from you, plus others."

That was a very unhappy situation. That was the only experience I ever had where I had to tell people to go back when in my own mind I felt the strike was justified. The company was 100 percent wrong. By the way, not one of our members went through that strike line. Not one person scabbed. All the scabs were from the outside.

So I do things now more in a diplomatic way and work the system as much as I can. Who knows how I would've handled this situation when I was younger.

With the climate of the country today, though, companies that make money will still ask for concessions, it doesn't matter. Emerson made a lot of money, but they're still asking for concessions. They want to make more. General Motors had a bad year compared with last year. They only made $1 billion, you know? I mean it's one of those things.

Outsourcing

Let me tell you something else about what these companies are doing. You know, people talk about a shorter work week and really when you have automation and robotization coming along, which you're going to have more and more of in the next ten, twenty years, shorter workweeks obviously make sense, except for one thing. We deal with the rest of the world. So if we were to say, "O.K. we want forty hours pay for thirty hours work . . ."

something I used to say back in the 1940s, that's fine, but then it made sense. It doesn't now because if you do that, the company is just going to move overseas! They're going to do what they call "outsourcing," which means stealing your job, O.K.? And that's what's going to happen. There's going to be more and more of that.

So shorter weeks are not the answer anymore. The answer has to come through legislation, and while I don't think this bill right now, HR 4800, is a solution to all problems, it's a help. And it gives a signal to the other countries, "Don't keep screwing us." I argued against free trade back in 1964 when we were losing all of this country's will and know-how and everything else that the government sent offshore. I made a big to-do about that for years, but people wouldn't listen to me. I even had fights internally with my own union about it. I was always in opposition to free trade, because it was just plain stupid.

I would believe in free trade if there really were free trade, if these multinational corporations weren't allowed to just take the money overseas, and keep reinvesting it there because if they brought the money back they'd be taxed. So if we had laws that prevented giving the know-how to another country, and let them raise corn or rice or whatever damn thing they were going to raise, rather than becoming an industrial country when their people don't even have enough to eat, yeah, I'd be for free trade. I'm not for free trade now, it's horseshit. That's the way I feel about it.

The Members

Everyone today is concerned about job security. That's the number one item in everyone's mind, and you hear it over and over again. The older guys say, "We'll get out if you give us a bigger pension." It doesn't necessarily follow that they all will do it, but I think they say it anyway because they feel the pressure from the younger guy who wants to move up the seniority ladder.

But we did get an early retirement plan at GE and in Westinghouse. We took some of the steam out of the pressure cooker somewhat because we worked out an agreement. I'm not saying this to brag, but I was the one that really pushed in the direction of giving extra money to the high seniority people to get them out. My argument went along the lines that you're going to save, in many cases on rates, because the younger guys don't get the same rate of pay. And secondly, people get sick when they're in their fifties or sixties much quicker than a person in their twenties or thirties, and so you'll save on insurances. Well, they bought it and quite a few people took advantage of the plan.

Some of our locals, like myself, are very social conscious. But you'll probably also hear a lot of bigotry from some too. In fact, I think the reason

Reagan was elected was because they thought he was a bigot as well. They were just very comfortable with him on the race issue, and he gave them a lot of signals.

It's like when I was chief steward in my plant. There were some openings in the wire department, and I tried to get some of the blacks who were working as porters to apply for the jobs. All the dirty jobs in that plant were done by the blacks—porters, or general helpers, things of that sort. Now some of them didn't fill out the applications because they just couldn't read or write, but some did after I pushed them—and pushed them very hard. I remember the big boss saying, "Why do you want to bring these Goddamn niggers up here?" and that was his position. He was prejudiced.

Well, we got them those jobs. I just pushed and pushed, and got them in. I said "Under the contract, the first shot goes to those who are in the plant, and these people deserve it." So they went ahead with it and brought three black fellows up into the wire department, and two of them succeeded.

But the shocker for me was, really the shocker, was all these guys in the assembly department who loved me, really loved me, suddenly went into a revolution because these two blacks were there, whom they called "niggers." But the strangest thing happened. One of the most hostile guys in the wire department, he and another jerk, the other fellow was probably a little worse than he, wound up after some months sitting down and playing checkers with one of the black guys. But, oh God, I had guys come to me who liked me and said, "Gee, Bill, you've hurt yourself politically," and all this other stuff. It was all bullshit, and I'd tell them so. I used to argue with everybody over that issue, you know? I'd get a whole bunch of them around, and tell them what I thought.

6. "Look for the Union Label"

Sol C. Chaikin

Remember, where there are no free trade unions, there are no human rights.

Sol Chick Chaikin, born in 1918 in New York, attended the College of the City of New York and graduated from Brooklyn Law School in 1940. He immediately went to work as an organizer for the International Ladies' Garment Workers' Union (ILGWU), and later served in a variety of posts including business agent, district manager, director, international vice-president, and secretary-treasurer. In 1975 he was elected president of the union.

In recognition of his efforts on behalf of human rights throughout the world, President Jimmy Carter named Mr. Chaikin a member of the U.S. Delegation to the Commission for Security and Cooperation in Europe to review the Helsinki Agreement. He is also associated with a variety of organizations concerned with international affairs, including the Trilateral Commission, the Council on Foreign Relations, Freedom House, and the International Rescue Committee.

Both Rutgers University and the City University of New York have conferred honorary degrees of Doctor of Humane Letters upon Mr. Chaikin, citing his community activity and service to the public.

He serves as a trustee of Long Island Jewish Medical Center, Brandeis University, and the Fashion Institute of Technology. Mr. Chaikin is also chairman of the board of the Jacob Javits Convention Center of New York.

At its national convention in June 1986, Mr. Chaikin retired from active service of the ILGWU and was elected president emeritus.

The International Ladies' Garment Workers' Union (the "ILG") was founded on June 3, 1900 in New York City by delegates of several craft unions within the ladies garment industry. During the 1920s the ILG was racked with factional disputes among Communists, Socialists, and Anarchists, which severely depleted the union's finances and membership.

In 1932 David Dubinsky was elected president, and under his leadership, the ILG settled on a more democratic course, with a commitment to a comprehensive program of social unionism. To enhance the quality of life of its members, the ILG pioneered the establishment of union health centers, mobile health units, recreation facilities, portability and reciprocity of health and vacation funds, and other social services.

As a result of increased American purchases of foreign produced apparel through the 1970s and 1980s (in 1987, nearly sixty percent of women's and children's apparel purchased in the United States was foreign made) the ILG's membership suffered significant declines. Membership fell from 351,795 in 1977, to approximately 173,000 in 1987. The ILG includes 401 locals and represents workers in thirty-seven states, Puerto Rico, and Canada.

In response to the significant loss in membership, the leadership, especially Mr. Chaikin, have steadfastly demanded federal government enforcement of antidumping provisions, retaliation against countries that subsidize exports, and revision of U.S. tax laws that encourage overseas production by American business.

* * *

I must tell you that I have been preparing for my retirement for about six or seven years. I thought if I were reelected, served, and survived until now, that I would retire on the occasion of our national convention of July 1986. And everything I've done since making that decision had the future years of the union in mind. For example, I advanced the interest of capable, competent, dedicated younger people, and saw to it that they had the right opportunities, so that the ILG would have a cadre of effective leaders for the future.

I thought of myself as well. I knew that I just couldn't go out to pasture. I had too many interests that I wanted to pursue but didn't always have the time while I was an active president and a senior member of the AFL-CIO's Executive Council. Now as president emeritus—our union is unique in the sense that every retired president who's served an appreciable length of time in the office becomes emeritus—it's possible for me to pursue some of these other activities.

To begin with, I'm the chairman of the board of directors of the Jacob

K. Javits New York Convention Center. . . . Now that takes almost a day a week of my time between board meetings, discussions with political leaders who have some oversight responsibilities, meetings with the executive officers of the center, setting policy, and reviewing complaints that we get either from the public or from the people who use it.

I have also become a director of a bank. Now that's a very great departure for a union leader, and it came about in a very strange way. But back about six or seven years ago, I had been invited to make a major presentation to about 600 deans and senior management faculty attending a meeting of the Association of Deans of Collegiate Schools of Business. It was a surprise when they asked me, since I was the first union officer ever to be invited to address the group. So I decided to accept the challenge and spoke to them about what I considered to be some of the difficulties, indeed dangers, of interlocking directorates, and about morality in business and the importance of teaching ethical values. I stressed to the group that they had a huge responsibility in inculcating positive values among their students, who will eventually become the captains of industry.

The third thing that I talked about was the danger that I saw in the evolution of corporate ownership. Theoretically, stockholders own a corporation, at least that's how it was meant to be, and it's their duty to elect the board of directors, who then in turn choose the executive officers of the corporation. But as the corporate entity evolved, officers of corporations have become members of the board of directors, and in many corporations these so-called "inside directors" are a majority of the board and become a self-perpetuating group.

I said in my presentation that this was wrong and a perversion. I know that stockholders don't exercise their rights as owners, I don't kid myself about that, and that's why I believe it is the responsibility of every corporation to have a majority of outside directors on their boards. These outside independent directors then could judge the performance of the executives of the corporation, and fairly set their salaries and bonuses, etcetera, and protect the rights of the owners.

Well anyway, when I retired from the ILG I got a call from a friend of mine who heads one of the big investment banking houses there on Wall Street and who asked me to come down and have lunch and just chat. He asked me, "What are you going to be doing with yourself now?" And I told him about some of my activities, about being a trustee of Brandeis University and of a medical center in New York City, that I had been doing some lecturing, and raising funds for a medical care project in Israel, and my service as a member of the executive board of the Franklin and Eleanor Roosevelt Institute.

He probably didn't think I was busy enough and asked me, "Why don't you come to work with me?" I said, "No way, I just gave up the best job in America and I'm not looking for another job." But what he had to say turned out to be very interesting. The thing that he wanted to get me involved in was the bank which his company had established, actually one of those "nonbank banks"—a custodial trust company. When he introduced me to some of the people involved, it turned out that one of them was a former professor of management who heard my presentation about the paucity of outside directors, and so that's how I became a member of the board of directors of the bank.

The Exercise of Authority

Although we live in a democratic society, it's a paradox that some of the components of our society operate in a nondemocratic posture. That's one of the reasons, for example, that I spoke to those deans of business schools about the importance of outside directors. But I also realize that making an automobile is not a democratic procedure and that there has got to be an exercise of authority. The buck has to stop somewhere, and someone has to say, "No, we'll do it this way." You can't always have a democratic vote. It's true for a board of trustees, and I have no hesitance in saying that it was true of this union when I was president. Let me give you an example of why that has to be.

A manufacturer located in New York traditionally has the nice end of the business. He raises the capital, buys the fabric, hires the designer and salesmen, and all of the things that would go with it. And while he would probably also cut the fabric needed for his designs on his own premises, when it came to sewing those pieces together into a product, he'd send them to a fellow across the street whose only virtue is that he has space, sewing machines, and workers. That fellow is known as a contractor, but he's not the only contractor working for the manufacturer. The manufacturer would probably also send 5,000 garments to a contractor in Massachusetts, and 3,000 to one in Pennsylvania, and maybe 7,000 to a contractor in Virginia.

As you can tell we are very different from other trades in this regard. For example, it doesn't matter one goddamned bit what the Boston bricklayer business agent, or cement finisher business agent, or carpenter business agent, negotiates on wages to the building trades people in Worcester, Massachusetts. It doesn't matter whether they get $16 an hour, $26 an hour, or $8 an hour, because the carpenter in Worcester knows what they get in Boston has no real effect on the availability of work in his town. If you want to build a building in Worcester, you're going to build a building in Worcester, and the fact that a carpenter in Boston might work for less doesn't mean much. These products are not sold on a national market, they're not mobile.

You can't just build a building in the desert of Arizona for cheap wages and put it on a flat car and move it.

However, that's what can happen in the garment industry. The manufacturer is free to send it to California, Mississippi, or Pennsylvania. Our goods are mobile. Now, how is a union to cope with a situation of that nature? Well, you need somebody to be the coordinator, the "judge," and the "enforcer." And in our union, technically, that's the president. If you didn't have someone doing it, you would have extraordinary cutthroat competition among the employees on wages and benefits just to get the work, and all of the work will go to the lowest paying factory.

Individual and Management Rights

We've told our employers, compete on style; compete on merchandising; compete on deliveries; compete on who is able to raise capital for less; compete on manufacturing efficiency, your own talent, your effort, your knowledge, drive—but no way do we want you to compete on the backs of the workers.

But they're not listening, and that's the reason we're suffering in the garment industry today. Sixty percent of all ladies' and children's apparel sold in America comes from overseas, where naturally we have no control. There's no way I can tell the workers in Hong Kong they must not work for $1.08 an hour, no way I can say to the workers in China you must not work for the equivalent of $.21 an hour.

Management says it's their right to go where the costs are less. Well, if it's a right, the exercise of it has caused a lot of trauma, and distress, and despair, and frustration in this country. But most of them don't give a good goddamn that they're weakening the fiber of America. I had a guy say to me, "Chick, I'm no longer an American company, I'm an international company!" I said, "Sure, but the first goddamned time somebody overseas takes control of your factory, you're gonna run down to the State Department and tell them to send troops to protect your property." You can couch it in any terms you want—that they have a right to do it, that they have a mission from the Lord Almighty to do it, but these rights are not unrestricted.

Let me explain something. I recall when all of the labor and social legislation was coming out of Washington during the period of the New Deal. Do I have to repeat to you the damned slogans that these same manufacturers used against the establishment of wage and hour laws? They screamed, "Liberty! Freedom to contract!" and hollered, "What do you mean the government of the United States demands that if I'm in an industry affected by interstate commerce that I have to pay a minimum of $.25 an hour to the worker? Don't I have a God-given right to hire that worker for $.20? or

$.15?" And that's what they paid in 1933, '34, '35. I mean people worked in garment shops in Fall River, Massachusetts, for fifty-six hours a week for $3! So management quoted all of their so-called God-given rights, but a community has rights and obligations as well.

There are obviously individual rights, but they have to be measured within the general community needs. You've got the right to free speech, but you can't just yell "fire" in a crowded theater. Somebody'll beat the living shit out of you and throw you in jail! You've got the right to free speech, but you can't incite to riot!

Another example of where a community's obligations ought to take precedence involves a landmark case going on right now in New York on the homeless. About six or seven years ago they emptied out a lot of mental institutions in New York state, they were "de-institutionalizing," and a lot of these people wound up on the streets of localities which don't have the resources to take care of them. So all of a sudden we have not only homeless, but mentally ill homeless. People of America sleeping on the streets, defecating on the street, ill and diseased. It was such a disgrace that Mayor Koch of New York City ordered city personnel to go around and pick up the homeless who were not capable of fending for themselves. Can you believe the Civil Liberties Union offers the defense that those homeless have a God-given right to be on the street! No way.

The Image of Labor

Since retiring I've been doing quite a bit of lecturing on various labor related topics. For example, I've gone to Fordham Law School, the Jesuit Council, the Harvard Graduate School of Business, University of Minnesota, Columbia Graduate School of Business, among other places. I do these "PR" things to keep me alive and also to demonstrate that the labor leadership is not somebody with horns and forked tail.

The labor movement though has always had difficulty with its PR. All the media loves that stuff about Jimmy Hoffa and Jackie Presser, they love it just like they love a juicy murder. Look how the media wrote up the reaffiliation of the Teamsters, not as something based on trade union principles, but as "a hope of the Teamsters that the prestige of the AFL-CIO will interpose itself between the government's reported efforts to trustee the international." I didn't hear a commentator say that there were any positives in the Teamsters' reaffiliating, like making the house of labor stronger, or that it will end some of the raiding, and so forth. All they did was talk about the negatives!

I want you to know that about five years ago, Lane Kirkland, as a result of conversation around the executive council, was asked to open discussions with the Teamsters about reaffiliating, and there were even some discussions held with the Teamsters then, but they were not interested in it. Yet, if the reaffiliation took place then, few in the media would've written negatively about it. Jackie Presser, the Teamster's president, back then was not under indictment, he was the fair-haired boy in the White House . . .

We've never, never, never thought seriously in terms of public relations. Certainly not in the sense of hiring somebody, as Lee Iacocca has, to put his best face before the electorate and the consuming public. We've never thought in terms of merchandising either our ideas or our own personalities.

For example, very few people know that we refused to have anything to do with the so-called trade union movement in Egypt because it was a coopted movement. But after President Sadat of Egypt made his extraordinary visit to Jerusalem, George Meany sent me and an official delegation to Egypt because he thought the changes taking place in Egypt ought to be encouraged.

And few people know that I was sent to Buenos Aires by President Carter and Meany to see what we could do to help those in the Argentinian labor movement who were moving away from the Peronista ideas, and to see if I could get some of their leaders out of jail. I even had a list with about ten names of missing labor leaders for their government's consideration. They found and released a couple of them before we left the country, but claimed no record of the others. Perhaps they didn't, because they were using freelance vigilante squads to pick people off the streets and do away with them. Remember, where there are no free trade unions, there are no human rights.

And on another occasion, President Gleason of the Longshoremen and I went to Chile for a solidarity visit with the labor leaders there. While there, I spoke with Chilean president Pinochet for three hours, encouraging his government to reestablish full human rights and a free trade union movement in Chile.

And few people know that Meany together with six other trade union leaders would meet often with the top industrialists in America. We did it very quietly and unofficially, and without publicity. I remember going to the Exxon headquarters to meet with Cliff Garvin, who was then the head of Exxon, Steve Bechtel of the Bechtel Corporation, Roger Smith of GM, and Reginald Jones of GE to talk about things of mutual interest. We'd talk about legislation, we'd talk prounion, antiunion, probusiness, antibusiness. We didn't particularly persuade each other but we were on a first-name basis, and we explored mutual problems very quietly, very circumspectly. There's more to what goes on with labor and management than meets the eye.

Anyway, a lot of our activities are just not known by many people, nor do they really know labor's leaders. For instance, George Meany was a remarkable exponent of American trade unionism. He was honest, loaded with integrity, very bright, always mindful of his responsibility not only to the membership of the AFL-CIO but to the general community, and he was a stalwart defender of democracy and fighter for freedom and human rights everywhere.

But he never tooted his own horn, and he would probably consider it degrading to hire a press agent to do it. He was his own press agent, just as I was, just as John L. Lewis, David Dubinsky, my predecessor in the ILG, Walter Reuther—would he have hired a press agent? These are people who had just supreme confidence in their ability to articulate and communicate their ideas. They were confident in their leadership, and in their intelligence, there's just no question about that. Iacocca wrote his [auto] biography. It was ghostwritten. Perfectly all right, no problem. And the same with Iacocca on television selling Chrysler automobiles.

But let me give you a graphic difference between ourselves, and others who advertise themselves. In 1975 I became president of the ILG, and for many reasons decided to do some advertising to tell people a little bit about our union. We wanted to talk about American-made products and union-made products, and to convey the message through the so-called "union label" song. So, we hired an advertising agency who suggested using national network television for our spots. I thought it was beyond our capacity, when one of them asked, "President Chaikin, have you ever considered television?" I said, "Television? Who the hell can afford television?" Well, we went into it and eventually spent $18 million. You have to realize that's not a great deal of money in advertising. Procter & Gamble spends $18 million in three or five days of the year.

Anyhow, the difference between us and others is that when they asked me to be the spokesman on the program, I said no way. The campaign had nothing to do with me, my face, or my name, I wanted people to know the International Ladies' Garment Workers' Union. The members were paying for it, and it's theirs. We never believed we needed to embellish the story that we had to say, or had to "commercialize the institution." We don't have a product, we have an idea. We're not selling soap.

So we've never compared ourselves to Lee Iacocca, who sells cars, or himself, or himself in an effort to sell his cars. Perfectly all right. He's merchandising a product. . . . However, I am perfectly aware of the difficulties that we have had in getting our idea across without going down that route.

Looking Back

Since we just talked about leadership, let me tell you about some of the labor leaders, the great ones in an historic sense, whom I've had the privilege of knowing. As I already said, George Meany was a towering, towering person.

Solid, stable, little cant, and no hypocrisy. Oh, I was a great admirer of his. Even U.S. presidents would cower before Meany.

Let me tell you something about that. I was very friendly with Jimmy Carter, friendly enough so that in 1980 he asked me to second his nomination for the presidency of the United States. . . . Well, he was having a difficult time with Meany and asked me, "Chick, how do I deal with Meany? Why can't we be more compatible, more interacting and forthcoming?" My response was, "I'm going to tell you how to do it, but you will not like it, and you will not do it." I said, "You have to treat George Meany as a sovereign power."

You see, George Meany used to be invited by Kennedy often to have lunch, dinner, a drink. . . . Lyndon Johnson used to call Meany often to talk about all sorts of things, and "Why don't you come over for a drink, George?" Do you know, and you can check this in Washington, that every meaningful foreign leader who came to Washington would pay a call on George Meany. He was a great friend of Conrad Adenauer—they were on a first-name basis. I know personally Adenauer used to send him a case of fine German wine every year through the diplomatic pouch. When Juan Carlos, the King of Spain, the young one, would come to Washington he'd always ask to see George Meany, just to sit and chat.

And there are leaders of other countries who wanted to see him, but if he was not convinced they were advancing the interest of workers and the democratic spirit in their own country, he'd say "no way." He thought Nassar of Egypt was a vicious dictator, and he had no use . . . for Juan Peron.

Meany also named every member of the Executive Council from the time I got on. He was a jewel.

David Dubinsky was a dynamic personality, volatile and very charismatic. He spoke with strength to his audience, who were mostly immigrants, substantially Jewish, many Italian and a smattering of others.

And Dubinsky was quite shrewd—but not in the sense of being manipulative—very creative, and had the great talent of attracting very bright people. He was a Socialist as an adult, but when FDR was running for the White House, he left the Socialist party and became a Democrat. He was anticommunist to the core, and battled them in New York City politics and even in our own union. I would say, on balance, he was a very unusual guy, and when I tell people about him I generally say, "David Dubinsky was a man of towering, towering virtues, and equally towering vices." Frankly, if he were white anglo-saxon protestant he would be nationally known.

I hold Walter Reuther in as high regard as David Dubinsky. Reuther was a student of Dubinsky's and they were very close friends. The ILG was very supportive of Reuther, and helped him become the president of the UAW. We gave him the money to support the GM department's 120-day strike in 1946. In fact, I've kidded Doug Fraser and Owen Bieber, [presidents of the UAW], about still owing us $100,000 plus interest compounded from 1946.

I happen to like Lane Kirkland very much—he's a close personal friend of mine. Lane is intellectually far superior than Meany, although you couldn't fault Meany in that department. Lane happens to be an exception, though, and while he writes magnificently, he doesn't speak as well as I would like, but he's improved over the years. Where Meany exuded strength and confidence, Lane is laid back, like the southerner he is.

You know, lots of people think that union organizations began in the 1930s during the height of the Depression. Far from it. In fact, our union was founded in 1900, and we're not the oldest union! There are a good couple of handfuls of unions that started in the 1880s, 1885, and it's remarkable how they were able to remain alive during that period when there was such extraordinary concentration of economic power and wealth in the hands of the industrial giants, like Carnegie, Rockefeller, and the railroad magnates.

And the struggle continued even beyond the first World War, when there was great political revulsion against unions, and even attacks on them as a kind of reflection of the Bolshevik revolution in the Soviet Union. Everybody was scared to death that unions might go in that direction and hurt the domestic tranquillity, and so unions were viewed as enemies. You had the Palmer raids and all of the other acts of suppression and attempted suppression. But we survived all that. And yet, some things haven't changed. There are some 33,000 unfair labor practices presented to the federal government each year, and every day somebody's being fired for union activity. While there are no Pinkertons, there still is some violence—sporadic, but thankfully nothing like it used to be.

Getting Started

I was the third college boy that was hired by David Dubinsky to work for the ILG. One of the others was Gus Tyler, who is our assistant president—that's his technical title, but he's really director of our educational department. He's the big brain, the house intellectual. The third fellow was Bill Gottenberg, who started our first management engineering department. We used to help contractors set up their machinery so there'd be a smooth flow of work and they'd be more efficient. It was an unusual department, but we've always been a unique union in all of the things that we've done. Our theory was that the more efficient the employer was, the better opportunity we had of getting an extra nickel an hour.

Well anyway, Dubinsky was afraid when I spoke to him the first time about a job that what I really wanted to do was be a lawyer for the union. And when I told him I wanted to be an organizer, he looked at me and said, "Why does a nice Jewish boy like you want to be a union organizer?"

Well, the answer was because my parents were members of the ILG and I used to get the stories of life in the factory, the difficulties, the exploitation, and the feelings for a class struggle all with my mother's milk. You know, when I was growing up and my parents' friends would come by, we'd give them a glass of tea and cookies, that was the extent of the hospitality you could afford back then. Conversation though would always relate to work. What the hell else did these people do that was of equal importance?

And so as a youngster, I became enticed by the socialist theory of production for use and not for profit. In other words, you only produce things that people need, not because you can make a profit. It was the old socialist theory of "to each according to his needs, from each according to his ability." It's really an idealistic concept, but I thought it was fantastic. However, when I got ready to attend the College of the City of New York, I asked myself a question, "If a worker gets everything he needs, and in return he works according to his ability, who's going to clean the shithouses?" I don't mean that literally, although that was my question. In other words, who's going to do the dirty, dangerous, gut-ripping hard jobs? Why would I pour molten iron, work in a hot, steamy, dirty, filthy steel mill, or, would I be a sand-hog and dig tunnels a hundred feet under Boston Harbor? Would I want to work as a riveter on those buildings going up in New York? I don't know if you are aware of the fact but guys doing that job would have to take a red hot, I mean blazing hot, rivet from the coals with a pair of tongs, and then throw it over to an another guy who was working on a steel plate maybe eighteen feet or more away.

Well, I looked at those jobs and wondered who would do it in a socialist world. I mean, you have to be a schmuck to volunteer, 'cause you are not going to get any more compensation than anyone else. That's why the Soviets started the system of *Stakhanovism*—you know what that means? There was a worker by the name of Stakhanov, a miner, who at some point produced more kilos of coal than any other miner. He was a super worker and they gave him a medal. Then somebody said, "Why shouldn't the other workers do as well, or almost as well?"—and so the system of offering bonuses and extra money began. So it was no longer "to each according to his needs." Well, listen, if I'm going to vie with somebody else, you know, compete with somebody else for material reward, I'd rather do it in a capitalistic society. Why should I let the state be the capitalist? So I was gradually weaned away from socialism.

But anyway, in my last semester of law school I realized that I really didn't want to be a lawyer. What I really wanted was to be a part of this new thing going on in America. It was from 1935 to 1940, the height of

FDR's push for administrative bureaus and labor legislation, and all sorts of fights before the Supreme Court over the constitutionality of these things. And I decided if I were going to be part of it, I had to be part of it through the ILG. That's why I wrote to Dave Dubinsky, and asked him for a job interview. After my interview with him, I had another interview with a vice-president later on, and we went through the same paces as it was with Dubinsky, essentially "Why does a nice Jewish boy, a lawyer, like you want to become a union organizer?" But lo and behold, on August 14th, 1940, I got a letter from this vice-president telling me to report for work on that Monday with enough clothes to last me for a week—the letter didn't say where I was going. I remember the day because it's the same day I learned that I was among the 350 or so—out of the thousands who took it—to pass the bar exam. The coincidence was extraordinary.

Well, my new job paid twenty bucks a week, plus $2.00 a day for room and board. It was a living wage at the time. Young lawyers in New York City would have to scrounge around for a job, and if they were lucky, they got a law clerk position that paid $5.00 or $7.00 a week.

There was no formal training for becoming an organizer back then— you just picked it up, depended on your ability to articulate, and behave in a way that exuded a little stability and some confidence. In fact, though, it was easy in those days to attract workers to you. In Fall River [Massachusetts], where I started organizing, jobs were scarce, but in spite of that, practically all you had to say was, "Aren't you interested in earning a couple of dollars more, don't you think you ought to have some measure of job security? Join the union and improve your conditions."

Salaries and Unionism

It's certainly harder for us to organize today than it was when I started doing it in 1940. We're victims of our own success. I'm embarrassed when football players who earn up to $800,000 or a million dollars go out on strike under the coloration of a trade union. Very frankly, I would never have permitted them to join the AFL-CIO. I just don't believe that people who are in a circumstance where they are being compensated enormously compared to the average median of earnings of workers should use a form of union organization as an element of coercion. They're behaving like medieval guilds, which I never liked. So I'm not happy with unions of professional ballplayers—I just have a prejudice, and it also extends to movie stars. Sylvester Stallone gets $7 million or $17 million a picture, or Liz Taylor— there's just no relationship between us and them. It's horse shit. There's no relationship between a Bill Cosby, who is reputed to have earned $80 million last year, and us.

Yet, I am also constantly amazed at some of the wages that are earned by union workers—operating engineers, electricians making $50,000, $60,000 a year—it's extraordinary where the average hourly industrial wage for about 7 to 8 million labor-intensive industrial workers isn't even $7 an hour. And that makes for my prejudice as well. I just don't see any community of interest between labor-intensive workers and them.

You know, it even troubled me that union officers' salaries were disproportionate to the ability of their own members to earn. I don't mind telling you that as I advanced in rank and in income, though, I didn't voluntarily return 25 percent of my salary to the treasury. There are all kinds of rationalizations, and I tell you frankly that I accepted them. You say to yourself that you deal at a higher level, you negotiate contracts with employers, you match wits with them, and the chances are you work longer hours than your management counterparts because they don't go around the country talking to stockholders every Monday and Wednesday as union leaders must with their constituents. So you say the guy who's across the table from you earns $720,000 a year, aren't you entitled to $110,000?

And I'm not going to deny that when workers come out of the factory, or off the bench, and become officers of a local union that their lives don't become a lot more comfortable. When you're a local officer you can come to work at 9 a.m. when offices open, instead of being on the factory floor at 7 a.m. in the morning wielding a sledge hammer, or working in some hot, dirty, stuffy building. You're not subject to the vagaries of economic boom and bust. You get a salary, whether it's a $300 a week, or $500 a week, or $800 a week, it's a salary, and you get paid fifty-two weeks a year. You're not subject to layoff. Listen, it's a capitalist society and we shouldn't expect unions to be egalitarian, a speck, a small island in the midst of all this materialism. So life does get more comfortable when you become an officer.

Political Action

On those trips when I went out to the membership I rarely heard anything from them about Central America, South Africa, or any other of the great social issues of our time. But they heard about them from me! First of all, our union has always been concerned with more than just wages, hours, and working conditions. In fact, a favorite phrase of mine was that when you joined the ILG, you became an industrial citizen. I also believed that it was equally important for the members to be political citizens, and always encouraged them to get out and vote. It's your town, your state and nation—you're a member of the world community, so vote.

The scandal about our American democratic system is that fewer and fewer Americans participate in elections. Ronald Reagan is the president, but I don't think 20 percent of Americans voted for him. He only got a majority of those voting in the last election. And that's a result of apathy, disinformation, and a large underclass that does not understand it's got a stake in what's going on. Let me give you an analogy. If the Boston City Council is discussing some important item, maybe it's that integrated school busing program, they'll get a thousand very vocal people coming to the meeting. But where are all the other residents of Boston? It's "Let George do it, I'll read about it in the paper, I'll hear about it." It was the same with Reagan, a lot of people decided they didn't have a stake, but they understand it now.

The Executive Council of the AFL-CIO

A political pecking order on the executive council? Sure, sure. There's a political pecking order in every institution, in every facet of communal life. I would say that in terms of the most important representatives on the council, and this is a result of their unions' size and quality of leadership, are those from the UAW; the Steelworkers; perhaps two of the vice-presidents who represent building trades unions; Food and Commercial Workers; AFSCME; the representative of the ILG, traditionally, started with Dubinsky and it continued with me; and the Teachers union with Al Shanker. These are the people who would be consulted with, privately, quietly. In the past, the Machinist union might have been called upon, but it wasn't for the many years that I was on the council because of the personality of Bill Winpisinger. I suppose Lane might call him occasionally, depending on what the circumstances were. I don't think Meany ever did.

I could name people who are also highly regarded. For example, among the Building Trades guys, it was Jack Lyons, former head of the Ironworkers. The Ironworkers I don't think ever had more than 100,000 members, but he was kindly regarded by his fellow building trades officers. He came on the executive council at a young age and survived everybody until he became ill and then, of course, he passed away. Marty Ward, who was the head of the Plumbers' union, George Meany's union, is another who was highly regarded, a decent and level-headed guy.

Before I left the council I also lobbied to get a seat for Bob Georgine— he's head of the AFL-CIO's building trades department. Years before, that effort wouldn't have had a ghost of a chance because the council never had the head of a department serve on it. He comes out of a small union in the building trades, the Lathers, Plasterers, whatever it was called—they're not worth a hoot in hell in terms of power. He was elected to the executive council and he probably is the most influential of the building trades officers around and he'd be among those who would be consulted.

I suppose, depending on what the circumstances might be, Paul Hall, the former powerful head of the Seafarers, would be consulted. He was a friend of Meany's, friendly, very supportive, very cooperative. He's dead now, but he was a power when in office. If other unions had a strike and they needed manpower, he was always willing to help. Not by a long shot does his successor have the same stature.

When Jerry Wurf was the head of AFSCME, Meany thought he was a pain in the ass, often. And he was. Even within his own international, he had a very rough reputation. But he was very bright, very outspoken, and in many ways, depending on the issue, I think he would be one of those that Meany would chat with because it was a great and growing union. Today, Gerry McEntee, who's his successor, is part of the charmed circle because of AFSCME's size. But he's also very active, ambitious, and a fairly articulate guy, so he's part of that group today.

Just to show you how transitions work, George Hardy used to be the head of the Service Employees International union. He was looked upon as a good trade unionist, but a buffoon. He had a foul mouth, totally uninhibited in language, and I don't know whether he thought that was a badge of courage but half the guys on the council had little use for him. On the other hand, his successor at SEIU, John Sweeney, is very highly regarded. SEIU is a good-sized union and an important union, and Sweeney is an excellent chief executive.

Sometimes you hear someone criticize the Executive Council because they think there are not enough women on it. That's because only presidents of unions got on board, and until we contrived to break that rule, there were none. Today there is at least one female president and she sits on the council with two other women who are vice-presidents in their unions. But listen to me carefully, and make a mental note of this. Of the top thousand CEOs in America, not one is black, and two are women. And one of the women is the CEO by grace of her husband. That's Liz Claiborne. She came out of my industry and heads the corporation named Liz Claiborne, but her husband, Art Ortenberg, is the guy who built the business. I know and admire them both, and he's happy to be the vice-chairman of the board while Liz is president and chairperson.

In talking about the number of women and minorities in organizations, I want to tell you that I'm opposed to affirmative action quotas. However, if you talk about remedial activity, giving people an opportunity to eliminate a past deficiency, I'm all for it. Absolutely. Give them tutoring, give them special aid, and then let them compete. I don't buy moving people to the top of a list because of their minority status. I also oppose veteran preferences even though I could benefit by them. . . .

7. "The Wrath of Grapes"

Cesar Chavez

My fasting was mostly for our people—I wasn't trying to force the employers to do anything. I was trying to force our people to do something.

Cesar Chavez, president of the United Farm Workers of America (UFWA), founded and leads the first successful farm workers' union in U.S. history. Like other UFWA officers and staff, he receives a $10 weekly stipend plus food and living benefits.

Mr. Chavez was born in 1927, on his grandfather's small farm near Yuma, Arizona. At age ten life began as a migrant farm worker when his father lost his land during the Depression. In 1948, he met his wife-to-be while working in Delano, California vineyards. The Chavez family settled in the San Jose barrio of *Sal Si Puedes* (get out if you can).

He served as national director of the Community Service Organization, a barrio-based social and political organization, in the late 1950s and early 1960s. In 1962, after failing to convince CSO to commit itself to farm worker organizing, he founded the National Farm Workers Association (NFWA).

In September 1965, Mr. Chavez's NFWA, with 1,200 member families, joined the AFL-CIO's Agricultural Workers Organizing Committee (AWOC) in a five-year strike boycott against Delano area table and wine grape growers. In 1966, the two organizations merged to become the United Farm Workers.

By 1970, the boycott resulted in contracts with most table grape growers of the area. That year, to limit the UFW's success to the vineyards, growers in the vegetable industry signed "sweetheart" pacts with the Teamsters union. Ten thousand farm workers in California's coastal valleys walked out of the fields to protest the grower-Teamster agreements.

In 1973, when the farm workers' table grape contracts came up for renewal, most growers signed with the Teamsters, sparking the largest and most successful farm strike in American history, in which Mr. Chavez called for a worldwide boycott of grapes, head lettuce, and Gallo wines. By 1975, a nationwide Louis Harris poll showed 17 million American adults were honoring the grape boycott. In 1977, the UFW and the Teamsters signed an agreement that gave the UFW exclusive rights to represent field workers, and the Teamsters, plant workers.

From the beginning, the UFW adhered to the principles of nonviolence practiced by Gandhi and Martin Luther King, Jr. Mr. Chavez conducted a twenty-five day fast in 1968 to reaffirm the UFW's nonviolent commitment. The late Senator Robert Kennedy called Cesar Chavez "one of the heroic figures of our time" and flew to Delano to be with him when he ended the fast.

Mr. Chavez is currently leading an international grape boycott, begun in July 1984, called "The Wrath of Grapes." The theme symbolizes the threats posed to vineyard workers by the use of pesticides by growers and the threats posed to consumers by those pesticides as residue on food.

---※ ※ ※---

M Y motivation comes from my faith. I don't gloat over victories, and I don't let defeats detract me, because I've had a lot of those. In fact, in the first nineteen years of my work I never had one single victory. Yet, it never ceases to amaze me though what the union has done to me, or what the union has done for people. It has opened up unimaginable vistas for providing service to our members, and even those who claim to be members of the Farm Workers. And for me, and a lot of others, who might not necessarily be close to the church, providing service and help to people really is our biggie.

My fasts have been misunderstood by a lot of people on the outside who think it's the same thing as a hunger strike. The workers understood very well what they're all about, especially the Catholic workers, or let's say the religious workers—they understand that the whole idea of a fast is to make a sacrifice. While it's an extreme form of sacrifice, it engenders quite a bit of concern among a lot of people. And so my fasting was mostly for our people—I wasn't trying to force the employers to do anything. I was trying to force our people to do something. That's the difference. And that was what kept me going on those two occasions when I was able to do twenty-five days and twenty-four days. I don't think I'd ever have done it, or been able to do it if I said, "Okay I'm not gonna eat because I want the endorsement of something."

And the fasts were not something I consciously planned, maybe they're planned away in the deep recesses of my mind, but consciously I never planned any, they just happened. It's a calling, it's a need to do it, it's like I'm forced to do them. In fact, when I do them I'm against doing them because I have to stay in bed, and I can't work, or do things for the union that have to be done.

In-Service Programs

In-service programs were the way we built our union, and that's how unions were built a hundred years ago. They had all sorts of beneficial societies, burial plans, health and medical clinics, credit, and all that stuff, you know. And I see the AFL-CIO is going back to that, and I'm really happy because unions are basically a mutual society.

We've always done it that way in the Farm Workers. When a member of a union leaves the union, or a company closes down one day, or they throw us out, or whatever, the members are never left alone. They're continuing members of the union for as long as they want to be. We never say that you have to work to be a member of the union.

In fact, we have more people now working under contract, than we have people paying dues. Look, the University of Indiana reported that twenty percent of the farm workers that come to the Midwest on the Midwest migrant stream say they're members of the Farm Workers, but we don't have any record of them. And even in California there are people who say, "I'm a member of the union," but they haven't paid dues in ten years. Sometimes those people are even scabs, and our members will even point them out. But I always tell our people, "Wait a minute. Remember that the best scab has to be turned around. Otherwise we'll never win."

But all these nonmembers, nondues-paying members, will still come in and use our services. That puts a big drain on our resources. We have nonmembers in undocumented families, for example, who come into our clinic on an emergency basis to deliver their babies. But that's why we exist, see, to offer service to the people.

Union Spirit

Unions are basically volunteer organizations, but some unions have kind of gotten away from that in recent years. See, when that happens, you get in trouble, because then you don't have the spirit. The spirit comes because people put their time, and their effort, and their sacrifices into it. Now, we do have paid staff, but their jobs are to coordinate, not literally to do the job. It's just too big for them to do anyway.

To have union spirit, you have to get the members involved, and make them feel that the union and all the decisions are theirs. Because the moment they feel that the union belongs to the president, or belongs to the big shots, as they call them, then they won't do anything for a union. So in our union, for example, we let the members make the decisions, even though sometimes their decisions are not the best decisions.

And naturally, that can be a big investment, because often times they ask for things in negotiations that we know aren't there. But if you fight with them on it, you take the shine off them, and you shouldn't do that. However, if you let the employer tell them that their demands are unreasonable, then you can build spirit on that. It's really a very simple thing, and in fact I always tell our organizers, "Never ever put yourselves in between the workers and the company."

We've always used this approach, starting from the very first time farm workers in this country negotiated a contract. Back then, we were getting 65 cents an hour to work in the fields, and when we went to negotiate the members came in with their $5.50 demand. Well, we thought it should be something more like $2.00, $2.50, but we went ahead and brought the demand to the bargaining table. Schenley's negotiator was a very savvy guy, and when we gave the demand to him, he looked at it, and then gave each one of us his calling card, and said, "When you guys are serious, call me," and walked out.

Well, I just sat there, and I didn't say anything. For a half an hour there was a lot of throat clearing among the members who were there, and a lot of people shifting in their chairs. I didn't say anything until the question was asked, "What do we do now?" I said, "Well, we can do three things. We can forget it. We can go out and strike again, fight them some more and make them accept our demands, or we can negotiate to a more reasonable level." So that's how we do it in our union. I think if we had fought with the members or told them up front that we should go for $2.50, in the back of their minds they'd always figure, "Maybe this guy sold out." But you have to let them find out, because when they find out by themselves, then they think it's my union, it's mine.

My Work

There are a lot of reports that I'm involved in every aspect, every detail of what's going on in the union. That's just not true. The growers put that stuff out to some reporters to make us look inept. That there's no one in the union but me, that I'm the driving force of the movement, and everyone else is inept, or doesn't know what they're doing. It's all nonsense.

Look, the union's highly decentralized. This year I've been at the headquarters 10 percent of the time, and it's still running, so those articles about me are just not true. It would never work if I had to be running everything. And a lot of stuff, frankly, that goes on in the office is so boring I wouldn't want any part of it anyway.

My job is basically making sure that people have the authority and the means to do their job and they can support us. I coordinate things like making sure we don't get too many boycotts going at the same time. Really, my job is to leave our people alone so that they can feel like it's their job and it's their work. I support 'em or remove them, but I don't meddle around with them.

And I've certainly removed people. Never because they failed, but only when they weren't willing to work with people. I never removed anybody who couldn't do the job or failed, because if they couldn't do the job, they could be trained, and if they failed, we could try it again. But some people just get on their high horse, and are not willing to work along with others, and it's those who don't belong in an organization of people, they belong out there by themselves.

I do a lot of traveling and public speaking, neither of which I like to do. I prefer to be with the workers, that's what I'd like, negotiating, to be involved. But still, the traveling today is easier and better planned than in the early days. Back then I'd catch a "red eye" from California to New York, land in New York City without knowing anybody, and I'd get a bagful of dimes so I could call different people on the phone until I found someone who would invite me out to visit a union. I remember staying two days out at the airport making calls because nobody invited me. Nobody knew who we were! Now I don't do that, I have a place to go, a place to eat, but back then it was terrible.

Communications

In the first place, unions, and my union included, are still in the horse and buggy days when it comes to telling our members what's going on. Why should people come to meetings? They're boring, and they take time. So, I believe we should be using other ways to communicate with them. Look, if people can order things by phone, shop by phone, get entertainment, and so forth by phone or by TV, why can't they get something through their union in those ways? See if we gave a short-circuit TV meeting and people could respond to what's happening in the meeting using some of that new technology, we'd have a lot of people participating in the union.

But really, our single biggest problem is we can't communicate to the people. We were so worried at one time that we weren't even communicating with our staff as well as we should, that we established a system called the Wire. Every desk in our offices in California, and some in Arizona, has a little speaker on it that the person can turn on to listen to what's going on in my office if I've turned on my microphone. And I do that when I meet with some important person, or I'm talking about something new, or what's going on in some critical area.

We found that the Wire greatly increased the level of participation, enthusiasm, and generated a lot of new ideas because people were able to know exactly what was happening in headquarters. And it even helps me to stay in touch with our staff and members when I can't be with them. For instance, if a committee of workers is having a meeting about a grievance, I can chime in, and maybe tell them, "Hey, I remember we had a problem just like that years ago," and I'll tell the staff, "Look at so-and-so case." Or I'm saying, "Damn it, he worked with us about ten years ago and he has something I need. I need to get a hold of, I don't remember where he was at, I don't even remember his name, maybe John something, but he worked with . . ." and right away I get a call, "Sure, he worked with me, I was his manager." Or, "We worked together. I don't know where he's at, but so-and-so might."

The Wire has also saved us a lot of money and effort as well because the top leadership also has a speaker in their homes, and at 7:00 a.m. we have a "traffic" meeting when we talk about, "I'm going to go to Los Angeles to meet with so-and-so, and I'm going to so-and-so." And pretty soon, we find out that someone's going to La Paz, our headquarters, for instance, to get something while I was going over there too. Well, only one of us really needs to take that trip.

But it's not only with our people that we need to do a better job with communications, we really need to borrow from management some of their ideas on how better to get our story across to the public. See, management doesn't put salesmen out on the street to do their advertising, and we shouldn't either. We should be using the media more, but a media that we control. We should have a daily labor newspaper, a union network, and a union radio station.

Strategy

We have a special marketing department that markets the union to farm workers, the boycott to consumers, and does fund raising. See, we have to do things differently now than when we first got started, because standing in front of a supermarket just doesn't work any more for us. Things have changed such that you can't go to consumers with a message that's "Help me, help me."

Now we have to go with a message of "I'm here to help you." In fact, we just got through with a four-year study of what our mission ought to be, and it came down simply to food. We're concerned about the price of food, because at $2.00 or even $1.50 for a head of lettuce it's too damn much— the consumer is paying for all the mistakes that the corporations make— and further, we want to have food that's clean and safe to eat, no pesticides and toxins. So our marketing group is in charge of getting our mission, our concerns out to those who can make a difference. In the past, we used to try to reach anybody and everybody we could, and we'd have jillions of leaflets, but today, we just go to people very selectively. We know that we can win a boycott with 7 percent of the population supporting us.

The Support of Labor

We have excellent support from the labor movement in the United States, excellent. I think we represent to them just the classic struggle, maybe what they were years ago, and that's the struggle for recognition and minimum wages. So they generally come through for us with support when we need it. But we also do a lot of work for them, we help a lot, you know, any time, any place. When they ask us for help, we come in.

I really don't think though that George Meany understood what we were trying to do in the beginning. You know, he was hearing a lot of bad stuff about us from the palace guard, but once I was able to get to him and show him, he became quite a convert. And towards his later years he did some pretty outstanding stuff for us.

For example, there's a clause in the AFL-CIO constitution that says that the Executive Council can, by their vote, assess each member a special fee, I think it was 3 cents a month, to help with some cause. In those days there were about 16 million members, so we got through Meany something like $6 or $7 million. He did that for us. He never did it before and it hasn't been done since. We also had assigned to us at one time—Meany did this— like 90 percent of all the AFL-CIO field staff.

Hostile Environment

Governor Deukmejian of California is an obstacle to us more than anything else. We don't want to fight him because we don't win anything. And the growers are like most employers, if you show them some power, they respect you. Short of that, though, they don't respect anything. And the economic power I'm talking about is the boycott. See, they learned that every time they'd beat us up, or kill one of our people, we'd hit them right over the head with the media, so there's not much violence against us now as before, but we don't know what will happen once they start getting desperate, you know.

The toughest growers to work with though are not the big corporations. You see, if you show a big corporate entity some economic muscle, or you hurt them a little bit, or he perceives like you're going to hurt them, they back off. Their only hangup is money. But the other growers, the self-made, family owned businesses, they have no experiences with unions, and while money is an issue with them, they also have a lot of prejudice about dealing with a minority-led, and minority-membered union.

And as far as the Teamsters, we don't have any problems with them unless the growers bring them in. We can beat them hands down any day in terms of organizing. If we go into a field, people will select our union 10 to 1 any day, and there's no problem. The problem is when the growers make book with the Teamsters, and then tells the workers, "If you go for the farmers [United Farm Workers], we're going to fire you, but if you want a union, take the Teamsters." Those are big problems for us, and we can overcome them, but we have to hustle real hard, you know.

Looking Back

When I started organizing, my wife and I had no money—I mean we started from square zero. I'm talking about a dollar, we didn't have one dollar. It was just day to day, a bare existence. But I think that maybe contributed to the response we got from the workers, because they understood what was happening. When they came to my house for help, they saw our empty shelves, and so what happened was they developed a system that's still in the union. When people come to our headquarters these days, they bring food. In fact, we get the best fruits and vegetables that money can buy, I mean, that fingers can take. But what my wife does now is to take that food and she sends it everywhere to people who need it. She's become a food distributor. Pretty amazing.

8. In the Trenches— The Best Place to Be

Charles Dale

I really do miss the hell out of being an international rep—it's the best job. You're out there where things are happening, you're in the trenches. You're with people and you maneuver, and you manipulate, your mold people, arouse them.

Charles Dale became president of The Newspaper Guild (TNG) October 15, 1987, following the retirement of Charles A. Perlik, Jr. For eight years prior to his incumbency, Mr. Dale was TNG's secretary-treasurer; for 24 years prior to that, he was an international representative, bargaining and organizing across the United States, Canada, and in Puerto Rico.

In the early 1950s he helped organize the Canadian Wire Service Guild's unit at the Canadian Broadcasting Corporation, where he worked as national political editor. He served as the local's treasurer and later president.

While a TNG international representative, he was instrumental in bringing major units in British Columbia into the guild and played a key role in establishing joint bargaining with other newspaper unions on the West Coast and in Hawaii. For many years, until 1978, Dale was the president of the Federation of Guild Representatives, the bargaining representative for TNG's field and administrative staff.

Now a U.S. citizen, Mr. Dale was born in Springhill, Nova Scotia, in 1929 and studied at Victoria University in Wellington, New Zealand.

The TNG was founded in 1933 as a union of newspaper reporters. By

1937, however, it became the first industrial union in the newspaper industry when it extended its rank to all unorganized departments of news and editorial employees. Today, the guild represents 40,000 news and commercial department employees of newspapers, news services, magazines, and related media including reporters, janitors, advertising sales persons, circulation clerks, photographers, librarians, and keypunch and computer operators.

At the guild's national convention, TNG locals vote upon the components of a collective bargaining program, which sets minimum standards for negotiations with employers. A poll in 1986 of TNG members showed that 73 percent of members thought their jobs would be worse off without the union, and more than 80 percent were satisfied with their contracts. TNG is known for its internal democratic governance. Its national conventions are often tumultuous affairs, and it is not unusual for there to be six or more roll calls of delegates in order to reach a decision on an issue.

Notwithstanding its diminutive size, TNG has been a pioneer in the study of the effects of visual display terminals on the health of workers.

At the time of the following interview, Mr. Dale was secretary-treasurer of TNG.

———————————* * *———————————

THERE'S an attitude here in the United States towards unions that beats' the hell out of me. For some reason this society just ignores what the labor movement has provided for this country and its workers. Maybe someday it will no longer be a demeaning thing to join a union.

I really can't point my finger though on when this whole antilabor thing got started. The fact that labor has never had a good press is a good place to start. We are described as labor bosses, and our image is that of George Meany sitting at a pool in Florida holding a big, fat cigar. That hasn't done a hell of a lot of good for us, nor has the image the press conveyed of the Teamsters. There are just too many people who think that union leaders are ripoff artists, that they don't do very much for their salaries, and just get rich off the sweat of the workers.

I live out near Reston, Virginia, where all of these huge organizations are located, employing thousands of people. Virginia is a right-to-work state, very conservative. It's the deep South as far as I'm concerned, and if you look at how all those unorganized people are treated there by employers, well, its disgraceful. They pay minimum wage, or possibly a little bit better, give no medical plans, and if an employee gets a week's vacation after one year of service, or two or even three years of service, somehow or other they consider themselves lucky. It's appalling the casual way in which they get fired and shoved around. Those people have no security, no recourse if they get fired, they can just pick up their paycheck and leave—that's it. They're brutalized, harassed, discriminated against, humiliated, and still if you ask them if it would be a good idea to have a union so they could fight back, their response is either, (a) they're afraid, or (b) the bad images of the labor movement are thrown up to you.

By and large, those people don't see unions as a good thing. For them, the person who belongs to a union is somebody who drives a truck, shovels dirt, fixes roads, or drives a bus. They think unions are for a different class, and they're better than that. So it is tough getting through to them on how unions can serve a useful purpose in their lives.

Union Spirit

While that old time level of union fervor and commitment isn't as widespread as it used to be, you can still find it. There are people out there yet who see the injustices in the workplace, and they get involved. Fortunately, we have on our staff some young people who are not dedicated to their salary, or career, but to the cause. And I see those people as the great hope of the future. They're young, they're imaginative, and they can be a pain in the ass at times because of their energy level, which is a hell of a lot higher than mine as a result of my age, and the fact that I've been around the track so many times.

But I really don't know what it will take to turn around this country's antilabor attitude. A complete, rapid and refreshing turnaround for the labor movement might occur if the nation got hit with some real hard times. But the nation is probably too well-insulated against that sort of thing occurring. All of us in the labor movement are trying to be innovative, trying to do things that will attract the attention of the members, but I don't know the answer.

Organizing

A successful organizing campaign starts at the bottom, there's never been any doubt in my mind about that. Somebody in a plant, or in a newsroom has to say, "I've had it, enough." If they find there's more than a couple of them who are interested in unionizing and equalizing the bargaining strength in that relationship, then a union can go in and tell them what to do. So, by and large, it's the rank and file, the workers in the plant who do the organizing.

In fact, what growth we have achieved in the guild is coming principally from organizing new members employed on small newspapers, and occasional successes with papers like the *Milwaukee Journal,* which certainly can't be characterized as a small newspaper. What you find today are smaller newspapers, unorganized newspapers—the bigger unorganized newspapers are paying reasonably good salaries, and some, especially the smaller ones, playing upon people's fears that the newspaper might have to close down if a union comes in. That tactic scares off people, and it has been used more frequently, and with greater intensity, since the Reagan administration brought this antilabor attitude into predominance.

But Reagan alone didn't start it, that would be absurd. We've not really had a prolabor administration for one hell of a long time, possibly not since Roosevelt. Prime Minister Mulrooney of Canada is also antilabor but he's a smart enough politician not to be too obvious about it. Former Prime Minister Trudeau though was prolabor, and a genuine liberal.

I have great confidence however that the newspaper as we know it will not change—perhaps the format will change in some respects, but it's going to survive for an awfully long time, and The Newspaper Guild along with it. I am concerned though about the advancements in computer technologies and the issues surrounding work at home. With people sitting at home and feeding copy to the papers via a computer, we'll need to insure that they're actually working decent hours and getting a decent pay.

Mergers

For us, there is always the possibility of a merger with another union. We went through a batch of years with the International Typographical Union trying to work on a merger but that came to naught. I can't really see us merging outside the industry. I always had the dream of one big union for the newspaper industry, the pressman, the printers, the mailers, the drivers. That doesn't mean I'm suggesting a merger with the Teamsters, although someday I think that will be possible.

Getting Started

I started in the newspaper business in Australia, where my stepfather was a member of the Canadian Diplomatic Corps. I went to college there very briefly but couldn't continue because of some personal problems, and so I ended up working in a glass bottle factory on an assembly line. That's the worst kind of work that anybody could possibly do. I was at the end of an assembly line and the bottles just kept coming down. We wore heavy glasses and gloves and had to pick up and inspect each bottle for flaws. If there were no flaws we would put them in boxes, and if there were flaws, you rejected them. The only way we could get a cigarette break, or a coffee break, was by running up the line, throwing all the bottles into the discard bin, quickly lighting up a cigarette, taking a puff, stomping it out and then run back to your spot on the line.

Anyway, after they had ordered me to work a double shift, I decided to start making inquiries about other positions and ended up getting a job as a cadet reporter on the *Sydney Daily Mirror*. They probably hired me because I had done some work on my high school and college papers, and because they thought it would be a novelty to have a Canadian on their staff, although many thought I was an American. In Australia the newspaper business is very highly organized, and I started going to the union meetings and really got involved.

When I got back to Canada I took a position with the Canadian Press, which is the Canadian equivalent of the Associated Press. There was an effort being made then to organize The Newspaper Guild, and it really was desperately needed. The pay was awful, the conditions were rotten, many of the bosses were unbelievable bastards. I was making $32.50 a week, and had been promised I'd go to $35.00 at the end of six months if my work was satisfactory. I didn't get my pay raise so I insisted on having an interview with the president of the corporation. He was not the one who hired me, actually it was somebody else, but he put his blessings on it with a little interview and pep talk. So I went in to see him, and he told me that the reason that they couldn't give me my $2.50 pay increase was because if they gave it to me, they'd have to give it to everyone. At that point, I decided the hell with this, I wasn't going to work for this crappy organization. They'd broken all kinds of promises already, but the $2.50 increase was just too important to me, and so I quit.

I next went to work for the Canadian Broadcasting Corporation [CBC], and while there I met a couple of guys who also thought it might be a good idea if we organized a guild local, and we ended up with a TNG bargaining unit and a contract. Later, at one of the guild's conventions where I served as a delegate, I was asked if I would like to work for the guild for a year helping out with negotiations in Vancouver and organizing small papers out in western Canada. I thought that sounded interesting, so I took a year's leave of absence from the CBC, and well, that year has turned into thirty-seven years, and I'm still on leave of absence from the CBC.

And I've no regrets whatever about my decision to stay on with the guild. It has provided me with a good life—I'm not wealthy, but I'm comfortable. I have a nice house, a little money in the bank, maybe not as much as I would have had if I'd stayed in the job that I left—the CBC is paying as much in that job as I'm making now—but I've gotten an awful lot of satisfaction from this job because I've helped people. I used to tell people when they'd ask, "Why do you do this? You spend most of your time in hotel rooms, and on the road," and I would reply, in certain company, "You know, every once in a while you get a gigantic, multicolored orgasm on this job. You actually get to accomplish something of real value."

The Secretary-Treasurer's Job

There are many things about the job of Secretary-Treasurer that are a pain in the ass. One of the things that I especially dislike is the amount of paper work involved. I find myself sometimes buried with paper. For example, we have two pension plans and a group life insurance program. We have investment managers, counselors, and those people are constantly sending material here that has got to be reviewed. Just the routine of handling the finances of this organization gets to me personally. Every expense account has got to cross this desk. I have to look at every one and approve each one. And with the exception of payroll checks, I have to countersign every check that goes out of this office. That can be really burdensome. We have stacks and stacks of checks and you just don't put your signature on them. You have to look at the check, and if you have any questions about it you've got to get the answer. You have to find out what the hell this bill was for, why are we paying this person and so on. There's an incredible amount of paperwork.

So by and large I'll spend my day handling paperwork and on the telephone. I have a lot of friends out there who figure that they will get prompter service out of the international if they call me rather than somebody else in the organization department. I don't want to step on their feelings, so I listen to them, and then refer them to this or that person.

I also spend some time involved in collective bargaining when we have major problems, or not so major problems. Somebody in management might contact me and say, "We've got this problem . . ." and I've gotten involved. We have an awful lot of contracts out there and I probably get involved in 15 percent.

You know, over the years, lots of employers and I have developed a relationship—after all, we've grown up together. If I give my word at the bargaining table, I'll never break it. Some of those employers behave similarly. On the other hand, there are one hell of a lot of employers out there who don't respond in kind, who are in no way ever going to let a union into their buildings, no way ever going to let The Newspaper Guild in, and no way can they ever be trusted.

There are days though in this job when I would just as soon walk away from it. Sometimes I even joke about leaving my keys on my desk, with a little note saying, "See you." Like last Friday. I usually get to the office early in the morning and try like hell to get away at a reasonable hour. It never works out that way. I always seem to start very early and work very late.

Last Friday I was in the office at 7 A.M. and I didn't leave the office until about 8:30 P.M. The only time I left here was to go out for a luncheon appointment. When I left here, I said to myself, "This is ridiculous." It's not a case of wasted time. I don't spend a lot of time running around gossiping. Most of the time I spend at my desk, on the phone, dealing with paper, with office problems, and with various other union problems.

It's an unfamiliar role for me, and I had to do an awful lot of adjusting to get used to the job. You see, I was on my own when I was an international representative and in that job you principally act as a troubleshooter. It didn't matter that I lived in California if there was a bargaining problem in Washington, or a strike in Montreal, or a problem in Vancouver or St. Louis, if they figured that I was the one who should handle it, I went. I had a situation where I was assigned to two different strikes and was bargaining at *The Washington Post* all at the same time. To a very large extent I was sort of a parachutist and a fireman, but I pretty well set my own schedule.

I really do miss the hell out of being an international rep—it's the best job. You're out there where things are happening, you're in the trenches. You're with people and you maneuver, and you manipulate, you mold people, arouse them. It gives you a lot of satisfaction. They need something, they want something, but a lot of times they're not prepared to stand up and fight for it, so you have to arouse that group to the point where they are prepared to take a strike and go out.

And it's terrific to see an employer discover that this group of people who he thought of as pussycats are all of a sudden wildcats. I'm not being a braggard, but I was a good rep. In fact, my career success to a large extent is attributable principally to the exposure I got as an international representative. I spent an awful lot of time both in Canada and in the United States organizing, bargaining, and representing locals in strike situations.

Although the secretary-treasurer's position is an important and significant job, it's second banana. And there is no question about that, but it's not a role that I resent. I might if I didn't have the relationship that I have with the president. There is a certain amount of prestige and power that goes with the job but everybody knows who the president is, everybody knows where the power is, everybody knows where the decision making is. I would never, under any circumstances, run against Chuck Perlik, the current president of TNG. Our relationship is too firm, too fixed for that.

I've known Chuck since the time when he was an international representative. We're very good friends, and I keep hoping that he's not going to retire because he's a superb president. I don't kid myself into believing that I could fill his shoes. In fact, nobody should try to fill somebody else's shoes, you should walk in your own. But he's been damned good for this union and as a team we work beautifully together.

I have not really thought about being president either. But in the event that he decides to retire or just wants to give it up, I'll have to make my decision. I've got some people in mind though who could work as my teammate in case I do run for the presidency. What I have is a list of six people and I'll just have to get it narrowed down.

Running for Office

For all the time I've been a local and international officer, I've never lost an election. That's because I've never had any opposition. That's the best way to run. It's very comfortable not to have to go through the pain, effort, and agony of running for election, as well as the personal expense. Running for office has become very expensive and time consuming, and I don't know how much longer I can count on no opposition, but the honeymoon for me in this particular job has lasted since 1979.

There's a certain amount of naiveté among the membership about running for office. You get people who know you've been in the union for thirty some years and you've done just about everything there is to do—bargained contracts when they were rookies on the paper and been secretary-treasurer for years, and then they want you to stand in front of them and tell them what your platform is. That infuriates me—it's ridiculous!

I've paid my dues and I'm prepared to tell all of them simply that I'm running for office and want their support. I've done a pretty damned good job, the record's clear if you read the reports and look at the financial statements. For somebody who has been in the union for about a year and a half to ask, "What's your position on this, what's your position on that . . .?" They're behaving like they're power brokers, and it's demeaning.

I have a feeling though that there are a hell of a lot of people who really don't want to make the sacrifices required to serve as a union leader. Others look at a union officer and say, "He's got a nice, fat expense account, a nice office, a lot of perks, he gets a decent pay raise." That's how they see the job, but it's not that way. There are many things about this job, about the job of any union officer position, that are not particularly attractive.

You don't work an eight-hour day, or a five-day week. We can't count on being able to take a vacation if or when we plan it. We can't count on a heck of a lot of family time. We can count on events determining what our schedule is going to be. We can count on private family occasions being interrupted by emergency telephone calls which require you to get into the office or travel somewhere. You forget that you're supposed to be off that day, and you get yourself back in that harness as a union officer and deal with the problem.

Looking Back

I joke a lot about what people will say about me after I'm gone, that they'll say, "Here lies a man who never ate at McDonalds, knew the inside of every airport on the continent and spent an awful lot of time in exotic places such as Hawaii, bargaining contracts without ever getting any sand between his toes." If people do remember me, I hope it's as someone who gave everything he had, and I'm very proud of that—I give everything I have in terms of my energy, I can't give much more than that. No union paycheck was ever given to me that I did not earn. I've earned every dime.

I think the most rewarding experience I've ever had as a union officer was when I was representing our Puerto Rican members in bargaining with a big Spanish language newspaper. This goes back a few years, but these people were getting less than $2 an hour and they went out on strike for higher wages.

This was a real grassroots, down home, blood-and-guts kind of local. They were so desperate that most of the members didn't even go home during the strike, because they didn't want to jeopardize its success. So many would just slice open a cardboard box and sleep on it outside of strike headquarters.

Well, their strike lasted about sixty-three days, but the devotion of those people, their dedication to winning was inspirational. What they wanted was something like a $.20 an hour increase to get them up to $2 an hour. You know, I've gone out and bargained for $400, $500, $600 a week for reporters, but I have never gotten in my labor experience the kind of satisfaction as when I got those members $2.12 an hour. And I know that there are a lot of other people out there who need the help of unions to improve the quality of their lives, and that's what a union is all about.

9. Southerners Are Unionists Too

John M. Defee

I came from that old school where you stood on the shop floor and frothed at the mouth and your eyes turned white, and you did everything you could to get attention for whatever your cause was.

John M. Defee has been a union member for forty-eight years. His union career began at the age of twenty-three, when he was elected to the position of secretary of his local. He later served as treasurer, vice-president, and president of that local, and in 1963 he became a full-time international representative (1963–1969), and international vice-president (1969–1983). Mr. Defee became the international secretary-treasurer of the United Paperworkers International Union (UPIU) in 1983.

The first organization of employees in the paper industry occurred in 1765 in Stroudsburg, Maine. There, employees had struck the paper mill over grievances, and when these were not resolved, they burned the mill down. The origins of the UPIU was the organization of machine tenders/paper makers in 1884 in Holyoke, Massachusetts. From there, its history runs a fairly complex path through mergers of such organizations as the United Paperworkers of America; the International Brotherhood of Paperworkers; and the International Brotherhood of Pulp, Sulfite, and Paper Mill Workers. The present organization did not actually emerge until 1972. Today, the UPIU represents more than 250,000 workers in the paper industry in the United States and Canada.

* * *

I JOINED the union on December 23, 1941, and was elected an officer in 1948. I'm kind of proud of my record of advancements because I've had no formal education beyond high school. But I've done an awful lot of hard work that maybe other people would not have done. I'm constantly aware of the difference between that 9-foot cotton sack I used to pull and this pencil that I shove here.

But I've done it and I'm kind of proud of that. I was fortunate enough, I came from a good family that had a good understanding of human nature and the difference between right and wrong, and they tried to teach me that. And I've tried to maintain that position all these many years. So, with that kind of a background then, it's just good hard work. Of course I've had challenges but they just made me get out and dig for it, you know.

I got started in union work when I worked for International Paper Company at their paper mill in Bastrup, Louisiana. In those days we had what was called a Southern Kraft Multiple. It was made up of ten paper mills, and one bag mill, and we negotiated as a single unit. In about 1947 or '48, our delegate from Morehouse local 404 was in Mobile, Alabama, negotiating for a new labor contract. And when I heard about the way he was conducting himself, and the way the conference was going, I just wasn't satisfied. So I proceeded to write a long epistle with what I thought and I presented it to him. But since nothing came of it, I said, "All right, I'll fix that." Come, I guess, November, when we elected officers, I was a candidate for that office, and I was elected to it.

I did some politicking back then, and was probably mouthier than most. Yeah, I was considered an activist then, but I'm long past that now. I've definitely mellowed over the years, no doubt about it. And of course that bothers me sometimes too. I came from that old school where you stood on the floor and frothed at the mouth and your eyes turned white, and you did everything you could to get attention for whatever your cause was. But we're so damned sophisticated today until I can't hardly speak to a group! I feel that I'm either getting too loud, or using the wrong kind of language, something.

You have to believe in this work if you are ever to be successful. If you don't love the work, if you don't have a feel that you're improving the hours, wages, and working conditions of your fellow man, you'd better stay out of it, because union jobs don't pay a lot of money, contrary to what maybe some newspapers say, and some younger people think. It does not pay the kind of money that could hire a person to do the work that a local union officer does. We in the international, when we reach this level, we make a decent salary, but the salary is still pretty low. When I went to work as a local union officer, my salary was my month's $2.50 dues. That was my salary.

I worked for International Paper forty hours a week and worked part time, or spare time rather, for my local union. But those hours for the union, it was a thing that I enjoyed doing. We were growing, and we were improving our lot. And we were recognized as an honorable people.

Spirit of Unionism

People now, especially younger people, just don't see unions the same way. I don't think they've lost the union dream—they may never have had it. But part of that is caused by ourselves, people like me. See, I'd go home after, depending on the schedule I had, six hours in a plant, seven hours, eight hours, whatever it happened to be, and maybe had put in two or three hours working for the union, and maybe never mention that to my daughter. I might never talk to her a bit about what I'd been doing. Maybe growled at her because of something she'd done, you know? And so they grow up under those kind of conditions. I believe that we've failed miserably in enlightening our children on where we've come from.

My wife and I have talked about that a number of times. We, as parents, try so hard to make it better for our children than we had it until somehow we lose out and fail to instill in them those important things in life. Like, where the hell they come from, you know? Or where are they going to try to go and in the meantime how are they going to get there? It looks like we've somehow or other raised a generation here that feels that somebody owes them something. Somebody owes it to them, and they're not supposed to do very much to get it. And especially if they don't have any memory of the union having been responsible for their daddy's getting where they are.

They ought to be out doing their own thing, finding their own flags and causes. That's the part that bothers me more than anything else. We've maybe raised a generation of people that's not going to know how to conduct themselves in case we have a real economic problem. We've had some recessions, but when we get down to something like the mid-thirties, I don't know how our generation of today is going to cope with that. It's going to be a terrible problem.

When I first joined the union, many of the paper mill towns were owned by the companies. In those that weren't owned by the companies, the workers lived in flats and shacks and two bedroom frame houses without any doors on the insides of them, and if they had one bath in them they were lucky.

I have to think that the union was responsible to a great extent for improving the lot of the workers so that now they have, many of our membership have, two or more cars, two or more televisions, two or more boats, trailers, what have you. I'm glad, terribly happy for them. It does create some problems, though. They're not willing now to take the employer on in the same fashion that we were, because they've got so much more to lose. You take a man and his wife who are both working. He's up to his ears in debt, and he knows that if he misses another paycheck, he's going to lose all those twos of everything. And so you find it awful hard to say to him, "Look, there's got to be something wrong with you if you don't take this employer on," you know? Because you know he's going to lose it.

But I don't think they're too comfortable. I think every human being in this country is entitled to those comforts, better medical facilities, better hospital facilities, a better life. But I'll say this, it has created a situation that causes unions to have to operate so different as to be like another world. We are going to have to change our methods completely in an effort to represent this kind of person, see? The unions grew up representing the first guy I talked about. Today we are representing another group of people. And I'd be the first one to say that we have not yet learned how to do that.

I don't know what it will take either. I had a representative down in Texas two years ago tell me about some of the things that his members were demanding, and the way they were conducting themselves. I said to him, "Jim, look, you don't have to put up with that. You can straighten those guys out." He said, "Not if we want to represent them, we can't straighten them out. Because this is their way of life today. It's different from when you and I came into the picture." I think he's right, but we haven't got it yet. No union that I know a thing about has it. We're struggling, we're struggling . . .

Organizing

We absolutely do not have the secret. We're trying our best. We're going to put on a cooperative organizing campaign right here in the city of Nashville, Tennessee, and the surrounding area. But the thing that is so obvious to me is the methods we're going to use are the methods I used twenty years ago, with a few variations, you know? We have to have a radical change, something radically different from where we are.

But I think that if we can't get enough support to win an NLRB representation election here, I think we could probably start some kind of social program for that particular group, or maybe we could start some kind of insurance program, or some other things. Not that they would be required to be a member to participate in it, but if they wanted to they could collect some small fee or something and get some type of organization going, and it wouldn't have to be a union. Those are the things that go through our minds all the time.

You notice where the AFL-CIO is coming up with this credit card thing. It's not enough, it's not nearly enough, but it is a piece. All of us have lost some. We've lost about 6,000 members a year in our union. Take Steelworkers, Auto . . . mercy, IBEW, all that group. The only way they're operating it seems to me, is maybe on the interest earnings on their investments. I don't think they could possibly make it on the per capita that we get now.

The Members

Our members are talking about bread and butter issues these days. But we in the labor movement, in the international labor unions, and the AFL-CIO, recognize that's not all we can go to the bargaining table with. Bread and butter issues will never be improved if we're going to allow our companies to run away to foreign countries, work those people for less than nothing, bring that merchandise back to this country and sell it back to our people who've lost their jobs because of the move. Somebody has got to have lost their marbles—they're not listening very careful.

So many of our rank and file membership don't seem to understand it though. They can't grasp the situation. When they walk into a K-Mart store, and there's three shirts out there, one from Taiwan, one from China, and one from the United States and all three of them cost $17, they'd just as soon pick up the one from Taiwan or some other place, never thinking that this shirt over here wouldn't have cost them another nickel, but would've made somebody a job someplace in our country. Whereas these other two, laying over there for that same price, come from some distant country and made by some poor individual back there who wouldn't have hardly missed that job since he's making such a little bit.

I don't know, it's the lack of understanding of the economics of the world that causes that, and I don't profess to understand it myself. Maybe our people are somehow going to wake up to the fact that it's not all taken care of right in the mill town. It comes from distant places too.

Political and Legislative Support

A lot of people don't understand that all of the great union causes are still with us. The same things that Walter Reuther fought over are still here. We're in bad shape right now and we need strong leadership as much now as we've ever needed it. The political arena is such that we have absolutely no clout as unions.

The laws, what I call "umbrella laws for working people," were not written clear enough, or with teeth in them. Now, we get a new administration that says, "Hey, look-a-here, we don't really have to change this law. All we have to do is withhold the funds to make it work." And if they don't have the funds to operate on, then organizations such as OSHA and those kinds of things become inoperative. We really thought we had a good program going with OSHA. It ain't worth a tinker's damn right now, I can tell you. They might as well disband it, and quit putting what little money they are putting into it, because there's not enough to furnish a guy with an automobile and a per diem to get him out of home, you know? Managements are policing themselves in terms of health and safety like they did a hundred years ago!

All of these laws have fallen apart because we got a Labor Department under the directorship of people like lawyers and consultants. In the past it was always a laboring man who was directing it, now it's totally disrupted as far as trying to do anything for the working people.

Since we do not have enough political clout to be very effective, we find the things that we're negotiating are being legislated away from us. I can tell you some stories that are pretty sad in this business. Let's see, when was that last tax revision, 1982? Prior to that time, if a company sold to another company, and the selling company had a labor contract, the labor contract went with it. They honored the labor contract, and maybe the next time at the bargaining table they might make changes, you know?

Today, if I sell a company to you, you could take the position, "O.K. I will honor and recognize that union if that union has a 51 percent majority. But I won't recognize your contract, I won't recognize any of the conditions in it." We've taken them all the way to the United States Supreme Court on this one, and we've lost it all the way. It's the only time that I know of where a contract is not binding and that includes the time from the early 1700s when contract law developed in England. And even in this country, whenever a contract was written, that dude was binding. But no longer are labor contracts binding, they're just documents out there.

I don't guess that I could hardly put a date on when all this started. But you know, for every action there's a reaction. I guess that's the law of physics. And I find that the things that we were doing in the thirties, forties, and the fifties successfully are now being turned around. A lot of our problems stem from, what does industry call them, the political action groups?

See, we originated the idea of PACs back in the forties, and our membership made contributions to them for all these many years. A lot of times they weren't able to give much, but they made small contributions and as large a contribution as they could. So, along about in the sixties the corporations began to say, "Hey, look-a-here, let's do our little PACs." And they got so much more money than the working people have, they knock us nothing flat. So politicians may not be controlled by the financial world, but they're influenced tremendously by it. We can't match finances with corporations, and so we began to lose. We began to slide downhill in the political arena somewhere along about the mid-sixties.

We did have some terrific people in office until then, and they did an awful lot of work for the labor movement—their hearts were in it. But along about the mid-sixties the companies began to get a hold of them and make inroads, especially among the lower level elected politicians who had no real feeling for the working man. And then these fellows just moved up to the top offices. But everything is on such a technical basis now that it's hard to find the humanistic politicians any more. We'll present a political candidate with a book and he'll sign all the places in the right spot, you know? He'll get in office and about two years later, you wonder if he must not have seen that book? You take that book to show him where he signed it, and he'd say, "Oh, man, I didn't mean it!"

Of course, my man was Franklin D. Roosevelt. I might have been especially fond of him because of my military service. But we've had some good ones since then. Harry Truman, of course, was one of the great leaders. He had a tremendous interest in the people. We began to kind of fall by the wayside then until John Kennedy came along. Kennedy was another, and I don't know how he developed into this kind of a person, but he was another person who seemed to have the feeling of the working man at heart.

Lyndon Johnson was the worst scoundrel that ever lived, until he was elected vice-president. When he was elected vice-president he made a 180-degree turn and became one of the finest labor-supporting people as we've ever had. But until he was elected vice-president, he was an absolute scoundrel. And I'm from Texas. We fought him in San Francisco at the convention out there just as hard as we could fight him. But for some reason and I don't know why, but when he became vice-president, he began to twist arms for liberal programs all over the country. He actually made the greatest improvements in the civil rights area of anybody that's ever done that. But after Lyndon Johnson, we haven't done too well. I haven't been too happy with anything up there in Washington. After him was the downhill point for labor.

Our members support Reagan. When I say our members, I don't say 51 percent of our members, but to be a real problem, it don't take 51 percent! But we have a large number of our people who still think that Reagan hung the moon—the greatest thing that ever came down the pike. But we are constantly placing before our members, by our publications, the facts about him. Some of them read it, and some of them don't read it. And those who don't read it, just hear him on television, and he is a tremendous communicator. He does those things that sound good to our people, but at the same time he effectively takes away from them all of the things they need to support themselves in times of trials and tribulations.

A fellow told me the other day about a group, steelworkers I think it was, up in Pennsylvania. When Reagan took the food stamps away from so many black people, they thought it was the greatest thing that ever happened. But now, whether Reagan caused it or who caused it, the steel industry is in such bad shape they're all out there on the street drawing food stamps. Yet, they don't even consider themselves in the same category as that other group. And they're still Reagan's friend, great friend.

Old and New

Our labor leaders have done as well as they could under the conditions they have to work and fight under. You know, I go so far back until I can recall when the president and the secretary-treasurer of the Louisiana state AFL-CIO had to go to the bank and borrow money on their own signature to keep the organization running. And even though we now have more money to work with than the old timers, Louisiana went from a non-right-to-work state to a so-called right-to-work state. So, how do you figure?

I think Lane Kirkland is probably as intelligent a person as we've ever had as the president of the AFL-CIO. Now, I won't knock George Meany at all about being intelligent either, but sometimes I thought he was a grumpy old booger. He probably could have done a lot better than he did for us, but he was still a dedicated trade unionist—you couldn't take that away from him. But I do think that probably Lane Kirkland is a better educated, maybe a smarter man. And I hope that because he is so that we are able to fix some of the broken pieces that we've got.

Labor-Management Cooperation

We've been involved in some of those cooperative agreements where a company and a union jointly try to improve the productivity and wages of workers. Some of them are good, but there is another side to that coin though. You see those programs tend to work only in the large locals that have full-time local union officers who are on the same level as the corporation's management. They're the ones who can demand and get an equal shot.

Now, you take a local out in the boonies some place that's got fifty people in it, a hundred people, maybe even up to five hundred people. Its officers are more than likely working in the plant, and there's no earthly way for them to reach that level of the management team. But they're going to find that management will literally love them to death. Management will put their arms around a handful of them, take them out to dinner, and the next thing you know, they've got a "decert" [decertification] election on their hands. If a management wants to be unscrupulous, and they want to destroy a local union, that's as good a way as I know of to do it.

But we have entered into a number of these programs in the larger locals, and some of the smaller locals have tried but their programs have just sort of paled away. And we've lost about three plants where I feel sure management used the program for the sole purpose of decerting that plant.

Another thing that's been talked about is having a labor representative sit on the board of a company's directors. If our president was to sit on a board of one of these big paper companies, our membership first off would just oppose it terribly. They might after a period of time get accustomed to it, but our membership would feel their president would not necessarily be able to keep the interest of the membership in his best posture. I don't agree with them. I personally think that we ought to have more communications with the top management people, but our membership is still of the opinion that you can't do that. We've not yet reached that point of trust that Scandinavian countries have reached.

Looking Back

I probably will end my career as secretary-treasurer, unless something drastically happened, God forbid, to our president. I helped him get elected. We're a product of a number of merged organizations. He was a vice-president/regional director of his union with an office in Little Rock, Arkansas. At the same time I was vice-president/regional director of my union with my office in Monroe, Louisiana. We had the same states and jurisdictions. So we had known one another for thirty, thirty-five years, and fought with each other for twenty of them just constantly. But then in 1972 we merged and when we did, well I got to know him, and he got to know me, and we became friends. I respect him for the job he did while we were in opposition to one another, and I hope he does me too. I'm a little older than him so I have no doubt that he'll be here when I'm gone.

You know lots of secretary-treasurers find it hard being "second banana," and sometimes it does bother me—being totally and completely honest, it does. But I'm also a realist enough to know that somebody has to be the second in command, somebody has to be there. So I'm not envious, and I think I handle it pretty well.

My theme is now to get back to the old philosophy of "I love my union." I'm going out now to attend two regional seminars, and the instructions for my staff are to pack me at least one "I love my Union" bumper sticker for every person that's going to be at those meetings.

After I'm gone there will be one thing of me left here, that'll be a picture hanging on the wall. We're no different from corporations in that regard. After a chairman of the executive board or CEO of any corporation leaves, they wipe it clean and start over again. It won't be easy though to walk away. I tell everybody that talks to me in the business, "Well, if I don't have any competition next time, I'll probably stay around, but if I have competition I might just go." But that ain't the way it works, if I had competition, I'd probably stay.

10. Hard Work and a Bit of Luck

Edward Fire

Politics at the national level is so much more sophisticated than at the lower levels. . . . You've really got to prove you have the right stuff.

Edward Fire was elected to a four-year term as secretary-treasurer of the International Union of Electronic, Electrical, Salaried, Machine and Furniture Workers (IUE), at the union's twenty-first constitutional convention in 1984. He had been first named to the post by the IUE executive board in 1982 to complete the unexpired term of his predecessor.

Prior to that, Mr. Fire had been an international vice-president and president of District 7, IUE's largest district, since January 1981. The six-state district is based in Dayton, Ohio.

From 1965 through 1974, Edward Fire served as president of the 10,000-member local 717, Packard Electric Division of General Motors in Warren, Ohio; as secretary-treasurer of District 7 from January 1975 through May 1977; and as chairman of the IUE-General Motors Conference Board from June 1977 through December 1980. He was chief negotiator for the IUE national contract bargaining with GM in 1979.

Mr. Fire is a native of Lowellville, Ohio, and attended Youngstown State University. He served three years in the U.S. Navy in the Mediterranean area.

For a description of the IUE, see chapter 5.

* * *

IT may sound corny but the work of unions is focused on human dignity. We are just not going to let people be abused in plants. Lane Kirkland said once that all sinners belong in church, and all workers belong in the union. I believe that. And yet, it's not hard to keep unions out of a plant, it's easy.

We just don't have a decent opportunity to organize today—the cards are stacked against us. What companies can get away with in terms of the law is unforgivable. In effect, they can tell people, "If you join the union you're not going to have a job," and, "If you join the union and there's a strike, who's going to take care of your family?" and all that kind of stuff. We've got to take away the power that these companies have in terms of really intimidating and abusing people when they're considering to join a union. That's what we've got to do for the long-range future of unions as I see it.

But we still try to organize. We had a campaign at Eastern Airlines, and we got murdered. Frankly, if we win a plant of 100, 200, or 300 people now and again, it's a great victory, but we win nowhere in proportion to the amount of money that we spend on organizing in those campaigns.

And it's not just in organizing where things are tough. I just spoke with a friend of mine from Ohio about what LTV is planning to do because of its bankruptcy. They're going to take away health care benefits from their retirees and cut the pension benefits of their recent retirees. And those poor people who worked their entire lives for that company are just panicked. And look at how TWA is attempting to bust the Flight Attendants union. So there are enough issues out there for unions and people to get motivated over.

Frankly, unless the political climate changes dramatically in this country, I don't see the IUE surviving as an autonomous union a generation from now. We'll get to the point where we can't function autonomously because we won't have the membership. We just keep losing, and losing, as are most other unions. The UAW could lose 200,000 members and it's a problem. If we lost 200,000 members, we're done, that's it, we're out of business.

On Management

Management people are basically professionals. They're doing their jobs just as we are. The big companies are pros and you can fight at the bargaining table, but you can also go out and have a drink afterwards. That sounds like a cliché, but it's the truth. I don't hate these people, I like to argue with them and debate them. If they're honorable about bargaining, I respect them and might even like them on a personal basis. On the other hand, if a guy is a no-good son of a bitch, that's his problem and I won't spare any time for him.

One of the most humorous things I've ever witnessed in negotiations came from our side. There's a guy by the name of Frank Palma who's been the chairman of the shop committee of Local 509 of Rochester, New York, since 1955. He has been able to perpetuate himself in office all these years and he really is one of life's most unforgettable characters. He does his homework, though—there's just no question about it—he takes care of the store.

Well anyway, we were getting down near the end of negotiations in 1967 in Detroit, Michigan, and had been meeting for something like the last three or four days, twelve- and fourteen-hour days. At the end of one of these all-day sessions, everybody was tired and bedraggled and just sick of eating rotten sandwiches, just really worn out, when the door to the bargaining room opens and here comes Palma. He's just come out of the sauna bath, his skin is all blanched out and his hair is still wet. He was the only guy I knew that could stay in a sauna for an hour and fall asleep. And here he comes with his big Italian cigar sticking out of his mouth and he walks around behind our side and just sits down.

We were really spinning our wheels at that point, not getting anything done. Well, Palma had not been sitting there for more than five minutes, and gets up, walks behind our head negotiator and whispers loud enough for the company bargainer to hear, "We can't get anything out of those c-suckers, Homer—let's get the hell out of here." The company's guy, who was always cool and smooth, when he heard what Palma said, the guy just went berserk. His face got beet red, he was screaming and yelling, "We don't have to take that stuff, Homer!" and Palma was shaking with laughter. That was a real classic. Palma has a knack of doing those kinds of things but you can't dislike the guy—he's a rogue.

My Work

What turns me on in this job? I really feel good about the union when I see one of our organizations functioning effectively. That's satisfying. If I see a district council for example doing the job for its members at the bargaining table, having an active organizing program, communicating with their members, being involved in political and social action, I really feel satisfied. I would be less than honest if I didn't say that a nice round of applause for one of my speeches isn't also satisfying. That feeds the ego obviously, and you get gratification from that.

I'll tell you what I'm most proud of though. This happened in 1970. We were in national negotiations with General Motors when at the same time the UAW struck them. Of course, all of our members were quickly laid off and under the Ohio law you were not permitted to collect unemployment compensation. As a result, our members were ineligible for supplemental unemployment benefits [SUB] under the contract, and so the only thing that they got for ten weeks was $12.00 per week strike benefits from the international. So in our negotiations with GM, I think I was helpful on the committee in successfully getting GM to pay the difference between what the members would've received in unemployment and SUB. That came out to around a $300 lump sum payment.

I wasn't married at that time, and I was living with one of my sisters. She told me that the day our members got their checks, she talked to the manager of the grocery store and he told her that he'd never seen anything like it. People were in there spending their whole check just on groceries. Those people really must have been hurting, and I felt I was instrumental in helping them. That was literally a case of putting bread on the table, and I am really proud of that.

So having something challenging to do like that basically gives me a sense of satisfaction. I have always enjoyed going to the bargaining table with General Motors—it's always a challenge. You're confronting people who are among the very best in the business, and the challenge is to be able to win for our members a decent contract, decent wages, and decent benefits. General Motors bargaining is intellectually stimulating, because they're not going to try to beat you into submission like some antiunion companies would do. With them, the challenge is persuading and convincing you to withdraw demands and to accept less than what you want, and that's stimulating.

Getting Started

It was really accidental that I got involved in union work. I was going to college and working the second shift at a GM plant when a good friend who was a committeeman—in effect, a shop steward—asked me if I would take a job as his alternate because, candidly, no one else wanted it. So I did, and as I became more involved in the union I started to develop somewhat of a social consciousness. This was about 1960, when Kennedy ran for president, and I really became inspired with the whole idea of doing good, being a real do-gooder, you know, and I saw the union as a vehicle where you could do that. And so that's basically how I got started in working for the union.

The best politics for making it in a union career though is just working hard at your job. But I can't overestimate the element of luck either—being in the right place at the right time has a great deal to do with it. I've often wondered where would I be in terms of the labor movement if I had worked in a plant of 100 people, rather than a plant of 10,000. If you look carefully at it you'll see many talented people coming out of small locals, but it's usually the people in the big ones who get the attention and the opportunities. That's where the votes are, and that's the way it is in a democratic organization.

Personality is also very important when you're running for office, particularly at the local level. People want somebody who's sensible, articulate, intelligent, and not someone who's an ass, or pompous or anything like that.

But the element of luck has a lot to do with a union career. And for me, it occurred in 1962, when one of the candidates for a top office asked me if I would accept being nominated for vice-president on his ticket just in case the guy who he had tentatively on his ticket backed out and ran against him.

Well, sure enough, that's what happened, and so I ran for vice-president of the local, and was elected because I was on the strongest ticket. Once I got a taste of being vice-president, and functioning as president occasionally when he was out of town, I knew I wanted to become president. I ran against the incumbent and very frankly, I didn't win the election, he lost the election. It was strictly an antivote. We had just finished national negotiations, which I didn't participate in, but he did, and he took the criticism for some controversial things that were done in the negotiations.

There was also a third person in the race who I think probably took votes that would have gone to the incumbent had the third guy not been in the race. But in any event, I won by 200 votes out of something like 2,500 cast. So that's where the element of luck is in my career. I really wasn't that well known, I had only worked in the plant about six years when I ran for president. But once I became president, I obviously started working hard. We had two-year terms then, and in my first bid for reelection I had a pretty stiff opposition. After that it wasn't too bad.

After serving as my local's president, I became secretary-treasurer of the district council. I served in that job for about two and a half years, but as it turned out, the guy who was the chairman of our bargaining group in General Motors, and a good friend of mine, got up one morning and keeled over, dead of a heart attack. And so I moved into that position, where I was pretty much my own boss. Then, the guy who was the district president said he was going to retire, and so I ran for and got elected to that position, which was a darned good job.

My Work

A typical day for me involves a lot of paperwork, going over expenditures, approving requests for payment, paying bills, answering correspondence, meeting with the president or with the legal department or others on issues that come up. It's just generally administrative type work. I don't really mind the paperwork routine, but I don't get turned on by it. It just has to be done.

What I do enjoy more is going out to the members. For example, if one of our districts is having an education conference, I enjoy going out there and trying to get them fired up on political action, and that kind of thing. Recently, I went back to my old district and made a pitch for support of the merger with the Furniture Workers, and that I really enjoyed doing. Besides bringing that message, I got to socialize a little bit with good friends.

Staying in touch with the members though is not easy, and we don't do as effective a job as we can, or should, especially on political matters. For example, some locals have newspapers, others distribute leaflets, and a few others do absolutely nothing in terms of formally communicating to their members. Because of the size of our union, the international doesn't have video conferences or things like that, so we rely on our newspaper, which goes to the entire membership once a month.

Yet, a higher percentage of our members voted for Ronald Reagan than voted probably for Eisenhower. Historically, 70 percent of all union members were Democrats, 30 percent Republicans. But obviously, Reagan, who is antiunion, made significant inroads.

We haven't communicated effectively to our members about political appointments either. I would say 90 percent of our members have never heard of Donald Dotsun, the head of the National Labor Relations Board, a crucial position insofar as the institution of unionism in this country. And Supreme Court appointments—I don't know that we've communicated to our members that with Reagan as president, we're going to have in all like-lihood an antiunion Supreme Court. So basically, I don't think we've done a very good job of communicating to our members. The most effective means of communication in our country is television, and we're not really into it anywhere near the level that say businesses are. Yet, we did a survey of our members a year and a half or so ago and surprisingly, they felt we were doing reasonably well in terms of communicating with them.

One of the things that we have always done well in this union is providing education, conferences, and programs to our leadership. In fact we're having a meeting in the next couple of days of what we call our Social Action Committee. It's comprised of the education directors of each of our geographic districts, and the people who are involved in COPE [Committee on Political Education], the AFL-CIO's political arm. This is our top leadership group and we attempt to motivate them through these programs.

And we also regularly hold district council meetings where we give workshops. The districts then in turn go into local unions and put on seminars. We also go into local unions from this level and put on weekend training classes. The international has even gone so far as to take stewards and officers out of a plant for a couple of days, pay them for lost time, and give them special training. So I think that overall, we do a pretty decent job in terms of educating at least our leadership. But trying to get the rank and file involved is very tough.

The Members

For our rank and file the number one issue now is job security, holding onto their jobs. That's the name of the game today in collective bargaining, and it's what's happening in all the basic industries of our country. For the foreseeable future, the days of real lush economic packages are over.

But I don't really know whether that means givebacks will become more prevalent in the future. How the trade bill is disposed of will really determine that. But the Japanese aren't crazy—they aren't going to flood our markets, nor are other exporters to our country, because they realize that they're getting to the point where the American people have pretty much had it as far as the jobs that are being lost as a result of imports. So I think that we have to wait to see what happens with the trade bill before we can get some kind of a feeling as far as what will happen down the road on bargaining.

There is no question though that our members are concerned with job security. We survey our members at GM and far and away it's the number one issue. Comparable worth? It should be a priority issue, and it is with the activists, but not with the rank and file. Since the passage of the Civil Rights Act, there have been many opportunities for women to move into what had been historically male jobs. And they're doing that. They're going into the skilled trades in factories for example, and so that blunts the comparable worth issue.

In fact, I am pleasantly surprised to see as I've traveled around to IUE meetings that there are more younger women in local union positions. There's still a strong feeling in our country that the union business is a rough business, and that's a man's job, but I think that's breaking down. Unions generally don't move rapidly in terms of change, and yet in our own union, as I say, I'm really surprised at how many women are coming into leadership positions at the local level. I think it's terrific. We have more women on our staff than ever before in our history. But at the same time, I don't think that women have a chance of getting elected to a district, a conference board, or to the international level at this time.

The Secretary-Treasurer's Job

You know, most secretary-treasurers work in anonymity. That's just the way it is. You don't see my name in the papers—you see Bill Bywater's. In fact,

I was looking through some papers today and saw the name of the secretary-treasurer of one of the big unions, I don't even know the guy, or even saw his name before. But that's a fact of life in this job.

I really wonder sometimes whether I should've come to Washington. I can't say that it's been a disappointment, but in Ohio I was a big fish in a small pond. Now it's just reversed. I made my choice. I came here as the second-ranking officer of the international.

Number two is never number one. I have a good relationship with the president, but the authority is in the president's office, and that's as it should be. But that doesn't mean that I'm thrilled about being the number two officer. To a degree, I'm spoiled. As I said, I was president of a big local and had the opportunity to do what I pretty much wanted to do. If I wanted to be involved with the bargaining, I could be involved, if I wanted to be involved in COPE and legislation and those kinds of things, I could be. Obviously, speaking as president, I had a lot of impact.

But I probably will take Bill Bywater's spot someday. I hope I do, but who knows? Politics at the national level is so much more sophisticated than at the lower levels. You can never really just goof off in these jobs despite the fact that you become part of an overall administration slate. You've got to be working, you've got to fight for the issues and go out and explain your positions.

You've really got to prove you have the right stuff. For example, we had a dues increase two years ago and I did a lot of the work on it, particularly in presenting and selling the increase. That gets you respect. The time I spend at the bargaining table with the GM negotiations also gives me an opportunity to show my strengths in that area. And finally, being a good overall administrator shows my stuff. I know I'm a decent administrator.

One of the things about unions though that perhaps few people recognize is that we have a bureaucracy as bad as any other bureaucracy. So it's just not a question of cleaning house, you've got to work with what you have to a certain extent. In my opinion, there's too many people in the union who feel it's a nine-to-five job, just like they worked in a plant or something. That isn't the way it is—we want to be a good organization.

Looking Back

Great labor leaders? John L. Lewis and Walter Reuther. They are the two giants as far as I'm concerned in the history of the American labor movement. And while I was a local union officer in General Motors, I had the good fortune to get exposure to people like Leonard Woodcock and Doug Fraser [former United Autoworkers presidents]. Those guys had a tremendous organization, there's no question about it. Their staffs had esprit de corps, they were motivated, and in my judgment, that's what we really need to achieve.

I really think Lane Kirkland is extremely intelligent, an articulate, witty person. And I really like his way with words. I remember the 1981 AFL-CIO convention held right after Stockman spilled his guts to the *Atlantic Magazine*.[1] Kirkland said about Stockman, "Now we have the architect of this economic house of ill repute. Now that the bust is near, he says he was only the piano player, he didn't know what was going on upstairs!"

But sometimes I do think though the AFL-CIO really goes too far, and spends too much time, on issues that are not directly linked to the membership. Maybe not as much anymore, but when Meany was president, he used to worry about all these foreign policy things that really didn't have a hell of a lot of meaning for us. We were always saying when he was president he was on the wrong side anyway because of his policies. I mean, if he was alive today, he'd be urging Reagan to send the troops down to Nicaragua! But Kirkland is no dove either as far as that's concerned.

Personally, I think I'd like to be remembered as the guy who helped to revitalize the union, got it on the move and started to do some good things. I don't have any revolutionary ideas that perhaps others have not thought of, but I really do think it comes down to a question of motivating people. I know I have the ability to do that and if I get the chance, I will.

11. Protecting Fire Fighters

John A. Gannon

We encourage our locals to write no lock out no strike clauses into their contracts because we are in the life saving business . . .

John A. Gannon took office as president of the International Association of Fire Fighters (IAFF) on September 20, 1980, and was reelected in 1982, 1984, and 1986. A working fire fighter in his native city of Cleveland for more than thirty years, Mr. Gannon was an active leader of the Fire Fighters Local 93. He served as president for more than ten years, following previous service as a committeeman, steward, trustee, and vice-president. During the same years, he occupied posts as a vice-president of the Cleveland Federation of Labor, a vice president of the Ohio AFL-CIO, and lobbyist for the state's fire fighters at the Ohio legislature in Columbus.

John A. Gannon was born in 1923 and attended Miami University in Ohio and Glasgow University in Scotland.

The economic recession of the early 1980s took a heavy toll on municipalities' fire services. Cities and towns closed fire houses, reduced manpower, and resisted efforts to improve the incomes and security of rank-and-file fire fighters. With an improving economy, however, the IAFF, under the leadership of Mr. Gannon, began efforts to raise fire fighters' living standards, cut the heavy death and injury rates that have made fire fighting one of the most dangerous occupations,[1] and to bring about urgently needed advances in the safety and health protection of fire fighters.

During recent years the IAFF has placed strong emphasis on occupational safety and health objectives, including modernized clothing and equipment for fire fighters, improved research on the combating of fires involving toxic chemicals, the protection of both the public and fire fighters from serious chemical hazards, and the improvement of facilities for the treatment of burn victims of fire.

The IAFF was established in 1918 as a result of the merger of local fire fighter unions across the United States. However, through the early decades of the twentieth century most cities prohibited the organization of fire fighters and other public service employees because it was considered a threat to a city's sovereignty. With the passage of the National Industrial Recovery Act of 1933 and the National Labor Relations Act, the Fire Fighters, like other unions of public sector employees, grew steadily in numbers. Today, the IAFF represents 180,000 fire fighters—including drivers/operators, hosemen, tiller men, sergeants, lieutenants, and captains—in the United States and Canada.

———————————————— ✳ ✳ ✳ ————————————————

I'M up for reelection in August of '88 and I want it. I just haven't accomplished what I set out to do because of our financial problems. We've only just begun to rebuild, hire, and put in some new programs.

Getting Started

After I had been laid off from my job as a plumber, I decided to become a fire fighter. That was during the economic recession of the late 1940s. In fact, I got called for the fire department the same week that the plumbing company that I worked for called us all back to work. But it really wasn't a coin toss in choosing between the two jobs. You see, my wife remembered that during the Depression there was a fire fighter that lived on her street, and everybody looked up to him because he had a steady job during those years. Well, like I said, things were slow in '47, '48, and '49. It wasn't a depression, but at least the public servants were still working. And that impressed my wife and I, especially since we were expecting our second child. So I went for the security and the pension, and I joined the fire department.

Going to the fire department did mean I was going to have to work more hours than I did as a plumber, and for about half the salary of a plumber. Let's see, I was making $219 a week as a plumber working 40 hours a week back then, and as a fireman I got that amount of money twice a month with a 72-hour week. We were also 24 hours on, 24 hours off, and once every two weeks, we got what we called a "Kelly Day." That came from Chicago, where Mayor Kelly gave the fire fighters, years ago, an extra day off, and so they called it a Kelly Day.

A Union Career

As soon as I joined the department, I joined the union, and started attending union meetings. Attending meetings was a little unusual, most members didn't and still don't. But as a matter of fact, going to the meeting back then offered a way to get a little recreation because we weren't paid too much, and we couldn't really afford much in the way of outside entertainment.

But I didn't really get active in the local until 1960, when half a dozen of us were put up on charges for neglecting to pick up our new fire boots. See, the city had contracted out the boots to this one-man operation, and every time we'd go down there to pick up the boots, the guy would be out selling. It was always, "Be back in an hour"—that sort of thing.

Well, we didn't have that kind of time and the six of us would change off, "Well, you go down tomorrow, and I'll go down the next day." Finally, the chief called for an inspection and we didn't have our boots, and so they put us up on charges. We went to our steward, but all he said was, "Well, you guys are wrong," and he wouldn't handle the grievance. The department was all set to lay us off when I decided to handle my grievance, and then the other five guys said, "Handle ours too." So I went in and won the grievance, and I won pretty big.

Anyhow, the union got all excited about it, and I got pushed into running for trusteeship. Well, I won the election and served for two years; then I was elected as my local's vice-president for two years, and then president for ten years. In 1976 I was elected vice-president of the international.

Our vice-presidents are not full time with the union—they're paid per diem on assignments. But since I had the largest district (I had the Midwest—Ohio, Illinois, Indiana, Kentucky, Michigan) the position was just about full time for me. I was extremely busy as a vice-president, the militancy of our members was unbelievable. From '76 to '80, in those forty-eight months, we had forty-two strikes, and I had to work them all.

The problem then of course was that there were no collective bargaining laws. Ohio didn't have it, Illinois didn't have it, Kentucky had one but it was designed specifically for Louisville, Kentucky. The local there, Local 345, was able to lobby that through the legislature so the law is called law 345. The rest of Kentucky had no collective bargaining whatsoever. In Indiana, to this day, the locals and the cities meet and confer but they don't really have a law that allows collective bargaining for public employees. The only state that had a law was Michigan, and it had one for years, and it was a model law.

And so what you had most times were the cities treating the fire fighters as second class citizens. They'd refuse to pay, refuse to meet with us, or just stall—that kind of thing. Well, by 1976, things just came to a head. The fire fighters felt it was time to speak up, and to show strength. And that's what they did. I'll never forget the strike in Chicago. See, most of our strikes were typically resolved within three days, but in Chicago, it went on for twenty-two days.

Chicago mayor Jane Byrne attempted to settle it early on, but the local's president was enjoying his notoriety too much for that. He was on television every other day, and I guess liked it too much even to meet with her. She asked me to come over and meet her, and I said I would if there was a union member with me. She said that was fine, but when I asked the local's president, he wouldn't allow it. He said we had her on the run. He then called the members out to strike on February 14. Can you believe it? The fourteenth, in Chicago! Just like the St. Valentine's Day massacre! Well, a couple days later he got thrown in jail for striking, and then Reverend Jesse Jackson entered into the dispute and helped to mediate the situation.

Reverend Jackson could've broken the strike. He had about 500 members who pledged their support to him, and if he had decided to cross the line with them, well, that would've ended the strike then and there. You have to remember that about 500 members had already crossed the line, and Jane Byrne had hired 700 replacements. So if Jackson had crossed the line, it would've given the city enough personnel, and it would have shut out the rest of the strikers. But Reverend Jackson didn't cross the line, and in fact he did a good job as a mediator.

It's funny, but not too long ago, I was at a roast for Senator Bill Bradley and all the presidential candidates were there. At the next table over from where I was sitting the reverend was being interviewed, and he kept looking over at me. Then all of a sudden he yelled over to me, "Fire fighter!" and then came over and shook hands and said, "Remember I helped you guys in Chicago?" and then jokingly, "What I'll do now is to give you a shot at helping me." I told him that the best I could do in helping him with his bid for the Democratic nomination was to arrange for him to speak to our board, the same offer we gave everybody else, and he said that's fair enough.

Strikes

We encourage our locals to write no strike, no lockout clauses into their collective bargaining contracts because we are in the life saving business. We believe it's not to anyone's advantage to have strikes and lockouts. However, if the members are getting pushed around, and not treated properly, I think they ought to have the right to strike. But, because our job is life saving, what we've done at least in every strike that I've been involved with, is to have what we call a "flying squad." That's made up of strikers who have their own equipment in their own vehicles, and when an alarm came in, they would respond to it. And what they do is to go through a building and look for life, and do the rescue, that's all. In any case, they then reported to the chief what they did, and then went about their business.

But really, my feeling is that the threat of a strike is more valuable than a strike itself. However, if you don't scare the opposition, you'd better have all your apples in the same jar. You know when locals would call me when I was vice-president and say, "Well, we had a strike vote and 68 percent of the men want a strike," I'd say, "Don't do it—70 percent, don't do it; 80 percent, I'd still say don't do it." Until you get over 85 percent, or 90 percent, you don't have control. And to call for a strike when you don't have that support is a mistake, a big mistake. You get backdoored by those who don't want a strike, and it just creates more problems for you.

Making It to the Top

Well, my predecessor retired and the international's secretary-treasurer immediately announced his candidacy. I didn't really have problems with him, I even had supported him up until the last year. But we started quarreling just after that over some questions I was asking about the $262,000 deficit he was reporting, and some other things about our finances. I wasn't getting good answers to my questions, so I went out and asked two other vice-presidents to run for president. But they said no, that nobody could beat him, and they didn't want to gamble. I said, well, I'm not going to let him just walk in, so I decided to run.

I won by 220 votes out of 147,000 that were cast, and my opponent immediately challenged the results. He ran to the federal court but they threw it out saying that until we had used our own avenues, including the Department of Labor, and the procedures in our constitutional bylaws, they would not hear the complaint. That mess ended up costing the union about $100,000 in legal fees, and within thirty days of sitting in this chair, I found out that the deficit he was reporting wasn't $262,000, it was more like $700,000, and that wasn't counting the cost of the election or our convention expenses. So to make a long story short, the deficit actually amounted to $1,800,000. There was nothing illegal about the deficited amounts, it was just overspending, some recklessness, really no blame to be laid on anybody. The former president was just very liberal with funds—they were flying first class and just having some of the good life.

Well, the first two years in office for me were really tough, we had to get a loan from the Painters union in the amount of $700,000 for cash flow, just to keep the dogs away from the door, and we also had to go to the membership for a voluntary assessment. We also cut back in staff to save on salary expense, and established a line-item budget, so that we had better control over our departments. We are doing much better now though. We paid back our loan, and as a matter of fact, we've paid for our last two conventions in advance, and that represents better than a half a million dollars.

On Management

The cities started playing hardball with us right after President Reagan broke PATCO. It's just been take-away time since then. For example, there've been locals that had full family hospitalization, and the cities are moving them to single coverage. And a lot of our affiliates have gone through no-pay-raise years, or just gotten an insult of a 1 percent raise. And these are in cities where taxes are good. So we've gotten to the point now where we send economists into cities to examine their budgets before we begin negotiating. And oftentimes we're able to find out they're hiding money, or just not properly managing it.

For example, we found one city that kept most of their general fund in a checking account at a local bank. We figured that the amount of interest they lost by keeping it there would've doubled the salary demands that this particular local wanted. So when we got that information I called the mayor, told him what we had found, and that we wanted to meet with him.

Later on the city's finance director told us that the mayor would agree to our 10 percent wage demand if we agreed not to take any of what we found public. To that, I said, "Well, we've just had a meeting with the executive board here and their demands have changed." He said, "You dirty bird," but agreed to the demands, and we got the members 12 percent for two years. Darned though if the president of that local didn't call me about two months later wanting to go public with what we found because he was angry with the mayor over something. I told him, "What do you care? Next time you go into negotiations you've got the same clout!"

Stress

I think every fire fighter, at least one time in their career, has dealt with . . . a life and death situation. I know it happened to me within maybe four hours. We assisted with the birth of a baby, then went to a false alarm, and then in the next call, we had a fire and ended up putting a body in a body bag. It's definitely a stress job, and it concerns us a lot as to how our members cope with it.

One of the things we're especially concerned with is the incidence of drug abuse among our members. Years ago, we never thought about drugs, but it started popping up on our job after Vietnam. Veterans coming back and smoking pot would be put up on charges, and the union would have to go and represent them at grievance hearings.

While we always represent them fairly, our position is that we don't want hopheads around on scenes of life and death. You don't want a guy walking on a cloud when you want him working with you. But we also didn't like the idea that these people could be fired without proper representation, so we always have a representative at the hearing with the member. But we always tell the member that we won't protect him a second time. The first time you go along with the problem and you get the member into a substance abuse program, which we have in our contracts now, but if they do it the second time, they're on their own.

Same with alcohol abuse, which in fact had probably a higher incidence when I first came on. But I think the departments are more stringent about alcohol abuse today than they are drug abuse. For instance, there are some departments that maintain you can't drink alcohol up to eight hours before coming on duty. And if that's in the contract, the position of the union is that you live up to the contract.

Affirmative Action

We have increased the number of women and minorities in the Fire Fighters over the years, but it has been slow. I would say that when I came on the job in the forties there was maybe 1 percent minority representation, in the sixties, I think it went up to about 4 percent, and now it might be 10 percent. It's hard for us to determine the exact percentage because one thing we don't do is to ask the membership about their gender or race. We try to treat everybody equally.

However, we did have a federal grant to help us set up a minority recruitment program to increase the number of minorities working as fire fighters. What we did was to set up headquarters in a ghetto area storefront to recruit people. And we hired black fire fighters to go in the poolrooms and recruit applicants. After we recruited them, we tutored them maybe for two months on subjects pertaining to the examination for fire fighters, and while there was no guarantee that they'd get a job, a lot of them got good jobs.

When Ronald Reagan came along in '80 though, his administration cut our grant, and the next thing you know, we're in court with affirmative action problems. We did try to approve some monies to continue the program at our convention, but because of our deficit, it was decided that any monies we got from the members would go to save the union.

Looking Back

About twenty-two years ago in Cleveland, Ohio, we had a severe fire in which a lot of people got severely . . . burned. But as we were rushing them to hospitals for treatment, the hospitals were saying to us, "We don't have any facilities, take 'em over to the City Hospital, or take 'em over to the Metro," or something like that. Well, at that point I decided that we had to do something about getting a facility that could handle burn victims.

So I went to Metropolitan General Hospital, which was centrally located in the city, and convinced them that we ought to do something. They agreed and fitted out a bed for the treatment of burn victims. I then started to encourage our local to raise money to expand the number of beds, and I think our first contribution was maybe $8,000. Since then we've been able to raise more and more money for them, and now the hospital is finishing a wing devoted to treating burn victims. It also has several helicopters to service emergencies. But the really incredible thing is that they've decided to name the wing after me. That's an accomplishment that took a long time, but really, to have something like that named after you, it's overwhelming.

12. On the Road across Rural America

Tom W. Griffith

Paul Harvey's old story about people going to a convention back in the 1940s pretty much describes our members—they went to town with a $10 bill and the Ten Commandments, and didn't break either one of them.

Tom W. Griffith served as president of the National Rural Letter Carriers' Association (NRLCA) from 1983 through 1986. While president of the 70,000 member union, he served as the chief spokesman of the NRLCA negotiating team in the 1984–1988 national agreement deliberations with the United States Postal Service.

After service in the United States Navy, Mr. Griffith attended Colorado State University and shortly thereafter went to work for the Postal Service as a rural letter carrier. He is a second generation rural carrier. His father served out of the Eaton, Colorado, post office for thirty-seven years.

Mr. Griffith chose not to run for reelection in 1986, preferring to return to his native Colorado, and retiring after more than forty-one years with the Postal Service. Prior to becoming national president, he had served as an unpaid officer of his local union (1968–1975), a member of the national executive board (1975–1981) and national vice-president (1981–1983).

The NLRCA was founded in 1903 by rural letter carriers representing fourteen state associations. Today's rural letter carriers drive 2.4 million miles and service 18,000,000 rural American families on 43,000 rural postal routes. Rural carriers are "post offices on wheels," providing full postal service to the American public. Carriers are often considered part of the extended families of their customers.

———————————— * * * ————————————

Labor needs to hold its head up. We've gotten the things we had to fight so hard for, the fight for good working conditions, comparable salaries, and good fringe benefits. Now of course, management is going to employees and saying, "You got it all, what do you need a union for?"

I don't think their position is all that unusual nor should it be unexpected. It has to be that way to balance power between labor and management. As long as the pendulum is moving, whichever side it's on, if it's moving, that's healthy. If it gets stuck on one side or the other, that's dangerous. When labor becomes too powerful, it can choke off managers' ability to manage, and needless to say, a too powerful management can stifle a responsible and reasonable crowd. And it's the latter situation which we have now, the pendulum is really stuck on the management side. It's the new mood in the country—Republicans, President Reagan, PATCO, and the whole tone of "busting unions."

It's very clear from all the evidence for example that Mr. Reagan is dedicated to turning as much of public service employment as possible over to private enterprise, to the corporate leaders of the world. I can't decide whether it's because of ignorance, or vindictiveness, or what the hell the reason is, but this administration is determined to do just that. While they might not get rid of all government employment, they're making it so bad that nobody wants to go to work for the government. If my son or daughter, either one of them, would act like they wanted to become a rural carrier or a Postal Service employee, I believe I'd buy them off! I'd certainly counsel them to stay the hell out of the business, because at the present time there's no future in it. Worse than that, there's no pride in it.

I ride a lot of airplanes and one of the first things you talk about to the guy sitting next to you is, "What do you do?" I never know whether to tell them I work for the Postal Service, or I work for a labor union, because neither one is very popular in this country. If you tell them, "Well I work for the Postal Service" they'll start telling you about how bad it is and how bad the services are. And if I say, "Well I don't really work for the postal system, I'm a labor officer for one of the postal service unions," I'm really in trouble.

This whole thing probably started back in the early to mid-seventies when the Postal Service was in fact pretty terrible. Right now, the service, and the cost of the service to the citizens is fantastic, but nobody knows it. But neither the press nor the cartoonists will get off our backs. We're easy targets, we can't really fight back very well. And when Mr. Carter changed the Civil Service Commission to the Office of Personnel Management [OPM], that certainly didn't help us. The former was an advocate for Civil Service employees, but the OPM is an adversary. They're trying to beat us to death all the time on benefits and working conditions.

I heard one labor leader say that to get the mood back to pro-union in this country it's going to take a terrible recession or depression, because only then people will finally recognize the importance of labor unions. And I suppose that's true. Unions were born out of that sort of thing, and they'll be reborn, I suppose, if that comes to pass. But even if we don't enter into that great recession, labor unions are still going to exist, they're just not going to be able to hold sway in everything that they do. They're going to have to fight and scrap, but again, I don't think they ought to have their way with everything, only when there is a need.

PATCO

Reagan did set an example for public sector employees with PATCO, but the problem was really created by PATCO. I happened to know the PATCO people and it was a terrific union. But the fellow who called their strike led them down the primrose path. He promised them something that he couldn't deliver, something that wasn't true. He said, "We'll bring the air traffic industry to its knees. If we don't work, they can't fly, and if they can't fly, the citizens of the United States are going to gather around us and we'll win the fight."

In the first place, the strike was illegal. And secondly, you can't do it illegally and be successful unless you have 100 percent control. You got to bring them to their knees. I'm not an advocate of strikes, or strike clauses in contracts, maybe because I'm not that familiar with them. I wasn't involved in the Postal Service Union in the 1970s when they had the general strike, but I do know it was only successful because most of the people in the country understood that postal employees were poorly paid. The people were on the union side, and so the government couldn't do anything against the union.

PATCO was a different situation though. They had the bull by the tail, and just wanted a little bigger chunk of the tail. Had they went to binding arbitration, they may have won the case. I'm a believer in binding arbitration, it's always been included in the contracts that I've worked under and I think it works real well.

QWL Programs

We've tried to do different things to keep our relationship with management running smoothly, and at the same time improve the status of our people.

For instance, we initiated a quality of work life [QWL] employee involvement program with the Postal Service in 1982. It's doing well for us even though implementation on the part of management has been painfully slow. They've been in such turmoil over the last eighteen months, having gone through four postmasters-general, that the program has not really been a critical issue for them, and it has suffered some for that.

Our hope though is that the QWL program will reduce the costs related to handling grievances and arbitration cases. That's the tangible aspect of it for us. I also think we'll improve morale with it because every worker on the workroom floor wants a say about changes in work rules—if nothing else it makes you feel good. When the boss says, "Come on in, Charlie, let's sit down and see if we can work out something better compared to what we're doing," there's a lot of value in that.

Some claim that these programs are just a ploy by management to get more work out of the employee without putting anything in the worker's hip pocket in return for the extra work. I think that's sour grapes. There's worth to good working conditions and morale. I can even tie dollars to it because there is a difference in a person wanting to go to work in the morning and a person dreading it. If you're so unhappy in your job that you don't want to get up in the morning, that's going to carry over as a cost for your employer. But if you could switch it around, and have a positive feeling about going to work, that ought to be worth a couple thousand dollars a year.

In other organizations, employees have the chance to buy shares of their company, and that can build morale as well. We've discussed that vaguely and only briefly in past negotiations, but the Postal Service doesn't really want such a program. I really wouldn't want to buy any stock in the Post Office either. I think it would be a damn poor investment.

Collective Bargaining

Until the Postal Reorganization Act [PRA] of 1970, our organization was more or less a social organization. We had only one function really, and that was to lobby Congress. The PRA though forced us into a labor-management situation where we had to negotiate a national agreement. We learned fast back in those years, and were very fortunate that it was easy to make good strides then. It's not that way any more.

In the early years, the Postal Service really didn't know anything about the rural delivery system and we were just such a small portion of their operation. Anyway, there are only 43,000 rural routes, so that means there are 43,000 rural carriers and probably 35,000 substitutes that fill in on relief days. That's a drop in the bucket compared to the other postal unions like the City Carriers and Clerks, which are both 250,000 or more. So it was relatively easy for us to make strides in those early years because when we asked for a 10 percent salary increase for instance, it didn't scare anybody. On the other hand, you negotiate for a 10 percent salary increase for 250,000 people, that scares them.

Mergers

We do work with the other postal unions to try and coordinate some of our activities, even though there's been some shooting between us in the past. We've suffered a raid or two in my time, and we really couldn't do much about it then because of our size. But I made up my mind that I was damned if I was going to give up this union to them. I'm not interested in mergers unless the others want to join us! So I made a determined effort to cooperate and get on a friendly and personal basis with Vince Sombrotto and Moe Biller [the presidents of the National Association of Letter Carriers and the American Postal Workers Union, respectively]. There had to be some co-operation among our unions because we were damaging each other, particularly when it came time to negotiate.

In not too many years, though, I think I'll live to see it anyway—you'll see a merger among the postal unions. It'll be two crafts, inside workers and outside workers. Our folks, the officers of this association won't say that, and I wouldn't want them to say it, but it's going to happen.

However, if this union wasn't so healthy financially, so healthy membership-wise and the membership apparently so satisfied, I'd think about a merger now. But we're doing well, we've got plenty of money, and the last time we looked, 93 percent of the regular rural carriers were members of this organization. That's fantastic if you judge it against almost any other legitimate labor union that doesn't have a closed shop.

Getting Started

I started as a rural carrier working in 1950 and got involved in the union about fifteen years later when someone dragged me to a meeting of my local. When I got there, they said, "Tom Griffith, glad to see you, where have you been? We want you to go out for the elections next year as vice-president. Oh it's all right, you don't have to do anything—the vice-president don't do nothin." They were right—I didn't do anything! But after a couple of years I automatically became the local president and got a lot busier.

In about 1972 or '73, I reached the top pay level as a rural carrier. In fact, my salary was higher than my postmaster, and if I wanted more money

I would've had to go into management, and at least in the short run take a salary decrease. Luckily, the opportunity came up to move into union work on a full-time basis and to make a living from it. And so I was elected in 1975 to a national position that paid a salary better than my rural route job, and my career has evolved from there.

To tell you the truth, I don't know why I got in this work. My dad was a rural mail carrier, but we were raised antiunion. Out in Colorado back then they didn't know what a labor union was. Still don't, really. It's not a unionized state by any means, and really, if you go outside of Denver, there aren't any unions except the Farmers' union, and you know what that amounts to.

A Union Career

The appeal of being a union officer in the long run lies in the money and the ego trip. It's definitely an ego trip—there's no other way you can look at it. It's just like being a politician. A politician is well-rewarded financially, but hell, they've all got egos that you couldn't carry through a door! And we're no different—I'm no different. Some of us admit it, some of us can't control it, and for some of us, it ruins our life and everybody's around us.

I think that as far as a career goes, it's a whole lot easier being in management than working your way to the top in a labor union. You get automatic progressions in management and you can get advanced even if you're bad, just to get you out of the way. That doesn't happen in a labor union. You only progress through the labor movement because of merit. If you can't stand that, then you've got no business doing this work. It takes political courage, a lot of guts and self-confidence to make it to the top. Although the salaries are pretty good when you get up into the higher echelons, there's no tenure, or any guarantees that you'll be around long. It's a very highly exposed job—you've always got people watching you.

And there's a lot of work to being a union officer, and that's one of the reasons I'm really kind of looking forward to retirement. I'm not tired really of the work, maybe just the sixty-hour workweeks, and working almost every weekend, and every holiday, and being on the road so much.

Vacation time is something you don't have. I haven't had a vacation with my family and wife since 1977, except for maybe the three, four days at one state convention or another, or at the national convention. But even there you only get to see the inside of the hotel and the airport—that's it. You live out of a suitcase, and that's not good. So I guess if there's a downside to this job, it's the damned travel.

I've served as president since 1983. While the traditional term of office in this small union is two years, I broke that long-standing tradition by staying a third year really in an effort to do away with the tradition. I did not want us to continue to be crumpled by the terrific price of a turnover in this office—the loss of experience and the loss of continuity. I even toyed with the idea of staying another year or two, but in order to do that I would've had to stay another three years to get us through our 1988 national agreement. I just couldn't stay another year and quit and drop those preparations on somebody—that would not have been fair to the members. Anyway, if I did stay I would've been too old to do some of the things that I've got in mind to do, so that's why I'm retiring now.

All in all, it'll be easy to walk away from this job. I will miss doing parts of it, but I won't miss it so much that it's going to be a problem for me. I'll get up and find something else to do.

My Work

There's usually at least one crisis a day, and it could come from one of three sources. We've got Congress to deal with for benefits and that sort of thing; the Postal Service, which we deal with for the national agreement and working conditions; and then there's the membership.

And our folks aren't too shy about speaking their minds. You get those damned telephone calls, sometimes it will just ring off the wall, or you get those poison pen letters. We're a pretty intimate, small group really, and if you travel around like I have to attend different meetings, you get to meet an awful lot of people. They'll write or call and say, "Goddamn it, Tom, you're doing it wrong!"—not, "Dear Mr. President, I'd like to raise a point with you . . ." Because we have a rule in this organization that all calls or letters to an officer get answered by the officer, keeping up with the members can take a lot of time.

But our members are by nature conservative. The great bulk of them are from little ol' small towns out in the country, and are good churchgoing folk. Paul Harvey's old story about people going to a convention in Chicago back in the 1940s is still generally accurate for our members—they went to town with a $10 bill and the ten commandments, and didn't break either one of them. Oh, you'll find today that some of our members tend to have a little fun at the conventions, a few of them drink, a few of them chase girls and things like that, but a good portion of them are God-fearing country folk.

Another part of the job that takes time and effort is managing our staff and office workers here at headquarters. It hadn't been too many years ago we had a young lady around here who wanted to organize a union to represent the staff. She talked about salary raises, some benefits, and that sort of thing. I told her, "Well, we provide those things for you, but if you would like to, we'll start at zero, and negotiate a contract with you folks. If you think you can start a better contract than we can negotiate for our people with the Postal Service, fine, take your choice." You see, we've always given our staff the same amount of wage increase or COLA [cost of living adjustments] that we got through bargaining with the Post Office. Well, that was the end of the organizing drive, but we were glad to let them have their choice.

Looking Back

There are three or four things though that I'm really proud of doing here. The first is buying this building to serve as our headquarters and leaving this organization without owing a cent to anybody in the world. We own the building and we have no outstanding debts. Not too many years ago, I believe it was 1979 or 1980, our members' equity was $27,000. We didn't even have enough money to pay our national convention off that year. Today our members' equity is almost $3 million dollars, and I'm pleased that financially we've done a good job.

I guess if I feel good about anything, it's holding the membership together, putting them all in step, and being able to maintain ninety percent of the craft as members of this organization. You know, we had a bad contract in 1981. In fact, it was the only bad contract that I know that we've ever negotiated, and it drew such a division in our membership that we were probably more vulnerable than ever before to being raided by another union. Well, I was the chief negotiator for our current contract, and everyone seems to be pretty pleased.

I've also always tried to get the best for the membership. My style is to hire professionals to advise me and to do the work. I've hired a professional lobbyist, who I think is one of the best in town. Our general counsel is one of the top three labor attorneys in the city. I have a professional who runs our substantial health plan, which is up around $75 million a year in claims paid out. We print a national magazine that has a circulation of 65,000 copies a week! Each week we put that baby out, and we've never missed a deadline. I have a professional who does that. Whenever there are special projects or special needs or a crisis, or anything, I spend the money and go talk to people that know what they're doing, take their advice and then make up my mind. You know, basically, I'm a rural carrier. I know how to carry mail, but I also know that a good manager gets assistance when he's not an expert.

13. Anticipating the Unanticipated

Marshall M. Hicks

Unions are born out of necessity, and we don't need to do advertising, on television or anywhere else, to convince people that unions are necessary.

Marshall M. Hicks has been national secretary-treasurer of the Utility Workers Union of America (UWUA) since 1971. Prior to this position he was vice-president (1956) and president (1957–1967) of Local 258 in Adrian, Michigan; vice-president (1961–1963), secretary-treasurer (1963–1967), and president (1967–1970) of the Michigan State Utility Workers Council; and executive board member (1967–1971) and regional director (1970–1973) of the UWUA. Mr. Hicks, born in 1931, is a native of Claibourn County, Tennessee. He was employed by Consumers Power Company in Erie, Michigan from 1952–1967.

The UWUA was created through a merger in 1945 of the CIO-affiliated Utility Worker Organizing Committee and a former "company union" at the Consolidated Edison Company in New York City. Today, the UWUA represents approximately 60,0000 members employed in electric and public utilities, including electrical utility linemen; nuclear power plant operators; water, gas, and sewerage workers; and clerical and professional employees. The union has 230 relatively autonomous locals and represents its members in nearly as many collective bargaining agreements.

———————————————————* * *———————————————————

F IFTY years ago working conditions and pay in this country were deplorable. And if it were not for unions, we would still have those conditions today. But we still really have not made all that many gains for everybody yet, including workers in hospitals, nursing homes, banks, and insurance companies. And there are still too many places who pay the minimum wage because the law says they have to, and that's the only reason they pay that much. Look, when my son got out of college, he looked into becoming a probation officer, but with the salary they were paying, he wouldn't have been able to rent an apartment, or even to buy food. They were talking about $4,500 a year salary—you can't live on that. So, there's a lot to do out there yet.

Getting Started

I was drawn into union work because of an interesting circumstance. Shortly after I began working for a utility company, a group of the guys on my shift were talking about an individual who had previously been an officer in another local but was now working with us. During the time he had been an officer, it seems he used up a lot of the local's funds trying to get himself elected to another job. Most people in my local knew about it, and nobody really wanted to see him get started up again. So they were all talking about it, and I said, "Look, all you guys just stand around and talk about it—you ought to put your money where your mouth is. If you don't want the guy to have the job, then you ought to be willing to say, 'I'll take it.' " They all turned to me and said, "What about you?" And that's how I ended up a union officer.

In reality the opportunities for advancement in unions are limited, there really aren't that many full-time jobs. But moving up in a union's hierarchy isn't really a case of survival of the fittest—it's a survival of the willing. See, when I started out as a department steward, the position didn't pay anything. As a matter of fact, I probably lost money by doing it, because I gave up overtime assignments and other things I could've been doing. And even when I was the president of my local, I was only paid a monthly stipend of about $.10 per member. And with approximately 220 members, that wasn't a lot of money. In fact, I probably had to spend as much as a couple of hundred dollars in some months just on my own time. So given the time and monies involved, it's always difficult to find somebody willing to do the work of a union officer.

My Work

We're a little different than unions that have larger staffs. I not only do the work of a secretary-treasurer, I'm also the safety director, I do all our legislative work and political activities, make arrangements for educational conferences, and I also give instruction to local union officers about financial matters. It's a good, full day.

In this job you have to react to circumstances rather than make long-term plans. As a matter of fact, I had a serious argument with a group of other secretary-treasurers about trying to budget activities in this line of work. I don't think it can be done effectively because you really can't anticipate what might develop, even in my industry, which is fairly stable. There's just too many circumstances where you think you have an idea of what might happen, and then it turns out differently. For example, you never know when there's going to be a strike, when there's going to be long protracted negotiations, and you never know when an organizing opportunity is going to look fruitful.

I really do enjoy my work though, but every once in a while I kind of wonder what it would be like to just have one function. What I see for example when I go to legislative meetings are these other unions that have a legislative director with maybe three or four assistants. But I probably wouldn't enjoy it, because I'm not the type of person that can sit around and wait for something to happen, and then have other people take care of it. I like to be busy. My philosophy is that if you want something done right, do it yourself.

If there is any difference in my likes and dislikes among my duties, it'll depend on whom I am working with, and for what reason. For example, a lot of our small companies hire a lawyer to do their negotiations. Well, if you're working with one who knows what the final job is to be, and that's to reach an agreement, I won't mind working with him. But when you have to work with a lawyer who thinks his job is to put you out of business, then there is no joy in the work for me. It's just a matter of tough head-knocking.

I was involved in organizing when I was regional director in the field, and while I really didn't mind it, I would say it's not my most enjoyable activity. First of all, I'm not the type of person who meets people easily. I'm kind of quiet and don't talk too much, so it's very difficult for me to just go up to a stranger whom I've never seen before and start a general discussion. I can talk business with anybody, but just to become palsy with somebody is not really part of my nature. But I did do it as part of the job.

I really enjoyed working on grievances because that's something where I can help someone directly and individually. There is one grievance though that stands out in my mind where I wish I could've done more. It was the first time I made a decision on whether or not to arbitrate discharged employees. In the particular case the individual involved was bordering on mental retardation. He had a kind of a menial job of fixing up and picking up things around the shop, and was used mostly as a handyman to the superintendent rather than in actual production work for the company. Well this fellow was fired for stealing company property, and I've never settled within myself that we did right by him.

You see in the old days a utility company placed gas meters inside people's houses because outside meters would record less than was actually going through a meter when the outside temperature was cold. In the early fifties when temperature compensating meters came out and allowed meters to be kept outside, one of our jobs was to change over the meters.

So anyway, as workers brought those older meters into the shop they just threw them in a pile in a scrap box. This fellow, every night, and everybody knew it—the superintendent knew it, the foreman knew it—would take six or eight meters home with him, and take out a little brass plug from it. The next day he'd return the meter to the shop, but would sell the brass plugs. That's what they fired him for.

Well, I was convinced by the other members on the grievance committee that stealing is stealing no matter how small it is, regardless of how much time and service a guy's got or anything else. But the more I thought about it, I always felt bad about it because I know that guy didn't think he was stealing. He thought it was fine, because everyone saw him do it, and he never tried to hide it. He was never going to get another job, and the fact we couldn't do much for him has always bothered me. I hate to see those kind of things.

Looking back over all the things I've done in the union, I think the position I learned the most from was probably the time I was the vice-president/secretary-treasurer on the Michigan council. While I was there I got involved with the job evaluation process and learned to interpret duties and jobs and apply values to them. I also had the opportunity to present arbitration cases, and also cases before the NLRB and the Unemployment Commission in Michigan.

Image of Unions

You know I've never seen an article in a newspaper that said a union did a good job, or got a good contract without a strike. When I moved to the city of Jackson, Michigan as the president of our state organization, we represented something like 6,000 people at that time and somebody said to me, "You moved into this city and represent that number of people, and yet nobody knows it. If a guy gets named as manager of a local store or something, they have a big spread in the paper about it." That aspect of being a labor leader doesn't bother me. Notoriety doesn't excite me that much.

Unions are born out of a necessity, and we don't need to do advertising, on television or anywhere else, to convince people that unions are necessary. I've never really believed you can sell a narrow viewpoint like ours by just blasting it on TV day in and day out. The oil industry tried that and they're still not loved.

Commitment

Being a union officer and involved in your community are really matters for those who are willing. Union members, and generally, Americans are becoming a bit more selfish with their time. A lot of the things used to be done out of the fact that you wanted to belong, and you wanted the union to succeed and all that. Now, everybody says, "Look, I'll do it if I get paid. If I don't get paid, I'm not going to do it."

But I've always felt that attitudes of the general public are sort of like a pendulum, they swing in one direction, and once they get there, nobody really wants to be there, and so they swing back again. That attitude of unselfishnes will come back. In fact, I was just thinking last night "Where have all the flower children gone?" I was active in politics myself in '68, '69, and the early seventies. I guess they're thirty-five and forty years old now, and working as stockbrokers.

I remember during the period of time I served as county chairman for the Democratic party, I worked five days a week for the union, and then on Saturday I would meet with the treasurer of the party and we spent all day Saturday trying to plan out how we were going to raise funds, etcetera. We had this one friend who was fairly active in his union—not the Utility Workers by the way—who used to come by every Saturday morning because he knew we were in the office working. He'd push the door open and say, "Hey you guys, know where all your members are? They're in their campers and trailers and they're on their way up north!"

By the way, I think labor ought to take positions on social and political issues, but it should be done by the AFL-CIO. Their total objective should be politics, whereas our role in this union is to represent utility workers, get them the best wages, hours, and working conditions we can. We do take stands on social issues, but I wonder sometimes if we don't lose faith with the membership when we do. We'll make great demonstrations about some issue, while the member is getting his head kicked in by a supervisor. The member has to be saying, "There's my union out there, what are they doing for me?" And I sometimes wonder if maybe we don't get too involved in those issues to the detriment of some other things.

The Members

Our members' concerns have now sort of faded in regard to money-in-the-pocket type of issues. They're looking now at job security, their group insurances, and the value of pensions. Remember that the utility industry is a long-term industry and most people working in it stay until they retire. I've always thought there's a certain type of personality type individual who gravitates to this industry, and that's the person who's looking for long-time security rather than a get-rich-quick type of circumstance.

Looking Back

I probably take a simplistic view, but if I can do a good job for somebody and accomplish something, even if the other guy's mad or not satisfied with what I've done, I'll be satisfied as long as I know I've done my best. It hurts a little, but I'll tell you a little story about myself. I was once in a meeting with the top management of one of our companies, when a knock came on the door. It was a fellow from the local union in the town that we were meeting in and he said they needed me to resolve a problem.

Well, it seems that one of our members, an older black fellow who was probably in his middle fifties at the time, refused to obey a superintendent's order to take over a crew on that day. Of course, the superintendent wouldn't take no for an answer, so I went down to where they were working and asked the fellow what he wanted to do. He said, "I don't want to be the crew leader. I'll work for anybody they want me to, but I won't be a crew leader. It puts me in a higher income bracket and I'll have to pay more taxes and I wouldn't want that."

Of course that wasn't his problem. You see, he couldn't read or write and no one knew this about him. But to be a crew leader, you need to know how to do those things so you can fill out reports and follow maps. Anyway, under the contract as I understood it, a guy didn't have to take a promotion if he didn't want it, and I told him so. He then told the superintendent, "My union tells me that I don't have to do it, and whatever my union says is good enough for me." The superintendent said, "O.K., you're fired."

I went back to the meeting with top management and I really raised all kinds of cane with the personnel director of the company over the firing. He agreed it was wrong, and we worked it out so that the guy would come back to work, wouldn't ever be asked to take a promotion again, he'd get his back pay, and there would be no letter in his file. During the course of our conversation, the personnel director asked me whether in a case like this, "Wasn't it really the union's position that a guy is supposed to do what the supervisor tells him, and then file a grievance?" I said that was the general policy, to which he said, "O.K., just as long as we understand that, we'll put the guy back on."

So, when they wrote a letter to put the guy back, they said, "On the basis of the commitments made by Marshall Hicks, we'll put him back." Of course the local union wanted to know what commitments I made. There were none, but they went ahead and started to leaflet everybody at the next state meeting to have a recall or have me impeached because of what I had done. I did a good job, not something bad. And as long as I can say that to myself, in whatever I do, that's all that is important to me.

14. Doing Your Job—That's Campaigning for Office

Douglas C. Holbrook

A union career is for those people who really want to dedicate themselves to some very strong principles.

Douglas C. Holbrook was elected secretary-treasurer of the American Postal Workers Union (APWU) in 1983. He has held this office since being appointed to fill the unexpired term of his predecessor in May 1981. Prior to his present position, Mr. Holbrook was the president of the Detroit district area APWU local (and its predecessor, the Detroit local of the National Postal Union) from 1966.

After working as an auto worker in Detroit for two years, Douglas Holbrook joined the postal workforce in 1956 as a part-time clerk. In the Detroit local, he served as trustee, editor of the *Detroit Postal Worker,* and vice-president. He was also founder of SOAR—Save Our Annuity Retirement—a coalition of 40,000 active and retired federal employees in Michigan.

He was a member of the board of the metropolitan Detroit AFL-CIO for eight years. He was also elected to the Warren, Michigan, board of education from 1971–1980, serving three years as president and two years as vice-president.

Douglas Holbrook was born in Colburn, Virginia, in 1934. He attended high school in Virginia and studied labor relations and administration at Wayne State University.

The APWU, the largest postal union in the world, was established in 1971 as the result of the merger of five postal unions. Long denied the ordinary collective bargaining rights of private sector unions, a major and illegal strike in 1970 by 200,000 postal workers prompted Congress to pass the Postal Reorganization Act of 1970. The act created the U.S. Postal Service, an independent agency of the federal government. Today the APWU represents 365,000 members including clerks, maintenance craft workers, motor vehicle workers, special delivery workers, and mail handlers. Unlike other unions of federal employees, the APWU can negotiate over wages, hours, and some personnel actions. In recent years, the APWU has fought attempts to privatize the Postal Service.

--------------------------------- * * * ---------------------------------

I THINK labor's role in making this country what it is today has been undersold. Without labor, you would probably not have three classes of society, but, rather two—the very rich and the poor. Labor has given America a middle class, but a lot of middle class people have forgotten how they got there. They do not realize that we had to fight for those things they now enjoy. We went through with 150-day strikes against General Motors and the mining companies and made those sacrifices. But now the whole country is on the train of, "Let's see how much we can do for workers without labor unions."

When I started in the Postal Service thirty-one years ago, I was making $1.81 an hour, and the big goal at that time for working people (since I didn't know anybody who had a lot of money) was to get $100 a week. If you would just make $100 a week, you were making it! Obviously, things have changed, and they've changed in good part because of the labor movement.

Our achievements though are not without problems. For example, have we priced ourselves out of the market? At what point did the coal industry realize they could no longer operate and make it? What happened to steel? Or the rubber industry? There are no longer any rubber plants in Akron, Ohio. There are very few miners working in the coal fields of West Virginia, Pennsylvania, and Ohio, and even Virginia, where as a youngster I saw the United Mine Workers organizing miners.

The Industry

The same problems apply to us in the Postal Service because we are very close to being privatized. In fact, I was on "The Larry King show" recently with Congressman Crane, who is an advocate of privatization of the Postal Service and everything else. It is terrible that an elected official takes that position, and especially when they have never been inside of a post office to see what it is like.

Federal Express can make a profit because they have a specific business that they cater to. And the United Parcel Service can make a profit from the parcel post business that they took from us. But those firms cannot make a profit off the regular mail, so they do not bother with it. We have a different obligation compared to those firms. Our obligation is to service every American home in this country six days a week, and that means delivering 150 billion pieces of mail a year. It is a unique business; and there is no one else who can do it.

What people do not recognize is that we have the best mail system in the world. I have done a lot of television and radio programs where we have debated this matter, and I have had thousands of telephone calls come in to me from people who have got complaints. and that is only natural because you cannot handle 150 billion pieces of mail a year without having some of it go astray. But invariably somebody will call me and say, "I didn't get my Social Security check, and I didn't get this, and I didn't get that . . ."

But I never have had a call on any of these programs—and I've done programs from New York to California—who said that they did not get their bills!

Look, I don't like to go in the post office and see long lines. But I do not like to go in the supermarket either and see long lines. People will not complain about a supermarket or a bank; but when they go to a post office and have to wait fifteen minutes, they are ready to yell and scream at you.

But I think we have to do better every single day because after all, the public pays our salaries. That is something most people do not know. They think our money comes out of the U.S. Treasury. It does not happen that way. Our money comes directly from stamps sold at that window and services that we render. We do not receive any subsidies from the federal government, except for some funds given for the mailing expenses of the blind, nonprofit institutions, libraries, and colleges.

The Structure of the Union

Everything with us is determined through the collective bargaining process and arbitration, except those areas where we are covered under federal government employee legislation. That includes the areas of retirement, health care, and some other issues like veterans' preferences. But like federal employees, we are not allowed to strike. So, we are rather unique in the federal government because we are covered by both the federal employee legislation and the Postal Reorganization Act of 1970.

We are one of the few unions in the country that is experiencing tremendous growth, despite the fact we are "open shop." People do not have to belong to a union to work for the postal system. However, nearly 85 percent of all postal workers belong to one. It kind of comes around again to the philosophy of Doug Fraser [a former UAW president], who believes that unions do not organize, bad management does. And, that certainly is true of the Postal Service, particularly with the new board of governors that we have since the postal reorganization.

Collective Bargaining

We have to be constantly vigilant about the safety and health conditions in our operations because we have had a lot of new automation introduced into the system which has never been tested. The Postal Service just threw a machine in, and said "operate it." And that has resulted in thousands of people now suffering from illnesses that they should not have, particularly carpal tunnel syndrome and eye problems. And because we do not fall under OSHA, the federal government got away with it. The government is a wonderful institution because it exempts itself from all of its own laws.

I never understood how the federal government can pass laws and say "Everybody's covered, but we're not." YES, we have had people killed. We had a man killed recently in Texas; one in Detroit, Michigan; and we had a man put through a conveyor belt in New York City. We have more accidents than anybody in the world because management turns off switches, bypasses equipment, or pulls a safety system off a conveyor belt.

And I have been to some of our own operations in New Jersey, where they have built those buildings on swamps and dumps. People are going to be dying from cancer and other diseases probably not yet known to man because they work out of those buildings, and yet our employer does not seem to have paid much attention to that health risk.

Despite these problems I would not want to see us involved in any of these quality of work life [QWL] or employee involvement programs. For these programs to work, you have got to have integrity on both sides. See, the idea of QWL is to work collectively in building a better workplace, but management uses it to see if they cannot undermine a collective bargaining agreement and get rid of a union.

And the Postal Service is not really serious about QWL. If they were, there would not be the number of grievances filed every day by the Letter Carriers and Mail Handlers' unions that have QWL programs. Those unions have these little petty grievances coming up the line all the time, whether it is a cart to distribute the mail, or whether it is too hot in the workplace. And yet, these sorts of things are supposed to be resolved right down there at the lowest level according to their QWL program.

When management gets serious about QWL, and wants to do it in the right way—and their interests are the same as everybody else's—then it might work! Right now, there is no way in the world that this union can support any type of program of employee involvement, and our members accept that.

Image of Postal Workers

I am very proud of the Postal Service and the job that postal workers do every day. Yet, the Postal Service never really promotes the job that postal workers do. We have spent over $2.5 million in commercial advertising over the last two years just to bring our message to the American people. Now, you are not going to change American people's ideas for $2.5 million on television; and, we know better. But we had to do something about our image because Federal Express attacked us in a TV commercial that really made us look like we were a bunch of lazy slobs.

A lot of people look at us, postal and federal workers, as selfish individuals who do not care about this country. I resent that more than anything else in the world. It's just not accurate. Our people care, and want to be involved in the legal process. Not too many people know that we are forbidden under the Hatch Act to run for most political offices and from participating in many other political acts.

My Career

A union career is for those people who really want to dedicate themselves to some very strong principles. You do not go into it to have a party. We have 320,000 members out there, and their lives and futures are dependent upon how well we do here. You have got to approach the work from the standpoint that you really want to make some changes for the better—not only for labor—but for this country. Even people working in nonunion firms have benefited by us, because look, nonunion organizations are paying union salaries in order to keep unions out.

When I go home, I like to feel that I have been able to do something positive during the day and that I have been able to help somebody out. But, it gets tougher all the time, especially when you deal with people who say "We can't do this," or "It's impossible, don't try that." These people are anti-everything. I think being "anti-" is a disease people get. I really think that you have got to approach life from a positive position. You have to try to devote yourself so that at the end of a career, or even at the end of a day, you can look back and say . . . . it's just a little better because of what I did.

I have been a member of the union for thirty-one years and an officer for about twenty years—a nice, interesting twenty years. I have only had a few elections where I have been unopposed. And, that has made it challenging. But, I really do not have a lot of time for campaigning anyway because of the demands of my job.

But my philosophy is that if you do your job every day and serve the membership, that is campaigning enough! But, you can also lose an election by working too hard as well. For example, in the last year, we brought into the union over 50,000 new members—and they do not know me at all.

My career in the union started as a real accident. In 1966 while I was on the executive board of the local, the president resigned out of anger and the executive board elected me president. It was a tremendous challenge to be elected at the age of thirty-five—the president of 2,000 people. And because it was unusual, it took me a long time to be accepted by a lot of people, including the leadership at the national level.

Old and New

But there were bigger battles to fight than that! We did not have the right to bargain collectively, and our working conditions were deplorable. There were long hours, people getting fired, part-time flexible employees working twelve hours a day, and seven days a week, no breaks; and some employees were being discriminated against because of their race.

And through the late sixties and early seventies conditions deteriorated dramatically. Because mail volume increased tremendously at about that time, as well, safety and health became very serious issues. So, I think these were the pressures that actually led to the postal strike of 1970.

And, in fact, it was my local, which at the time was the largest union in Detroit, Michigan, that was designated to take the strike vote. We were one of many locals who voted to strike. That strike vote was shown on national television, which I did not mind doing because I was young and a real activist. I was also a bit foolish since I did not pay much attention to the fact that you could go to jail for striking the government! But, I did take that strike vote. And, of course I was immediately served notice that I could go to jail and pay a fine of $100,000 a day. Needless to say, that did not excite my wife too much.

It is ironic, but my son called me recently when he was working in a nonunion shop and said he was trying to organize his shop. It sounded like what I was doing twenty-five years ago. I told him before he did anything that he needed to talk to me to make sure that he was doing it right. We did not want him getting fired in a right-to-work state like Virginia.

Anyway, the postal strike was settled without anybody losing their job or going to jail—and that was under the Nixon administration. We were very fortunate then, because I think today if we had 200,000 postal workers out, it could very well end the union. In fact, we came very close to a major strike in 1981, just prior to the PATCO situation, where those people were all fired—12,000 of them.

My Work

It would be hard to give up this position. As secretary-treasurer, I get involved in the administration of the union in a way that I like to do. For example, I am involved not only in dealing with hundreds of people, but have recently finished the 150th seminar that we have done across the country aimed at teaching our new officers how to administer a local—but also in negotiations, and just about every decision that affects this union. I manage a budget of $40 million a year. So I have impact. The constitution provides for three top leadership jobs in the union, and I hold one of them.

I think the only way to manage is by "team consulting." You cannot manage as an individual who has all these dictatorial ideas. So, I like to bring out people and to have their input because they are going to have to carry out the decision. I have about thirty people, and they seem to respond well to that style.

A lot of them come up with tremendous ideas that really have made an impact and saved us a lot of money. In fact, we just went into a new program last year where we began to deduct dues twenty-six times a year, instead of twelve. The plan was costing us $80,000 of new money to implement computer-wise, and my executive assistant came to me and said, "I'm not satisfied with that." I said, "Great, how are you going to cut it down?" Well, he cut it down about $30,000—and is still whittling away at it.

That is the only way you can manage, in my opinion. You cannot be a success in a labor organization, particularly when you are working with other elected officers, unless you try to put a team together. Because if you were sitting up there as a person making those decisions only—without any input from anybody else—those other elected people have a constituency too, and they could destroy you!

15. A Feminist Unionist

Barbara B. Hutchinson

Most Americans are more progressive in thought than they are in action.

Barbara B. Hutchinson is the second director of the Women's Department of the American Federation of Government Employees (AFGE). A trial attorney with a strong civil rights background, Ms. Hutchinson was first elected to her current post at AFGE's national convention in August 1980. In 1981, she was elected a vice-president of the AFL-CIO's executive board, becoming the second woman ever to serve on the labor federation's policy-making body. Earlier in her union career, Barbara Hutchinson served as a steward and first vice-president of the Equal Employment Opportunity Commission, Local 3599, in Atlanta, Georgia.

Under her stewardship, the women's department conducts a biennial women's training conference, sponsors an outstanding achievement award for AFGE women, and helps pay some of the costs of litigating discrimination cases under the Equal Employment Opportunity Law. Among her other activities she is a board member of the A. Philip Randolph Institute and the Joint Council on Economic Education.

Born in Braddock, Pennsylvania, in 1946, she received a B.A. in political science from the University of Pittsburgh, and a law degree from Dickinson School of Law.

Unions of federal employees existed in the United States during the 1800s. However, the federal government did not extend collective bargaining rights to its employees until 1962, when President John F. Kennedy issued Executive Order 10988. Although EO 10988 empowered federal employee unions with the right to bargain collectively, they were prohibited (and remain so today) from using the strike to enforce their demands; nor can they in most cases negotiate wage levels, pensions, fringe benefits, subcontracting, and personnel actions.

As a result of Executive Order 10988, the AFGE, which was founded in 1932, grew rapidly. Today, the AFGE is the largest union of federal government employees, representing approximately 700,000 federal government employees around the world. A major challenge facing the AFGE is the number of "free riders," who, because of union security provisions, are represented by AFGE in collective bargaining, but are not members of the union. Actual membership of the union totals 225,000.

---

* * *

I THINK the stereotype of labor leaders is an accurate description of what the general population, as well as some of our own union members, think about us. When I was first elected in 1981 to the AFL-CIO executive council I was told that the council members were a bunch of old fogies who were out of touch with the rank and file and who just sat around smoking cigars. I heard this not from people outside the labor movement, but from people within, particularly women and some of our black trade unionists. I told them, "But I'm on the executive council, and I'm not an old fogey." I was only thirty-four at the time I was elected.

But the perception of what labor leaders are like continues despite the fact that if you analyze their track record, they are as progressive, or more progressive than the membership. For example, the AFL-CIO had to put aside its sort of informal rule that you had to be a president of a large union in order to sit on the council so people like myself could join the council. You know, most Americans are more progressive in thought than they are in action. But I think the action by the council goes to show that they aren't staid and outdated. If they were, they would never have made that kind of allowance.

I think we can work on our image, though. We really never have done anything about it. Somebody said that we're just "bums and used car salesmen." For all we know, the president of the United States may have been a used car salesman before he became president. So you look at all this stuff, and you have to just take the good with the bad. You don't get everything the way you want it.

The same is true for the number of women serving as labor leaders. Management has no more women in their upper executive ranks than the labor movement, and the same is true in Congress. We don't vote on qualifications, we vote on stereotypes. So that all the things that are espoused, such as equality for women and race, are not really reflected in our actions. Even within the labor movement, the members have not voted for women candidates for board and executive spots in droves, nor have they voted for women candidates to be presidents of their unions. Both Canada and Britain have outdistanced us in these respects.

At the same time, I wouldn't want to see unions establish hiring or promotion quotas to increase the number of minorities or women serving as union officers. That's not what affirmative action is for anyway. But in any case, it would be entirely inappropriate for the labor movement. Unions are not designed to be representative of their membership's identity, they're meant to be representative of the members' ideals, desires, and goals.

But I will say there's been a lot of discussion among minorities and women in the labor movement to go in the direction of having the executive levels representative of the identities of the membership. If that ever goes through, it would be like going to an electorate and saying "O.K., you are all black, so you're going to have a black person as your representative." When you cross that line, you're as bad as the segregationists, as bad as the Klu Klux Klan.

One of the things that we fought so hard to eliminate, and people died for, got shot, and bitten by dogs, was to eliminate someone mandating whom we would go to work for, and whom we would have to elect. So I would resist any attempts to select representatives by identity. At the same time, however, the executive council recognized that part of the problem of women and minorities not moving up in unions resulted from people resisting the elimination of discrimination. And I do believe women and minorities had some legitimate gripes in that respect. I know when I got elected to the council, there were a lot of people who were suspicious, who said, "Who is she? She couldn't know anything!" So I think that's why the council decided to seek out and get some women and more minority representation on the council. They wanted to eliminate discrimination that had become institutionalized in the labor movement.

This is why I believe the council is really a progressive group. They could have just flatly said, "the heck with you people, you run for office." That's exactly what George Meany said. He said, "You people get elected presidents of unions, and then you can be on the council." So you have to figure there had to be some hard talking to get a lot of people to accept the idea of myself and Joyce Miller back then getting elected to the AFL-CIO's executive council.

Life on the AFL-CIO Executive Council

It was tough for me at first sitting on the council. Although I represent an interest group in this union, on the council I also was representing different identity groups. And I felt very uncomfortable with all the expectations placed upon me from those groups who believed firmly in their hearts that if you didn't espouse their cause, nobody would.

Women, blacks, Hispanics, other minorities and the members of my own union all felt that I was their particular representative and that I was surely going to protect their interests. I had also to contend with those males who felt that there was no reason for affirmative action, and those women who would say you weren't progressive enough. For a while there, between '82 and '86, there was even an undercurrent of a split between black and white females. When the whole comparable worth issue came up, blacks didn't want you to deal with it at all because they felt that it was a "white female issue," while the white females were accusing you of racism because they thought you were not taking the issue up. I tell you I had my hands full.

Of course, the basic problem with comparable worth is that half the people don't know what it is, so they're afraid of it. They think it's just another way of giving women promotions over men. It's a very scary thing to a great many people, the same way that maternity and paternity leaves are now.

The Status of the Family and Women

On many of these issues, though, we are still a very traditional society, especially when it comes to family relationships, child care and the status of women. Our institutions still operate on the concept that there is a parent— a woman, of course—who remains home all day. Our schools, for example, schedule all appointments before closing at 3:30 P.M., and physicians make kids' appointments during the day as well. What this society has not yet recognized is that the one-wage-earner family is almost gone.

That will change as we move forward to the year 2000. The rumble I think we're seeing in the 1980s about child care, maternity, and other social issues indicates we're moving towards accepting the fact that women are not confined to the home. The women's movement of the sixties was only the prelude to the actual changes that are going to take place in the next twenty years. By the year 2000, I would envision that young women, say, twenty-one years old and coming out of college will have no idea of what it was like to face these kinds of barriers.

And it's already happening in the latest generation of women coming into the workforce. They wouldn't recognize discrimination if it bit them. For instance, I know a very young female lawyer, who was just out of law school and working for the chamber of commerce. She came up to testify on Capitol Hill against the bill on comparable worth for federal employees, and during a break in the hearings I asked her, "Why are you here?" She said, "Well, we just don't see any reason for this legislation. It could be devastating." I said, "Miss, no offense to you, but in 1969 when I first went to law school, I was part of the first class that admitted women in large numbers. I'm the reason you're sitting here today. The reason the chamber of commerce employed you was because I took the brunt of listening to people who said, 'Why are you in law school?' " And I also told her the chamber had lots of lawyers, but they just dragged her out because they wanted a woman to testify on the bill.

You know, when I went to law school in '69 the first guy I saw asked me, "How many women are in your class?" I told him eight and he said, "That's eight too many." All of the rumors and innuendo were there—women were in law school to get a husband, you weren't serious, and that you took the slot of some well-qualified man. Even when I first got out of law school, job interviewers would ask, "Well, are you going to have kids? What are you going to do with them while you're at work?" Well, that young woman lawyer was very defensive, but the point is, she had no concept of what comparable worth was really all about, or even discrimination—she never experienced it. She thinks everything's great. But the reason it's great is because people like me had lots of doors slammed in our faces, and we said, "That's enough."

I feel I'm more of a true feminist now, much more so than say eight years ago. Back then I was more of an institutional person, who said about women's problems in the workplace that we have laws—it'll be taken care of. But now I think that women have to really be committed to the cause. If they're not, nothing's going to happen. I'm a feminist in the sense that I'll work as hard as I can, but I want others to recognize that I'm not totally free from other commitments in life. Some women are, just like some men are. If you have a spouse at home who provides extra support and really works with you, then fine. But if you don't, then the rest of society and your counterparts have to accept the fact that those family responsibilities don't lessen your dedication, your commitment, or whatever. A lot of women just don't have that support structure that men have always enjoyed.

I used to laugh with my peers on the executive council, who were males when I first went on, who said they didn't mind traveling. I said, "When you go away, you pack your suitcase and you leave. When I go away, I have to pack my suitcase, make sure that I've cooked, make sure that the baby-sitter or housekeeper has everything that they need, and have all hours of the day covered. A trip isn't difficult for you, but traveling for me is expensive, and you need to recognize it and accept it." I think that women have to continue to make that point to our counterparts, male and female, because I've found women who don't agree on this.

It comes back to this whole idea that America has not accepted the concept of women at work. That's why I think women have to be committed because it's a fact of their working lives—it's not going to go away. Some women try to "do it all." Me, I tell them that I'm not superwoman. When my son fell off some gym bars at school and broke his arm, I got the call in the middle of a very critical meeting. So I wrote a note to the guy who was the chairman and said, "I must go. I will be back. Do this while I'm gone." That should be acceptable. In the past, it never was.

You know, I had a discussion recently with a young female media person who was at our convention who told me, "Oh, the ERA is dead. There's no need for it anyway." I said to her, "Legally, you're absolutely correct. But the ERA would have created the perception in this society that there's something in the Constitution that says it's wrong to yell out, 'Hey, who's that broad over there?' As long as you and other women like you keep saying there's no need for it, you're still going to have that kind of problem."

Racial Equality

By comparison to the gender problems in society, the racial side is a lot better. Now there are blacks who would disagree with me. They'd say that there are not enough blacks in leadership positions in the labor movement. But I bet there are more black male officers than there are black females. Black males have progressed faster than women, black or white, so on that score I think it's better. In fact, I think in eight years you're going to see a black vice-presidential candidate, and they'll be acceptable. But when that happens, it will of course be a black male. America's sexism is still too ingrained for any woman, black or white, to be accepted as a candidate. Women themselves haven't convinced themselves 100 percent that they're qualified—witness the reaction to Geraldine Ferraro. Until women convince themselves that sex has no effect on ability, we just tend to reinforce the belief of men that we're not ready.

By the way, I don't think America is ready for Jesse Jackson. Politically, he carries too much baggage. He reminds the folks of the times they'd like to forget, and will always be a reminder of the wrongs they did in the past. Even though he's extremely talented and articulate, he represents too profound a change.

But gender and racial barriers still exist in this country. And anybody who tries to convince themselves that they don't, is just deluding themselves. You can still walk into a labor union or a place of employment and find some type of discrimination, some lack of seriousness, aimed at you because you are a minority or a female. In fact, the number of discrimination complaints that are being filed with the EEOC have risen 200 percent since 1980. So our society's precepts haven't really changed all that much, even with things like the Civil Rights Act in place. We may eventually achieve the things we espouse as a nation, but for now, there is a big difference in what we say and what we do.

While most instances of institutionalized discrimination, the overt type, may have been eliminated, I think any female or other minority in this country could tell you that instances of covert or de facto discrimination are plentiful. So statements by William Bradford Reynolds of the Justice Department that there are no barriers in employment situations is obviously a farce. Clearly he probably has never had to face those kinds of barriers. After all he's a white male.

I hate to say it but this [Reagan] administration's record on women is the worst. They have fired many of the women they appointed who spoke up on behalf of women's rights. They made sure that they got rid of them. I find these people to be regressive. Someone called them "right-wing reactionaries," but I just find them regressive. They add nothing to the tenets of democracy. For example, we have a class complaint against the Department of Agriculture because they won't allow sick leave for maternity or pregnancy purposes. I also have a class complaint against the Social Security Administration because they refuse to grant maternity and pregnancy leave that exceed six weeks for women who are in their lower graded categories, no matter what their doctors say.

We've fought with this administration on women, minority, and all social issues since the day they came to town in 1981. They consider these issues irrelevant. Things such as child care, maternity/paternity leave, the food stamp program, which helps women who can't earn enough, jobs, unemployment, and unemployment training—all of these issues are just not on their agenda. In fact, they met with us when they first came to town in 1980, '81, and they said, "We're not interested in these issues. We don't need them any more. This country has eliminated discrimination on behalf of women and all other minorities."

One of their comments to us was, "If you people want them, you deal with them. We're going to get rid of all this stuff." They sat in a room and actually said that to us. After we met with them, I called around to some of the civil rights people, some of the women's rights people, and they had been told the very same thing—"You people are irrelevant."

And that's why the battle is so clear, and the struggle is so intense. They've made it crystal clear that they do not think that these issues are of concern to America. Whereas with some prior Republican administrations, you might have a difference of opinion as to how fast, or how slow you move on these issues, this one told everyone, "It's of no concern to us."

And their comments are really something. Take Constance Horner for example, the director of the Office for Personnel Management, who said, "All black women are overweight, have high blood pressure and smoke." Give me a break! Where'd she come from? I mean, the woman is supposed to be an executive! I can't prove it, and it's purely speculative on my part but I've always contended this group around Reagan is the same little group who was around with Nixon. He didn't work out so they got themselves another one.

I really think Americans let themselves be deceived by this administration, I really think we did. I've looked at all of the polls and their analyses of issues, and this administration is diametrically opposed to what Americans say they believe in. I even think the Republicans are beginning to find this administration objectionable. As a party they don't seem to want to be too closely aligned with this administration. I found it interesting that a secretary of labor resigned to go out and campaign for a candidate who is not the successor to the incumbent administration. I thought that was the funniest thing.

Getting Started

I grew up in a small steel town outside of Pittsburgh so my sympathies were always with the labor movement. My father was a member of the old Hod Carriers and the Black Plasterers Union. In fact, he refused to join the AFL-CIO when they eliminated segregated locals, because he said they didn't want him when he wanted them. But my dad was a committed unionist. He talked unions and A. Philip Randolph[1] all the time. So between my dad and the fact that the Steelworkers were the predominant union in Pittsburgh, I grew up with very positive, and progressive images of the labor movement. It wasn't until I was much older that I heard any negatives about unions.

I first got involved with the AFGE when I joined the Equal Employment Opportunity Commission in Atlanta, Georgia, as a trial attorney. I joined, got active, and became a steward. When I went to my first convention, someone asked me to run for my present position. They said, "Well, we just want to put a candidate up against the incumbent because we think that she's not doing a good enough job." Everybody that I consulted with said, "Oh, yeah, that's all right, you probably won't win. It's the first convention you've ever been to."

Well, the incumbent was not a lawyer. She had no background or training in EEO, and when you take a trial attorney from the EEOC with eight years experience, and put 'em up against a person without that background, it really wasn't an even-handed contest.

For a job though that was certainly unplanned, it's been an experience. I mean, after seven years I'm a vice-president. If you look at those guys from the AFL-CIO, they've been at it for forty years.

My Work

My position is a full-time elected post. It's part of the formal structure of this organization along with the committee of fifteen women who are elected in their regions, and work with me as an advisory group. But as are most women's departments in unions, we are understaffed here. So it's been a long, hard climb to get the membership to deal with women's issues and to get those issues on the bargaining table. In fact, I can still go around this union region by region and count places where it's working tremendously and count other places where nothing's being done. Surprisingly the southern region has had more success than any others, probably because of a progressive individual. It comes down to the individuals you have in charge—for instance, the New York region is abominable.

And although I've been here for seven-and-a-half years, I can't really say that we've made any greater progress than say AFSCME, who do the same sorts of things as us, but without a formal department. While both of our unions have the same positions on the issues, we don't have the public relations access or monies as they do. So as a consequence, our members will ask, "How come we don't do what AFSCME does? They have a great position on women's issues." You look at them and say, "We're doing the same thing, but if you want us to publicize it, give us some money." To that they usually reply, "Don't get personal." Now I'm not saying that you have to have a structured program to address these issues. In fact all you really need is a union leadership that's interested and makes sure these issues are covered.

I will say though that as far as our members are concerned, they feel that having a department makes a difference. And I do think that having a women's department in the AFGE has contributed to our having a greater percentage of local presidents who are women than ever before, and had something to do with increasing the representation of women among our convention delegates. At our last convention, about 40 percent of the delegates were women, which is a real change.

What is very trying about my job though is the nitpicking type of work that's required. The labor movement has the unspoken ability to talk something to death. And sometimes I feel that if we would just move a little bit more quickly and talk less, we'd probably be better off. But we have so much internal political machinery, that's so heavy, I find often that we are our own worst enemy. Whether we're making the kind of headway we need to make, I don't know. I look at it and sometimes I say, "Listen, we could solve this if you would just be more cooperative," but then we go back to being this big political entity. And in a political entity, nothing is simplistic, there's a lot of zigzagging.

16. Back to the Basics

Charles W. Jones

Things have gotten a lot tougher for unions. We just lost a major shot at organizing a plant and I believe management may have used subliminal messages in their slides and films during their final presentation.

Charles W. Jones is president of the International Brotherhood of Boilermakers, Iron Ship Builders, Blacksmiths, Forgers and Helpers (IBB). Born in 1923 in Gary, Indiana, he attended the Harvard University trade union fellowship program from 1946 to 1947. Prior to his election as president in 1983, Mr. Jones served as a district representative, research director, and international vice-president of the union. Among his other activities, he is an elected member of the metal trades department and industrial union department of the AFL-CIO executive council.

The International Brotherhood of Boilermakers, Iron Ship Builders and Helpers of America (the forerunner of today's IBB) was established in 1880. In 1951, it merged with the International Brotherhood of Blacksmiths, Drop Forgers and Helpers (founded in 1889), and in 1984, with the United Cement, Lime, Gypsum and Allied Workers International Union (founded in 1933). The present membership is diverse. The union represents 100,000 members employed in shipbuilding and marine work (for example, in naval and commercial yards), boiler and electrical manufacturing, drop forgery, warehousing, the cement industry, and railroads, as well as blacksmiths and office, technical, and professional workers in the United States, Canada, and the Panama Canal Zone.

✳ ✳ ✳

ORGANIZED labor in the United States has shrunk to 13 million from about 19 million members, but so have the number of good jobs in this country shrunk. Our members didn't go because they were mad at us. They left because there were no more jobs in their plants, or in construction and shipbuilding. Their jobs have all gone overseas. Union after union lost—the Steelworkers, Auto Workers, Machinists, and the Boilermakers.

Our members are having to work for some hamburger place or to pump gas. Like I saw a young fellow working at a gas station who had a Machinist emblem on his jacket, and I talked with him a bit to see whether he was moonlighting or what. Here's a guy who was a skilled aircraft mechanic but had lost out because of the merger mania, and now he's out pumping gas.

And the service industry is going to be next. That includes lawyers, doctors, PR and advertising people, everybody in banking and everything else. They're a house of cards unless this country becomes a producing nation. What is even more frightening though about all this is that we've lost not only jobs, but we're losing the skills that go along with them.

During World War II, this country was known as the "arsenal of democracy." Yet today, we don't have a decent shipbuilding industry, and we are quickly losing the know-how, the skills, needed to have one. Take a look at Sun Ship [now Penn Ship] in Chester, Pennsylvania. We had 40,000 employed there in World War II. But just a few years ago, that shipyard had less than *400* people working in it. At that point the state of Pennsylvania came up with some dough, $10 million, to keep the yard alive and humming. They have some work now and we have maybe 800 to 1,200 members in there, but do you know that yard had to go out and scrape around for skilled people. Look at what happened when the Electric Boat Company, a defense contractor, in Groton, Connecticut heard where some machinists became available. The *Wall Street Journal* reported how Electric Boat figured they would go out and grab these thirty or fifty people but they soon found out though that everybody in the whole area had the same idea, and the competition for those workers was extremely competitive.

Getting right down to it, there is a very serious skilled labor shortage in this country as a result of those jobs going overseas. And we cannot train people unless there is work to train them on. You can't train a shipbuilder without ships. And anybody who says we can have a strong national defense with a vanishing industrial base, is just engaging in wishful thinking. I don't know if we've got enough people to run the artillery, let alone do high-tech research and development.

The Boilermakers are still training our people, though. In fact, we're not only training our members, we're also training instructors and foremen as well. But you know, we're going to run out of money and everything else if we don't get some jobs.

The "Stay-in" Strategy

One of the things we have been trying to do, though, is to retrain American trade unionists to fight smarter, and use what law we have left to try and keep what we've gained. For example, when a company serves us notice that it wants to renegotiate some feature of a contract, we'll meet him, but we won't, if possible, negotiate to impasse over what they want to take back from us. Impasses lead to strikes and lockouts, and that's not what we want. So what we'd do is simply stay in and continue to negotiate, and show the employer that he has had it pretty good all these years with us and our nice, stable agreement that governed the conduct of things in his shop. We call this our "stay in and fight back" strategy, or solidarity for short.

The *Wall Street Journal* called what we do a slowdown, but it's not, because you can be fired for slowdown. All we do is simply utilize concerted activity to show management how good the present contract is. It's not a slowdown, things just don't go as well as they always did with a signed union contract.

For example, in one of our shops our members will call for an emergency grievance session with management in, say, Department 12, and when they get down there, they'll be called to Department 14 for another grievance meeting. Now you take that combined with all the members in those departments showing up as the grievance committee, and management goes bananas. And of course under our strategy, our members do only what they are told to do. It's not a slowdown, it's just doing things we're told to do—nothing more, nothing less—efficiently.

But at any rate, where we are using our solidarity strategy, we are very careful to tell our members about the things they have to guard against and not do, so they won't be disciplined, discharged, or locked out.

We tell them not to do any sit-down, of course, and if they're told to go home, go home. We tell them no hit'n run strikes. But if they do have a dispute, a legitimate grievance, follow it through. If it's something involving safety and health, for instance, follow it through, and if necessary, warn management that you're going to strike over that grievance. But we also tell our members that if they do go out, not to strike too long, do it for only a half a day. That's so management can't replace you. We once struck an employer for only one day and he was ready for us with replacements—we had played the game too long.

I tell you this strategy is a hell of a union builder. I heard of a bunch at McDonald Aircraft who gave everybody a whistle and when anybody had a grievance, they were told to blow on it, and then everybody else would do the same on their whistle. In another shop, the members walk in to work in a single file in the morning with a U.S. or Solidarnosc flag, and the guys coming out will take the flags and carry them back into the shop.

Now the *Wall Street Journal* article also mentioned sabotage as maybe something we do. I tell you that we do *not* screw around with sabotage or vandalism. That sort of thing can only get you into trouble. And it's not the kind of thing that unions do. Sometimes people do it. Like when there's a picket line, somebody will inevitably come down to it, drunk and with a gun in his pocket. That's not the union, it's a person. But sabotage is not only a question of breaking the law, it's also very impractical. Because if you were to settle with a company on the day that some equipment was torn up, that broken piece of equipment is going to keep somebody off the job. So sabotage just cuts down the share of the pie for someone, and it's not worth it.

Generally though, I'd say that our strategy does require much more stamina and wits than going out on strike. A strike is more or less passive, you just go out there, march up and down and shout for a week, then wait and wait. We've tried to educate our people about strikes, that they don't cost an employer all that much, and that they don't last very long unless your employer wants them to. Under the new tax simplification bill, for example, if an employer loses money during a labor dispute, he can go back three years and recover every bit of the taxes that he paid towards the losses, and if that isn't enough he can go ahead fifteen years. So when we strike it has to be in our best interest, and not over some piddling matter, or because it advances somebody's intraunion political interests.

The Members

What matters to our members are bread and butter issues. Now they are interested in some social issues, but they are not all shook up over Nicaragua or the Iran situation. It's the basics that they are concerned with. For instance, because many of our members see their children getting jobs where there's no health and welfare, they are becoming more interested in seeing the country move to some kind of national health care program. As well, and probably for the first time, they're interested in the minimum wage, because they feel somebody in the White House is trying to push them back to the minimum wage.

I think what's happening now is that people who never saw a bad day in their lives are beginning to understand what the labor movement is all about. They're beginning to see increasingly difficult times. The fact is that there were a whole lot of people who used to look at a package, say a three-year package of $3.50-an-hour increase, and tell their union "Shove it, it just ain't enough. We want more." Today, some of them are quite aware that it's not a question of putting a nickel in and hitting the jackpot every time.

Organizing

Obviously, things have gotten a lot tougher for unions. We just lost a major shot at organizing a plant and I believe management may have used subliminal messages in their slides and films during their final presentation. The kind of thing a department store might use in its background music to send a message that's not discernible to your ear, but is to your consciousness. You know, something like "shoplifters will be prosecuted." Well, I think this company went out and photographed all the plants they had closed, of people on strike, picket lines and all kinds of bad situations. They buried their pictures in their films and used a lot of "boom boom" music, and just hammered away with it all at the people in this plant.

I just suspect the subliminal signals were used to make the employees think they would be forced on strike, be dominated by union dictators, and so forth. It's really incredible the things they throw at us. Would I use subliminal tactics? I don't even know how to do it, but I might learn to use it. You know, if the other guy makes the rules, I'll play by them.

But what would happen if trade unions were destroyed, or made weak and ineffective? What would fill the vacuum—government? bureaucracy? socialism? some other foreign ideology? A strong labor movement is essential for a strong America.

On Management

The whole antilabor thing has only intensified with the Reagan administration. The battle has been there for a long time with managements trying to beat our brains out in collective bargaining even back in 1958, 1960, 1961. There's no question that no matter how good the times are, that anywhere they can fire, intimidate, or whatever, they'll do it. They've resisted organizing activity not only in the South but in a whole lot of other places.

It's my belief that managements of today would really like to see a return to the days of the shape-ups. If you want to see that in action, you go to Savannah, Birmingham, or Los Angeles, and watch blacks and other minorities standing on a street corner, like cabbies in a taxi stand, and watch people come by in trucks and pick up four or five of those people to work that day. Or women drop by there to pick up somebody to do the lawn work that day and so on.

It was like that in the old days in the shipyards, steel mills, mines, or construction sites, where the boss would come out to the gate and said, "You, you, and you, come on. The rest of you wait because if these guys don't work out, we may need you at noon, or sooner." So here's the Sword of Damocles sitting on the gang box waiting for a job, or for you to screw up, or get killed or something. Do you know that the steel mills used to have one shape-up area for blacks, and another one for whites in Gary, Indiana? That's the way management would like to have things—individuals bidding against each other for jobs.

Most people are more or less educated only to the popular fallacies about trade unions. The media refers to all union leaders as "union bosses," and they call the management people "management representatives." Union proposals are "union demands," and management positions are "moves" for more flexibility, competitiveness, and what have you. But what the average person doesn't hear about are all those people from the Stetson University, and the law firms of Granville-Alley, Hamilton and Bowden, who were the ones who started these union-free environment consulting groups that Meany called "goons in pinstriped suits with attaché cases." Well, they are. They use some of the meanest, most vicious tactics I've ever seen to beat up on people who want to be a part of a union.

Political Action

But the labor movement is beginning to make a comeback. It's not anything dramatic. I don't think you're going to see things like a major committee developed to organize this or that and sweep through the country with the government's or the public's blessing. As I say, people are beginning to recognize why the labor movement began in the first place. It was to bring some strength and protection to those who had none.

What I do believe though is that labor has to make it pretty much on its own, it cannot depend much on politicians for help. You just have to do the best you can with 'em. I could go talk to a guy who would vote 90 percent against our interests, but he'll help us on a bread and butter issue if for example shipbuilding is important in his area. And yet I may go to a guy with a shipbuilding port in his area, but if nobody in his area gives a goddamn, he'll tell me, "You're fighting a losing battle."

In my opinion, Truman was the last great friend of labor in the White House. I think of the candidates running now for the U.S. presidency [1988]. The guy we could get the time of day out of would be Simon. I doubt if we'd get it out from Biden, Gephardt, Dukakis, nor any of the others. I just don't think they would do much for us.

I want you to know that there are people in the union who think it's none of the leadership's business to talk about politics. But it is our business. The only reason for our existence is to protect the members' interests, and the only way we can do that is if we can galvanize them into collective action through organizing, collective bargaining, and politics. You know the country ought to be delighted we don't want to start a third party and run the government. I don't even know why the Democrats want it. But we don't want it—why would we want to take over this mess?

Getting Started

My father and uncles were union people. My father in his earliest years was a Teamsters' business manager, but later on he became a Boilermaker. So I was around the labor temple a lot when I was a young boy. But I was one of seven children, and decided early on that things were tough enough around the house without me, and so I went off and got into the Civilian Conservation Corps, which not too many people know about today unless they've read about it in a book. I stayed with it for about four months until I got a chance to work on a boiler job in Jeffersonville, Indiana. I didn't get membership in the union right away—they said I was too young, and so I decided that without membership, I had no future as a Boilermaker. So I went off to California, Alaska, and Canada, to see what the rest of the world looked like. By the time I was eighteen years old, though, I had become a Boilermaker member.

I became an international representative at age twenty-four, and did that job for ten years. Then I was research and education director for about three years, then a vice-president for twenty-three years, and now I've been the international president for nearly three years.

You know, people look at us in the labor movement like we're some kind of misfits. But I don't really give a damn about that. As long as I'm satisfied I'm doing a job that I like to do, and want to do, that's all that matters. I don't really care what the hell anybody else thinks about my work. I am proud to be a part of the labor movement because unions have raised the standard of living and quality of life in America, and not just for union members, but for all people.

17. The Social Activist

Allen H. Kaplan

So my feeling is that being politically or community active makes you a whole person. If nothing else, it keeps you honest; it keeps you humble.

Allen H. Kaplan is the sixth national secretary-treasurer of the American Federation of Government Employees (AFGE). He was elected to the position in 1986. For the previous sixteen years, he served as national vice-president of AFGE's seventh district, representing members from Illinois, Michigan, and Wisconsin.

In 1967, shortly after beginning his government career with the Office of Economic Opportunity in Chicago, Allen Kaplan helped organize AFGE Local 2816 and served as local treasurer and chairman of the grievance committee. Prior to his federal sector work experience, Mr. Kaplan was an employee of the Cook County (Chicago) Department of Public Aid, where he helped organize the Independent Union of Public Aid Employees and served as president of the 2,000-member organization.

Also, while working for the Cook County Public Aid Department, he helped organize the National Federation of Social Service Employees and served as its first executive board chairman. The NFSSE—with a membership of over 10,000—represented locals in Chicago, New York, Los Angeles, San Francisco, and other cities. As chairman, he assisted strike actions in Los Angeles and Gary, Indiana.

A Marine Corps veteran, Mr. Kaplan graduated from the University of

Wisconsin, majoring in history and English. He also studies law at night at the Chicago-Kent College of Law, and campaigned as an independent candidate for a seat on the Chicago City Council.

For a description of the AFGE, see chapter 15.

--------------------------------** * **--------------------------------

M Y first impression of AFGE was a funny one. I was working in the War on Poverty program in Chicago at the time, and the other employees decided to organize a union. Since I had been active in another union elsewhere, they asked me to help and I agreed. So we called the district office of AFGE and asked them to send us an organizer to show us what we had to do to get recognition. All I remember was that the guy who came out was a short, fat fellow who had spaghetti stains all over his shirt. I think he had a sixth grade education and we were all college graduates. So we said thanks very much, leave us the forms, and we'll call you.

Well, we didn't call them back, but we did organize an AFGE local. It was very easy to in a sense, because our work in the program was aimed at organizing poor people in depressed communities of the Midwest. So, it just didn't make sense not to organize ourselves. In addition, personnel issues had never been a priority of management, and so we felt we needed a union to advance our interests.

Well, that experience turned out to be such an intensive learning experience for me, I think I earned the equivalent of a Ph.D. in unionism. I served in every office in that local, except that of president. Later on in 1970, at the age of 32, I was elected a national vice-president for the district that covers the Midwest states, and I was reelected to that position eight times. I've also run for the presidency and for executive vice-president of the AFGE but lost those races. I won my present position narrowly, so I've won some and lost some.

You like to win every election, but there are precious few full-time paid positions in a union, and always more people who are capable of filling them than there are positions. Take my district, for example. They're having a special election to fill my vacancy, and there are half a dozen candidates running and they're all good. They're all experienced, and solid, and most wouldn't run while I was there because they felt I was doing a good job. But they were as capable as I was.

I mainly got elected to my present position because the incumbent wasn't doing some of the basics of the job, and the membership was dissatisfied. So I'd say the vote was more against his performance than for me. I guess the members just felt a change was necessary. I had been around a long time and had lots of contacts around the country of people who had supported me in earlier campaigns and, they came out again for me. So really, had my predecessor done what he should have, he never would have been defeated.

I really do enjoy, though, the electioneering and politicking involved in running for office. It's fun. This last campaign was fairly low level. I only decided to run in June, which gave me two months to get things together, and we spent less than a thousand dollars in the campaign. I've been active in politics a long time, and have even run for public office, so my feeling is that being politically or community active makes you a whole person. If nothing else, it keeps you honest; it keeps you humble.

And maybe that comes from being a product of the sixties. I majored in history, was active in the civil rights movement, the antiwar movement, etcetera, and it just seems I was always interested and involved in social movements. I think my service with the Marine Corps also deepened my commitment to social and political action. It was such a radicalizing experience for me that when I came out, I was determined not to let people I had met in the corps have any say in running the affairs of our society. I had never been confronted with that kind of irrationality. Officers who came out of the South, for example, thought I was crazy when I'd discuss racial integration.

My Work

My role now as secretary-treasurer is a functional one. For instance, I maintain the membership roles, and when people send their money in, I have to see that it's accounted properly, and that there are no mistakes. While I miss being out in the field, I'm still in a position to influence policy as a member of the executive board and by working with the other officers here in Washington, D.C. That certainly will be easier for me now than if I were still out in Chicago. I'll see these people every day, so my role as an activist will continue. Perhaps my day-to-day stuff won't be the same, but I carry my activist philosophy with me.

In this job I supervise six departments—insurance, finance, computer operations, service, library, and building, and I'm expert in none of them. There are about fifty employees or so in all these departments, and since I've been in the post for only about a week, what I'll try to do as soon as possible is to learn what their functions are, what the problems are administratively, and then work out ways to achieve my objectives. Whatever I do though, I'll do it with the cooperation of the staff—there's just no other way to manage. People have to be made part of the process. Unless the staff wants me to be a dictator, I really don't believe in that approach. It's just counterproductive.

I really did enjoy my job as vice-president but it had gotten too easy for me. Things were running well and I knew the job so it wasn't a challenge any more. I used to have to create and reinvent challenges for myself in order not to go stale. The problem for an incumbent who is elected relatively easily—about half the times I didn't have any opposition—is to stay relevant, and on the cutting edge of what has to be done. So leaving that position wasn't particularly hard because I left a record of how a district should be run. Whoever wins out there will more or less follow the basics of what we did, organizing, political action, representation, and adding in their own ideas to those. They'll add to what I built.

Organizing

I really enjoy being involved in organizing. While nearly three-quarters of those eligible federal government employees are under recognition in one union or another, the problem is that we only have about 25 percent of them as members. To turn it into 100 percent we look to a combination of things. One, we do mass activities such as national demonstrations over issues of importance to get people thinking union and coming into the union. While that's sort of hard to do right now—there's still the aftermath of PATCO to deal with—there are two big issues that I think could attract nonunion employees. One is pay. We've been getting a raw deal on pay since Reagan's been in, and we've been losing real income. The other is job security. There's been a lot of contracting out of federal work to the private sector, and that's a major concern to a lot of government employees.

We could also increase membership through just nuts-and-bolts local organizing. You take a bargaining unit member and use them to reach every nonmember by letter, phone, and personal contact. It works, but it's just a slow, laborious process. If we could get what most of the state governments have—that's an agency shop—I'm sure we'd bring in lots of people. But that won't happen under Reagan. If there's a change in administration, there might be a chance for it.

Institutional Relationships

Although we can do organizing, we also have to develop the right type of relationship with management. A cooperative approach makes a lot of sense to me and I'd like to see more of it, by us in the AFGE, and the whole union movement. But I'm also not averse to strikes. I was involved in a couple of public workers' strikes and I think basically it will come to a point where the public sector employees in the United States will need a strike to come of age. We're still not taken seriously, and as long as we haven't exercised that option, we won't get full respect. The Postal Workers went through with a strike in the early 1970s, and what they achieved by it, compared to the rest of the federal workforce, is night and day. They've kept par on pay and benefits—we haven't.

If we were to strike, it would have to be on the basis of something that affects every member of the union. Pay and working conditions are those issues. Our members' attitudes towards social issues, comparable worth, poverty, farm aid, Central America, South Africa are like those in any other large organization—they're split down the line. Some people are for aid to the Contras, others are against, but no one's against fair pay.

By the way, I do like the idea of union-owned businesses. Now, I know a lot of labor leaders would say "Our business is to represent the members to management—we don't manage, we don't own," but I still think it's a good idea. I especially like the model of the Histadrut, the Israeli Labor Federation, where in the twenties, because Israel didn't have certain industries, the union created them. It creates somewhat of a conflict of interest within the Histadrut, but they've taken the approach that as an employer, they'll be a model employer, and set the pattern for the private sector. I think if you take that kind of philosophy, these things can work.

And another effective model is Japan, where their unions, management, and government work closely together in planning for the future. Instead of the adversarial relationship as our unions and managements advocate, they rely on a cooperative relationship. And generally where that sort of relationship does occur, like in Japan, western Europe, and the like, productivity, morale, and all those kinds of things are better.

The Members

Most of our members are really not actively involved in union affairs. Saul Alinsky, the social activist, used to say that if you have 3 percent active and organized, you have a good organization. Essentially, all unions are built on volunteerism, and so a low percentage of people actually involved in union affairs doesn't necessarily bother me, as long as it isn't too low. It's hard to get 20, 50 or 70 percent of people doing something, particularly in large units.

In fact, we lost a lot of good local officers and members to the ranks of management. They get offered a position and go. If you examine it carefully though, you'll find that union leadership positions actually offer very good training for managers because an officer will learn a broad spectrum of rules and regulations, and how to deal with people. And while it's a good strategic move on the part of management to promote union officers, it's also good for the rest of us because those people will carry their union philosophy with them, and make their work environment a better place.

Looking Back

When you do this kind of work you have to steel yourself to the fact that you're not going to win every organizing campaign you're in, nor every arbitration case you handle. But as long as you've given it your best, which I've tried to do, you can be proud of yourself. Maybe there have been some campaigns where I could've worked an extra hour, or done a little more preparation on a case, but in most instances I did the best that I could do.

18. Continuing the Legacy of Social Services

Joyce D. Miller

When we set up the retired members center it was because those retirees had made a contribution to our union. You just don't say "goodbye" to them after that. Companies do that—unions don't.

Joyce D. Miller is vice-president and director of social services of the Amalgamated Clothing and Textile Workers Union (ACTWU). A graduate of the University of Chicago, where she earned a bachelor of philosophy and master of arts, Ms. Miller served as the education director and director of social services for the Chicago joint board (1967–1972), and executive assistant to the general officers and director of social services of the Amalgamated Clothing Workers of America (ACWA), the predecessor organization to the ACTWU (1972–1976). She is a vice-president of the Executive Council of the AFL-CIO and national president of the 20,000 member Coalition of Labor Union Women (CLUW), an organization that promotes the role of women in the trade union movement and their rights in the workplace.

The ACWA was founded in 1914 by members of the United Garmet Workers who were disenchanted with the management of their union. Under the leadership of its first president, Sidney Hillman, the Amalgamated provided an array of social services to its membership, including medical facilities, insurance plans, and low-cost housing cooperatives. The union also extended loans to failing factories and entered into joint labor-management decision-making programs in order to maintain jobs in the clothing industry.

Today, the ACTWU represents 284,000 members in the United States, Canada, and Puerto Rico. It has also successfully organized workers in the tough-to-unionize South. In fact, the movie *Norma Rae* depicted in a Hollywood sort of way the struggles and ultimate success of the ACTWU at organizing workers of the J. P. Stevens Company. Of course what the movie did not show was that the organizing campaign took nearly seventeen years and included an innovative "corporate campaign" by the ACTWU that isolated the company from the business community.

———————————————————— ✳ ✳ ✳ ————————————————————

I DON'T think many of us on the AFL-CIO's executive council really knew that the Teamsters wanted to reaffiliate with us. But when you look at it, there are more pluses than minuses. We'll have 1.7 million more members in the AFL-CIO, they'll bring us great political expertise, their political action money mostly goes to Democrats, and despite all the negative images of the Teamsters, they do a good job in organizing.

Of course, on the negative side is the corruption. Whether it's labor leaders or business leaders, if someone is corrupt, they ought to be indicted, charged, have a trial, and if they're guilty, go to jail. And I believe that labor leaders certainly have to adhere to a higher standard for themselves because they do represent others.

Unfortunately, though, many people extend the Teamsters' negative image to all labor leaders. But that misconception stems from the fact that in our grammar schools and particularly in our high schools, there is so little provided students about labor leaders and the contribution of labor to this country. For example, I don't even think many college students know it was the labor movement that really led the fight for public education in this country. In fact, I don't think that they know anything about the contribution of labor to this country. And it really is sad that students can get to that level and still be in such a cocoon about labor.

But we are trying to rectify people's image of labor in a number of ways. For example, the AFL-CIO is initiating a program of getting information on labor into high school textbooks. We're also spending $13 million on a public relations television program to get our message across. I think the whole world probably knows about the International Ladies' Garment Workers' Union (ILGWU), and the "Look for the union label" advertisement. Labor has to do a lot more of this type of thing.

We just have to get into the media more with what we are accomplishing. Let me give you an example. From 1962 to 1972, I worked in our Chicago joint board and helped to build a quality child care center, a magnificent retiree center, and a quality health center operated right in our building. We provided our members supplementary insurance benefits, and an education fund program so their children could go on with their education past high school, which was a first-of-its-kind program in this country. Yet, when I said to a reporter, "You're always writing about anything negative labor does. Why don't you come and do a story on our union? We have all these great activities for our members." You know what he said? "That's not news." For the media, it's a juicier story to write about a labor leader who's gotten into trouble than one who's doing good things.

And because of what's in the media, most people think that unions are always on strike. The fact is that the overwhelming majority of labor-management contracts are settled amicably. Look at what Owen Bieber, president of the United Autoworkers (UAW), was just able to do with the UAW and GM. Everyone was predicting a strike, but he got a wonderful settlement at GM, and a wonderful settlement at Ford. Labor leaders are extremely responsible. They're certainly not goons, or knee-jerk kind of people who scream, "strike, strike." In fact, I believe that if you actually did a factual comparison of who was going to jail today from government, industry, or labor, I don't think the labor movement would come out any worse. We might even come out better than those other groups.

But in our society the integrity and quality of labor's leadership has always been suspect. That's nonsense. People in labor truly have social consciences, and they want to improve life for their own members, as well as make a contribution to the greater society.

For instance, the AFL-CIO's executive council, and for that matter the entire labor movement, has been terrific on issues related to working women and families. You know, I have really three separate jobs. My Amalgamated job as director of social services is my real job—I'm elected and I get paid for it, but I also have the honor of sitting on the Executive Council of the AFL-CIO and serving as the president of CLUW [Coalition of Labor Union Women], and that's a nonpaying volunteer job. And let me tell you, CLUW is planning for May of 1988 a demonstration in Washington on work and family issues, and labor is supporting us 100 percent. The executive council is even putting money into it. There are also individuals like John Sweeney, president of SEIU [Service Employees International Union], who talk about family issues all the time. AFSCME and the IUE [International Union of Electronic, Electrical, Salaried, Machine and Furniture Workers] have done yeoman's work in pay equity; the UAW has a wonderful program on sexual harassment and other issues affecting working women; and the Amalgamated established child care centers and was a key union right from the start in helping to get CLUW established, even before the women's movement took off. And the list just goes on. So there has been a lot of concern and effort expended by those in the labor movement on behalf of these issues, and remember that their achievements affect other people, not just those who are organized.

Labor has been very responsive as well to bringing women into leadership positions. When we started CLUW in 1974, you had no women on the AFL-CIO's executive council, and very few women in leadership positions of their unions. Today, you have three women on the executive council of the AFL-CIO, and I don't know a major international union that does not have women at the top level. You have now four presidents of unions who are women—Lenore Miller of the Retail, Wholesale and Department Store Workers Union; Susan Bianchi-Sand, head of the Flight Attendants; Patty Duke of the Screen Actors Guild; Colleen Dewhurst of Actors Equity; and Barbara Esterling is the executive vice-president of the CWA [Communications Workers of America].

And there are also women in many unions doing collective bargaining. It's not enough, but it certainly is progress. Don't forget, the women's movement really just started in the sixties, so there's been much improvement. And I think twenty years from now you'll see many more women doing collective bargaining and serving as presidents of unions.

Getting Started

I always had for whatever reason a social conscience. But when I was at the University of Chicago, there were a couple of professors who were just excellent in terms of their work with labor, and really turned on many of their students, including myself, to the labor movement. So when I was getting ready to write my master's thesis, it was arranged for me to go—it isn't in existence now—to the Michigan AFL-CIO summer school camp. From that experience I wrote my thesis on the role of the resident school in labor education, and from that, decided that I wanted to be an education director for a union. I really never had any other ambition. And in fact, that's where I began in the Amalgamated in 1962, as an education director for the Chicago joint board. I then served as social service director and administrative assistant, and in 1972, I came here to our national headquarters to do nationally what I had set up in Chicago.

My Work

I really feel terrific when we are able to bring out a program that helps our unemployed members, or one that helps people in their daily lives, in dire disasters, or supporting them when they have problems with their kids, or with their families. It's great when we can help a kid get a scholarship, or we're able to reduce our members' hospital bills, or help them to consolidate their debts.

We've set up a committee that's working on drug testing and alcohol abuse, and we're now doing an educational program on AIDS. We were also the first union to set up a blood bank program so that our members would always be able to draw on the blood that was put in by everyone.

Most of the ideas for our programs come from society, just by reading the newspapers, and from looking around at people's needs. We started the child care center in Chicago because we knew that our members had very little money, and that they had to have a place to put their kids. The idea for the education-by-right program came because there were people wanting to send their kids to school beyond high school and they needed help. When we set up the retired members center, it was because those retirees had made a contribution to our union. You just don't say "goodbye" to them after that. Companies do that—unions don't. You just know that there are people out there—they work every day in an apparel factory, they go home, they have problems.

One idea I have, but I don't know how to implement it nationally, is to help older people fill our their Medicare and Social Security claims because I know how difficult that can be for them. That would be a wonderful service if we could provide it, but that's just a germ in my head. Now that I have the idea, the next step will be to toss it around with my staff, see what we can do, how we could implement it.

But the Amalgamated has always been progressive and out front in terms of social programs. That hasn't really changed since the time of Sidney Hillman. In the earliest days of the union there were dance programs and art classes, and always an education director.

Now these sorts of things give me tremendous satisfaction. I've never gotten up out of bed, and this is true, in twenty-five years and said to myself I'm not happy to go to work today. My problem is just the opposite, taking time off from work is a tough one. And I think it's true of most union leaders. They truly do love their jobs, and their jobs become their lives. In fact, it really isn't like you have a job—it's more of a commitment. There are no such things as hours, there are no such things as real vacation time. I mean I'm entitled to five weeks vacation but if I take two weeks, that'd be a lot. You do pay a price with your family though.

Commitment

We continue to fight for all sorts of social issues for everyone's sake. We're out there in the vineyards fighting for equal employment rights, safety, and fair pay legislation, which Washington says are all solved. They're not solved, and we're fighting the whole policy of the United States government that says individualism counts, unions don't matter, affirmative action doesn't matter, occupational safety and health don't matter. The labor movement has paid a terrible price in the past eight years with the Reagan administration. All we want now is a president who's sympathetic, or at least neutral, on these issues and doesn't send a signal out that it's okay to bust unions.

19. The New Realist Craft Unionist

James J. Norton

I love the job and I want to put my imprint on this organization, but I don't want it to become my organization.

James J. Norton is president of the Graphic Communications International Union (GCIU). The GCIU, an organization of 200,000 members, traces its roots through the consolidation of unions in the printing industry over the past twenty-five years, including the Amalgamated Lithographers of North America, the International Photoengravers Union of North America, the International Brotherhood of Bookbinders and the International Printing and Graphic Communications Union.

Prior to his election as president in 1985, Mr. Norton served as recording and financial secretary of the GCIU for two years, and secretary-treasurer of the Graphic Arts International Union for five years. He also served as president of the Boston Photoengravers Union for four terms, and spent twenty-three years as an international representative servicing the New England states.

Among his other official duties, James Norton serves as a member of the executive council of the Industrial Union Department of the AFL-CIO and the executive board of the Union Labor Life Insurance Company.

Mr. Norton was born in 1931 in Boston, Massachusetts.

———————————————————* * *———————————————————

THIS may sound corny, but we're all products of our environment. And the biggest change in our lives, at least since I came out of school, has been the impact of advertising. Television wasn't available when I was in school—entertainment at home was a radio. So that advocated a simple life. Advertisements were not about roadsters, but durable cars in which you could take the family out on Sundays. But you see an automobile advertisement today—the damn cars are being driven about sixty-five miles an hour. Occasionally you see a family, but in most of the car ads that I've seen, the driver's going like a son of a gun. He has to be someplace in a hurry.

So I think advertising has influenced the kids of today to look for the fastest and most direct route to a comfortable environment. They just don't seem to have the same kind of commitment to things that we had when we were their age. Working at a job and putting some money away into a savings account to buy a house, setting aside money for education—that was the old way of doing things. The new way is to get your parents to do it, or buy a piece of real estate, turn it over quickly, extract some equity—making money with money.

There certainly are lots of people who are being disenfranchised by this streamlining method of making money. Jobs are going overseas. Environmentalists tell us that we have to be concerned about the wildlife we're losing, because extinct is forever. Well, how about the textile jobs and electronic jobs we've lost, they're also extinct. That's been fostered by American investments overseas. You've seen the horror stories of computer operations in Taiwan and the Philippines that are doing our work with people who can't even speak or understand English. Yet they can connect the keys on the console with the letters on the paper. And all of the billing of the airlines now is being done overseas.

I have come to the conclusion that unions cannot save industries. If a plant or a segment of the industry is being bypassed, that's it. Take for example those people who used to work with the old photoengraving method. That method became very expensive after the war ended because of the improvements and commercialization of the photo offset process. By the early fifties you could produce a product by offset that was comparable with a colored product from a photoengraving. That was great, because you suddenly found yourself putting colored pictures in newspapers with daily regularity.

But once industry veered away from photoengraving, there was nothing that this union could do to help those people. You couldn't go to a plant and say to the owner, we'll work for $3 less an hour because he still couldn't make a profit even if he paid us $3 an hour. Just no way he could stay in.

When that kind of thing occurs, there's nothing a union can do. You can reduce the amount of pain that's incurred with it, but you can't control it.

On Management

We're battling employers who are much better equipped to resist organizers today than they ever were in the past. Employers are quick to tell employees, "If you go with the union, that's the end of the job, that's the end of the plant, because eventually it'll put us both out of business." The young guy may not be too much impressed by that kind of a threat, but the middle-aged person, if he reads at all, or if he watches the news, has got to be somewhat indentured to the closing of a plant usually being associated with a labor union.

The management association has done an excellent job with this, because I've met with them privately and they told me, "Look, I'm closing the plant in that town." And I say to them, "Can we do anything about it?" "No, no, the decision is made." And then they begin to feed inflammatory issues back to the local townies that the union's demands are such that they're going to have to consider alternatives. It's a regular public relations effort on their part to cast the blame on the union. And they've even told me in advance, "Sorry, we have to do this." It's just become part of the relationship that you have now.

All these plants made money for years when they were under union contracts, but they can make more if they're out from under a union contract. So that's why they use these tactics. They'll share the profits with the stockholders, not with the employees.

Management associations didn't need Reagan to do this. Too many of our guys think it started with the strike of the Professional Air Traffic Controllers (PATCO), but it was happening before then. It only started to become fashionable and patriotic with PATCO. That's when it became a situation of "Throw the bums out."

It's a bad bad impression that unions have—bums, unpatriotic, lost jobs. You sort of get the feeling that unions have done something terrible to this country. What I'm afraid for is that some kids, who have seen their families affected by plant closings, will in fact attribute it, as they get into their own businesses, to the higher cost of operation with unions. And there is some linkage there. You see, when I was a kid, people reacted to John L. Lewis as if he were a traitor. He prevented the mines from working when our boys were being killed in Bataan and the Philippines. Now, today, you recognize what Lewis did, he just took advantage of a situation, and brought the Miners into some decent paying conditions at the time.

Collective Bargaining

But not everything is so bad, there are some good things out there. First, we've broken that cycle of the annual wage increases. Now that was suicidal. Unless you organize the entire industry, you can't have the organized employers paying too much more than the unorganized employers. Eventually the work will simply be lost because of competitive prices. That's forced all of us, including the rank and file, to recognize that it's simply a matter of arithmetic. You can't pay out more than what you take in, and you can't take in if it's costing you more to produce it.

For instance, photoengravers and photographers used to get four weeks of vacation after a year's employment, and that was great when everybody was organized. It's not true now though because if you take a new employee on, and give him four weeks vacation, you're doing something that probably nobody else in the country is doing. You can't do that anymore—you have to be competitive. Yet people say, "Well if you don't have anything that's an incentive for people to associate with the union, then you're not going to get them to become members." Well that's true, you have to have something that is going to be an asset to an employee for them to make the choice to belong to a union. But you're not going to do it today on the basis of what unions used to promise people. You have to tell them to think in terms of longevity on the job, and that this is a career and you're getting associated with a union that is telling you in advance what to expect—then you'll get them interested.

I applaud Kirkland's and Donahue's [president and secretary-treasurer of the AFL-CIO] efforts in going to conventions and talking about how competition is not just in the United States, it's all over the world. Tom Donahue, for example, is going down to South America to attend a very hostile meeting of management people, some of whom don't even operate in America. And he's going to talk to them about American labor's concerns about jobs we've lost to overseas. He's not going to get anywhere with them, but he believes that if we want to play in the ballgame, then we have to send the players, and at least tell them what our concerns are here in the United States for what's happening overseas.

So what I think Kirkland and Donahue are trying to do is get labor to appraise itself realistically, and I believe we're beginning to do that. We're certainly looking at the industry and saying segment A—what's the future of segment A? If it's the packaging industry, the packaging industry has a good future. If it's going to be the plastic industry in packaging, we better have another look at that and start talking with some of the employers in the plastics industry. The overuse of plastic becomes an environmental concern and that's beginning to have a definite impression on Americans.

Looking Back

I graduated from high school in 1947, and in 1949 I started an apprenticeship. I had a chance to go to school. I could've gone up to St. Anselm's College in New Hampshire, but we needed the income at home so that ruled out going to college.

But I remember being sworn in at my first union meeting. There were about sixty people in the hall and they were talking national politics. They made a reference to the U.S. president and I thought, "Jeez, this is quite an organization." The meetings were on Tuesday nights and we had fine turnouts. You'd find fifty or sixty people there always, but then Milton Berle came on the TV on Tuesday nights and we had to shift the union meetings.

What I'm suggesting is that things have drawn people away from unions. Part of attendance at union meetings in those days was a certain amount of entertainment and social activity that you now do elsewhere. The magic formula it seems to me is scheduling the meetings at the members' convenience. For instance, I used to go down to meetings in Florida, where they held them on Sunday mornings right after mass—mostly Catholics down there, so they'd schedule meetings right after mass—so that the wives would go home and the guys would go to the union hall. If you went to the 9:00 mass, you met from 10:00 to 12:30, and then you watched the Dolphins. Those people found the formula.

I lost the first election I ran in—that was for the position of scribe in my local. The scribe, who wrote for the magazine had died, and nobody wanted the job because he was so very good at writing. But I didn't really know him, and I used to like to write, so I ran for the position. I used to be a cartoonist and had visions of injecting a cartoon into the magazine. But the guys told me, "Look, you're a great kid, but you're too *stubborn*," so I lost the election, but won it the following year.

Leadership

I'm not an autocratic leader like some. A labor union can't be a one-man operation. If it is, it can only suffer. I've only had this position officially now since November, 1985. I got here because nobody ran against me. Nobody ran against me because they thought I couldn't be beaten. That's not ego, that happens to be a fact.

Since I've been here though I haven't developed a single program on my own. In fact what I've been doing mostly is trying to eliminate some of the ones that I don't think are beneficial for our future. You have to pull the plug on them and put that money where it would best be spent.

You can't accommodate everybody—there's just no way to do that.

Even when local unions want you to come to their meetings, you tend to go to meetings where you think you can have an impact, and you associate impact with numbers. So I tend to go to the big cities even though I believe there are more thinkers in the smaller cities. Some people get annoyed when they hear that. But I find if you want people to bounce things off, it's not necessarily the larger cities you go to. Although there are one or two there, it's the people from the suburbs of cities like Detroit whose jobs have been impacted by foreign competition, and who've seen the damage that it has done to families.

Looking Forward

I love the job and I want to put my imprint on this organization, but I don't want it to become my organization. I do want to get it, though, in the direction where it will succeed.

We'll do well in the growing industries like rotogravure, packaging newspapers, and in commercial printing. But we'll need to establish cooperative efforts with our employers to determine the most productive approaches to work and guarantee success for both them and us.

We're talking to some of our employers now, and each time I meet with them, they are prepared to meet again. I'm not viewing that as acquiescence to my goals, but at least they're willing to talk. Employers who won't talk with us, I don't have the time to try to cultivate them.

But we've got to bring in more members. And we have to deal with the members' concerns with security—"Can we hang onto what we have?" And so we'll also keep an open mind regarding possible mergers. In fact, we missed out on one with the International Typographical Union by an eyelash. I believe the Teamster pressure caused them to go to the Communications Workers of America. So that degree of competition in the labor movement is still there, and it keeps us sharp.

Reflections on Some Teamsters

By the way, I've met with Jackie Presser [late president of the Teamsters'], and he's a very impressive guy. He's a people person, but he's also a concern. A concern, because I think he works in a counter-direction to the AFL-CIO. But he has some good qualities—leadership and the ability to move people— and if those could be channeled in the direction of the house of labor, he could be a tremendous asset. Look, he has the ability to persuade people that the government is attacking him personally, rather than on his record. You walk away thinking, "He may have something there."

And look at what Bobby Kennedy did to Hoffa. I liked Bobby up to a point, but he had a crusade, a vendetta against Hoffa.[1] Perhaps it was justified for what Hoffa did—jury tampering, that's just inexcusable.

Yet Hoffa justified what he was doing under the guise of creating some good. That's of no value. The Teamster members who say, "Well he got me something and therefore everything else that he did is not that important"—that's no good at all. I met Hoffa after he came out of prison and I heard a couple of speeches he made with respect to prison reform. I believe that there was some credence to what he was saying and that he believed in it. How far he would have gone with it remains to be seen. But was he a good leader? Sure, he was a damned good leader. So was Hitler, but for heaven's sake, his leadership didn't do anybody any good.

20. Unions on Center Stage

Frederick O'Neal

Yes, labor is a special interest, but our special interest is the 240 million people in this country.

Frederick O'Neal was born in Mississippi in 1905 and has been an actor and director in the theatre, motion pictures, radio, and television since 1927. In New York City, he studied at the New Theatre School and American Theatre Wing. He also helped organize the Aldridge Players in 1927, the American Negro Theatre in 1940, and the British Negro Theatre in London in 1948.

Mr. O'Neal has been a visiting professor at Southern Illinois University and at Clark College. He was president of Actors' Equity Association from 1964 until 1973 and has been international president of the Associated Actors and Artistes of America (AAAA) for the past eighteen years.

Mr. O'Neal has been the chairman of the AFL-CIO civil rights committee from 1970 to the present; vice-president of the Catholic Actors' Guild; and a member of the advisory council to New York State School of Industrial and Labor Relations of Cornell University. Some of his many awards and honors include a doctorate in humanities from Lincoln University, 1976; honorary doctorate of humanities from Tougaloo College, 1982; honorary doctorate of human letters from St. Johns University, 1981; and NAACP Man of Year Award, 1979.

The Associated Actors and Artistes of America (commonly referred to as the 4As) is the international union or "umbrella" organization for performing artists in the field of entertainment. The 4As does not have locals nor does it accept individual membership. Rather, its members are nine autonomous national unions, including Actors' Equity Association, American Federation of Television and Radio Artists, American Guild of Musical Artists, American Guild of Variety Artists, Asociacíon Puertorriquena de Artistas y Tecnicos del Espectaculo, Hebrew Actors' Union, Inc., Italian Actors Union, Screen Actors Guild, and Screen Extras Guild. Representatives from each of the nine unions form the council of the 4As. The elected officers of the various unions are unsalaried.

───────────────────────── ✳ ✳ ✳ ─────────────────────────

MEMBERSHIP in our affiliated unions has grown considerably since I became a union member nearly fifty years ago. Unfortunately though, the employment picture for our members has not changed significantly over that same period. Those in the field of entertainment still have one of the highest unemployment rates in the country.

Take for instance Actors' Equity. It's the union that represents performers in the legitimate theatre, on Broadway, off-Broadway, community and resident theatres, and so forth. The unemployment rate of Actors' Equity members is almost exactly the same as it was years ago, and this is true of the other major affiliates as well. This has occurred because the number of new people entering the profession has outpaced the increase in employment opportunities. Although there are no accurate figures, I estimate the unemployment rate among Equity members to run between 60 and 65 percent at any one time. That means that these artists are not earning a living through their professional talents. They are either taxi drivers, secretaries, or bartenders, etcetera, when they're not working in the entertainment field.

One of my ideas to increase employment is to organize touring shows, and have them sponsored by liquor and tobacco companies, firms which are not allowed to advertise on television. These shows might employ thirty, forty, or even, sixty people, and I believe that if we had enough of them, I think we could increase employment substantially. At the same time the shows could become a very effective means of marketing the products involved, and there is a very good chance the company will make a profit from the tour itself.

From the unemployment figures I've quoted, one can understand the frustration and confusion of these talented individuals. Often they stop by to talk with me and receive whatever advice I can offer. Just three days ago, a brilliant opera soprano was here telling me that she didn't know where to turn for help in moving along in her career. I sent her to the head of the American Guild of Musical Artists, who then sent her to an audition. She called me later and said, "It's terrific, they're going to employ me!" These are some things that make you feel good about this work and being a part of this organization.

You will be interested to know as well that elected officials of the 4As and its unions are unsalaried. One of the reasons for this policy is that these people are still working in their craft and do not devote their full time to the positions. But, we also decided long ago that if there was a salary involved, it would keep rising and rising until you got to the point that people would run for office because of the money involved, not because of what they could do for the membership.

The Contribution of Labor

As a union member, one of the things that concerns me is the lack of knowledge among the public as to the importance of the labor movement in our society. I told a group of union members recently that "I'm proud of my union membership. I'm proud of it because unions are one of the most important, if not the most important, institution in our society." I said to the group "Who do you think built this building that we're sitting in now? It was union workers, the carpenters, electricians, plumbers, and so forth. Who do you think built this chair that you're sitting in? Who do you think tailored the clothes we're wearing? Who grew the food that you had for breakfast this morning?" If you're not lying on your back clipping coupons, you're part of labor.

We've been accused of being a special interest. Of course, we're a special interest. When we go to the Congress to talk about a national health insurance, we're not just talking about union members. Most of us, if not all, have it already. When we talk about housing problems, Social Security, who are we talking about? Yes, we are special interest, but our special interest is the 240 million people in this country!

Wherever you find a country with a weak or a nonexistent union movement, you find problems. I was in Peru some years ago, and now that's a country that has not allowed a free union movement to develop. When I got off the plane, I saw barefooted children in rags, parents not much better off, and families living in mud huts. At the same time, we went to the home of one of the country's officials, and there in his garden was an exact replica of the city square. He had the cathedral, the fountain, the government house, everything—an exact replica. I said, "I don't mean to be nosy, but do you have any idea what this cost you?" He said, "I hope I never find out."

Now in that country you had extreme poverty on the one hand, great wealth on the other, and a complete absence of a middle class. When that occurs in a country the red lights go on. It's a strong union movement that fosters a responsible middle class.

Therefore, in my estimation, the trade union movement is the most important element towards the maintenance of stability in our society. And I believe the AFL-CIO is doing a marvelous job in supporting working people. For example, the federation is beginning to offer new and creative sorts of benefits to the members such as a low-interest credit card, low-cost insurances, and the possibility of borrowing money for their mortgages or whatever, from an investment trust fund. It is not just sitting by idly. And there are some things which we'd like to achieve—for example, a universal health insurance, like they have in Britain and other countries.

Lost Jobs

The United States is facing a serious challenge from overseas. I think the one thing that we have to correct is our balance of trade. Every country, except us, protects its own interest. We seem to be helping everybody but ourselves. Some years ago, I visited a Toyota plant in Tokyo and the personnel director was telling our group that their employees make pretty good salaries, but nowhere near what U.S. workers make. I learned however, that when their workers go to lunch, the company pays for it. An apartment there is $25 a month—it's a company owned apartment. That same apartment in Detroit costs over $500 a month. We've got to have some kind of trade agreement that takes those things under consideration. So I say, "Even though it costs me more, I'm going to buy American made goods."

My Work

Because of my schedule here, I haven't done any acting in about ten or twelve years now, with the exception of a little voice-over once in a while for television. I just don't have the time for weeks of rehearsal in order to do theatre, television, and that sort of thing. But I do miss it all very much. I'm just too active with organizations such as Muscular Dystrophy, Sickle Cell Anemia, the National Committee on U.S./China Relations, United Nations Development Corporation, board meetings and so forth of the American Arbitration Association to do much acting.

Getting Started

One of the things which motivated me to go off more in the direction of labor, rather than staying in acting was McCarthyism. I was a target of some of that, and decided to do something about it. I'll give you an illustration of what I mean. On 9th Avenue and 41st Street in New York City, there used to be a little theatre—not a regular theatre, but they used to be able to do plays there anyway. After a performance of *They Shall Not Die,* some actors came out of the theatre and a group of goons attacked them. That area in fact was referred to as a bucket of blood back then, because of the number of such incidents that occurred there. But anyway, as I understood it, the police stood by and did nothing, even laughed at what was going on.

Well anyway, there was a meeting about the incident and I spoke up against it. For that, I understand the network put me on their list of communist sympathizers. They said the meeting was communist supported. I didn't know about being put on a list until my agent told me, but when she did, I said to her, "If they have this kind of information on me, you tell them that they'll probably get some more. Because any time actors are attacked and people stand by and do nothing, police stand by and do nothing, you call on me. I don't need to work in an industry that blacklists for these things, I can still dig a ditch." It was the principle I was concerned with.

As long as people tell the truth about things I can deal with them. It's the kind of two-faced thing that I can't deal with. For instance, when I go to affairs in California, it's usually the same people all the time, and they just talk about the people who are not there. But the minute those people arrive, it's "Dahhling!" I can't stand that kind of hypocrisy, or the kind of prejudice that you meet in the east and north, the "Some of my best friends are black" sort of thing.

In fact, I can better deal with southern prejudice, because whatever a southerner thinks he'll tell you to your face. Some of the presidents that I respect most were from the South—Truman, Johnson, Carter. I think Carter will go down in history as being one of the most honest presidents that we've ever had. We didn't always agree with him in the labor movement, but by golly, he told you what he thought. And there was no question about it. If you could change his mind, it was a real change, it wasn't something that was superficial. The same thing is true of Lyndon Johnson.

I've learned that you have to rise above the hatred and the offensive behaviors aimed at you. For instance, I was on an elevator with a friend of mine when a white woman got on whom we knew, and we also knew how she felt about us. Well, when she got on the elevator, it was in the winter time, I took my hat off. She, of course, put her nose up in the air. When she got off, my friend said to me, "You take your hat off to that so and so." I said, "No, I didn't. I took my hat off because of what I think of myself. That's something she'll have to deal with." My father told me that while it's important if people think well of you, what is most important is respect and confidence in yourself.

21. The Professional Newspaperman As Unionist

Charles A. Perlik, Jr.

I've only been opposed three times. Serious opposition? Well, my opponents thought so.

Charles A. Perlik, Jr., served as president of the Newspaper Guild (TNG) from 1970 to 1987. Mr. Perlik was secretary-treasurer of the guild from 1955 to 1969 and an international representative for three years prior to that. He is second vice-president of the International Federation of Journalists, which represents over 117,000 working journalists in more than thirty countries throughout the world.

Charles Perlik is a member of the Society of Professional Journalists, Sigma Delta Chi; a member of the executive committee of the World Press Freedom Committee and the board of directors of the Committee to protect Journalists, and a member of the board of trustees and former chairman of the Council on Hemispheric Affairs.

Mr. Perlik was born in Pittsburgh, Pennsylvania in 1923. After three-and-a-half years of military service during World War II, he attended Medill School of Journalism, Northwestern University, where he received a bachelor of science in journalism in 1949, and a master of science in journalism degree in 1950.

For a description of the Newspaper Guild, see chapter 8. This interview was conducted while Mr. Perlik was president of TNG.

————————————————— ✳ ✳ ✳ —————————————————

I STARTED working for the Guild in '52, and in all my years as an elected officer, I've only been opposed three times. Serious opposition? Well, my opponents thought so. It turned out that the first one was the most serious. I was a rep on the field staff then, and had only been working for the guild for 3½ years, and a colleague and myself decided to try to upset the incumbent administration.

He really chose me out of a flock to run with him, but I guess it was a wise political decision for him as I look back—simply because I had done very productive work in organizing large segments of new members in Canada, which at that time was almost virgin territory for The Newspaper Guild. That's where I carried votes for both of us and that was pretty much the margin of victory. I stayed with him for fourteen years as secretary-treasurer, and we were really unopposed most of the time. When he retired in '69, I ran for the presidency. It's a longer story than I'm indicating, with all kinds of changes along the way, but anyway, I won the presidency with a margin of something like 58 to 42 percent. In '71, it was 70 to 30 percent, and since then I haven't been opposed.

Sometimes you hear people in the locals complain that their union leadership has been in for too long, they're getting older, and why don't they retire? Well, I would respond, I guess, predictably. It seems to me that people who make that case want a boost up or an assist in fulfilling ambitions that they don't have the capability of achieving. So, what are they suggesting? That we should throw the election? Give them a head start? Twenty-five hundred votes?

I was elected to run this union within the framework of the policies of the convention and the board, and that's the way I play it. I have no hesitation to invoke those policies, and that gets my ass in a sling sometimes with membership groups, that's for sure.

But I don't even think it's right that the president of the United States is limited in terms. If a U.S. president is doing a good job, he should run for as long as he is doing a good job, or until the people of this country make the decision for him to do otherwise.

Bear in mind where the Twenty-third Amendment to the U.S Constitution came from. It came from the reactionaries just after World War II. They hit not only the political structure of this country, but they also hit the labor movement right in the gut with the Taft-Hartley Act. This isn't the only country with postwar conservative reactions. Britain kicked out Winston Churchill, who up through the war was one of their great heroes. And I suspect that if the Russians had an opportunity, they would have done the same with Stalin.

So, those are the laments, I think, of the people who are out and want it. Age doesn't make any difference. Why don't they do something about it anyway? Why don't they go to a meeting? Why don't they run for office? Why don't they challenge? What they're saying is that it's either ineptitude, maybe even corruption and certainly indolence, and I don't accept that. I think I have to run every day of the week, and every day of the year for office. How do I run? I get out among the members, I go to council meetings, I go to local meetings. I go wherever our membership is congregated.

To do it right you have to listen to the tone. To give you a classical example, we have a certain contingent in The Newspaper Guild that wants us to merge with somebody. Fine and dandy. I'm an advocate of mergers, too, not with just somebody, but with a union who could do something for us. We think we have a lot to contribute to any union we would merge with. If I go out in the membership, however, I am never asked: Why don't we merge? Who are we going to merge with? What are we doing about merging?

What are they saying to us? They're saying to us, "When are we going to stop the erosions in our contract? How can we stop the givebacks, how can we stop the two-tiered wage systems, how can we stop the demands from the employers for us to start paying for our health and welfare benefits, which for the last thirty, forty years they've paid all of?"

Old and New

The same issues, the same concerns, that motivated people thirty or forty years ago are the issues that motivate people to come into this union today. We never get an organizing inquiry that doesn't have at the root of it, "My wages are lousy, what can you do about it?" And if you look at the wages in the newspaper industry, you can understand why you get that. I spent some time recently at the Poynter Institute for Media Studies in St. Petersburg, Florida, which is a management established think-tank operation. They bring all kinds of people in the industry to discuss and talk about all kinds of things. This time it was a group of journalism professors, fifteen of them, and they were there to acquire expertise and knowledge in teaching a management course for newspapers. So commendably, Poynter at least brought in me, a labor guy, to give our point of view.

We spent most of our time trying to find a solution to the problem of getting a decent starting salary for graduate journalism students coming out of their courses. Jobs for their students—I guess every professor has that yardstick to confront him—but it's abominable in our industry. Two-hundred, $250 a week! Somebody with a bachelor's degree, depending on the university, in the science of journalism or the arts of journalism, whatever the hell it's called, to get paid that kind of money.

And so I asked them, "What do you tell the industry people?—You see

them all the time." The profs said that they claim that they can't afford it—
it will raise the cost to the advertiser. I said, "Hell, they're all monopoly
situations, where are the advertisers going to go?" They might go to radio
or television, but they can only go there to a limited extent—only the hucks-
ters can go to radio and television. Did you ever see a serious department
store ad on television? Of course not. Sure you see car ads and that sort of
thing. There is no way you can duplicate what they can do with the graphics
and the magic of cinema. But newspapers? Well, the professors just won't
take them on. They belong to the same country clubs, they consort in the
same crowds, and they don't want to go to a cocktail party and have their
ass reamed out, for Christ's sake, because they raised the advertising rates.

On Management

Our employers are bad, badder, and baddest! I think the worst one at the
present time of a national character is Gannett, I don't think there's any
doubt about that. Their organization is run by a very successful, very ego-
tistical, and very determined man, and he's got the wherewithal to get done
much of what he wants to get done. He's got a lot of allies helping him do
that, in the national government and in the National Labor Relations Board.
But Gannett knows just how hard to push things and get away with it. And
they've taken some absurd, some obscene positions. They won't agree, for
instance, to a minimum wage structure. Whoever heard of a labor agreement
without a minimum wage structure that means anything?

They also have taken this obscene position with respect to outside activities. They would have you think that somebody who works for that
organization is a eunuch as far as citizenship is concerned. They claim you
don't have a right to participate in civic activities, you can't run for office,
you can't assist in a civic endeavor, which is nonsense. There's no reason to
believe that a newspaperman or -woman can't do most of the things that
any of us can do as citizens, and still be effective as newspapermen and -
women.

Getting Started

My father was a salesman for Swift and Company in Pittsburgh, where I
was raised, and I can recall meetings of his cohorts in our house in the
summer. I really didn't realize at the time why they were there until after I
got involved in the union. What he was doing was forming a union for
salesmen for Swift and Company. That effort was successful, and the union
is one of the first in the country for salesmen. But my dad paid a price. Swift

and Company conveniently promoted him to assistant manager, and left him there for the rest of his career, some thirty years. From that point he only got the routine wage increases which their contracts with the salesmen forced them to give him. They never went beyond that, never went below it—he was in purgatory in that sense. He retired eventually from Swift and Company with a pension. Unaccountably, Swift, back in the thirties and the forties, had a private pension plan for its employees. There weren't many companies that had pension plans in those days.

When I started to go to work myself I went to my first job in the news industry, which was with the old International News Service [INS]. I was going to the University of Pittsburgh my freshman year and I got a job as an overnight copy boy. I was in that job three or four months and a dayside copy boy came up to me one day and said, "We have a union here, would you like to join?" I said, "sure," and I joined. It turned out after many many years later that young kid who came up to talk to me was Alan Kistler, now the Director of Organization and Field Services for the AFL-CIO. His career went many, many different ways, and so did mine.

Well, I lost my job at INS because they moved the state headquarters from Pittsburgh to Harrisburg, and they had to lop off people, and what the hell, a kid who's nineteen years old, a student—I was a small sacrifice. Then I went to Northwestern University, went into the Army, came back out of the service and decided I didn't want to go back to finish my degree right away. So I went around the city of Pittsburgh looking for work as a copyboy, because I figured that's all I was qualified to be. I was twenty-three years old then, and that was old for a copyboy.

But I didn't get a job until I got a call from the bureau manager at United Press [UP] in Pittsburgh, who said, "We don't have a job as a copyboy here, but would you like to be a newsman?" I said why not, and I went to work for UP as a beginning newsman at $32 a week. I was working there four or five weeks when I got my paycheck and saw that my salary was up to $40. I said, "My God, what a wonderful place to work. Here I am four or five weeks, I haven't done much for them, but they gave me an $8 a week increase." Just about that time, though, the steward sidled up to me and said, "Did you get a raise in your paycheck this week?" I said, "Yeah, yeah." He said, "Do you happen to know why?" I told him that I hadn't the slightest idea, and he then proceeded to tell me that the union just settled a contract in New York. Well, that kind of opened my eyes as to how things worked, and I became a member right there.

I decided six months later to go back to school, which meant leaving Pittsburgh and returning to Evanston, Illinois and Northwestern. United Press did not have a practice at that time of giving you transfers. You could quit, reapply in Chicago if you wanted to and if you got hired, fine and dandy. I was fortunate to get a job there on the overnight radio desk, but it turned out that school, work, and a new marriage was a tough schedule, so I left the job, and went to school full time.

After I graduated from Northwestern, I tried to get a job in Chicago, but just couldn't find one. So I took a job with the *Buffalo Evening News* with about six or seven of my immediate or nearby classmates, some of whom are very distinguished people now in the newspaper business, including the editor of the *L. A. Times*, Bill Thomas, and so forth. We all came out of that class. Murray Light, who is now the editor of the *Buffalo Evening News,* was among them.

My guild experience up to that time involved only my association with what was called the "Associate Member Program." This was designed exclusively for journalism students to put us in touch with the working press. So I knew some things about how the guild was operated and how journalism students could be served by it. But when I got to Buffalo, New York, I found a union with about sixty-two members and two bucks in the bank, or vice versa—it really didn't make any difference. The local hadn't held a meeting for seven months, and when my wife and I went to the first meeting that was called, I was elected president, she was elected secretary. So we decided to make something of it and because of some success in organizing units around the city, the region, and bargaining with the *Buffalo Evening News* I got invited to join the American Newspaper Guild staff—we became TNG in the early seventies—and here I am.

The Industry

I like my job, but I liked it a hell of a lot better thirty years ago. And that's mainly due to the beatings we've taken in the last half a dozen years, despite the fact that the industry had no need to make the financial recovery it claimed from our contracts. So we've been trying to keep the spirit of our people alive, and have them recognize that this is just a passing phase. The pendulum will swing again, indeed it will.

It started swinging in the wrong direction for us about '78, '79. Just before then, in '76, the pressmen at *The Washington Post* struck, ill-advisedly, and without asking anybody else for advice or support. They got whipped royally, not even in an hour. From that, New York publishers, St. Louis publishers, Montreal publishers, Vancouver publishers, all decided it was the time to take on the pressrooms. And so they did, and they all succeeded. We spent millions in those strikes supporting those pressmen, who never realized their day had come, and that they had to cut and run, and get the best deal out of it they could. Instead they decided to be out on the street, and they struck the worst deal. From that time on, the vulnerability of unions was confirmed.

But the real erosion of the unions in the newspaper business began with the technological revolution that destroyed the ITU [International Typographical Union]. That began twenty years ago. It didn't hit its climax until the ITU in New York settled its famous ten-year contract in which it conceded the right to automate the composing room.[1] Now once New York falls, like so many other things, everything else is going to tumble. It doesn't work in reverse. Once you get a decent settlement in New York, you would think that would flow west of the Hudson River. It doesn't always happen that way. But if you don't get a decent settlement in New York, you know damn well you won't get a decent settlement somewhere else.

Technological Changes

Technological changes, electronic newspapers, and those issues related to people working at home won't cut into our membership. First, the technology that allows that has got limited application for us. It's available and useful and attractive to the specialists, the columnists, the movie reviewer, the music reviewer, the book reviewer, where you have to have long periods of contemplation and so forth, but it's impractical on the news side. It's not so much working at home that gets us into problems—it's what's happening in the transmission of news coverage on the spot that has more bearing on the newspaperman. But we really don't anticipate much effect from that either. Just because you can take out a piece of equipment from your briefcase, punch out a story, put it on a telephone wire, and it feeds back into a computer in some building, well, that's not much different than sitting at a computer here, or sitting at a computer twenty feet away.

I don't think the electronic newspaper really has any future. It was a big threat, a presumed threat, perceived threat, six or seven years ago, and a couple of the biggies in the industry thought it was the coming thing—Times-Mirror, and so forth. They tried to peddle it, but they both shut down their activities because nobody is going to buy a newspaper that appears on the television screen. You can't take it to the bathroom, you can't take it on the bus, you have to sit and read a newspaper. Not only that, you've got to pay more for an electronic newspaper. You pay a quarter now for *The Washington Post*, but to get an electronic service on your machine, it's $15–$20 a month plus auxiliary services. Until something is done to make it a hell of a lot more flexible, it's not a coming thing.

The Voice of Labor

There is no one voice to labor on political or social issues. Take a look at labor's reaction and posture on the big international issues of the day. At the moment everybody is on the same side with respect to South Africa, but they're split six ways from Sunday on Central America. While TNG is a part of a coalition supporting human rights in El Salvador and Nicaragua, starting with President Kirkland on down, [on] the Contras vis-à-vis the Sandinistas there are very wide differences of opinion. I'm not particularly happy with the Sandinista side because after all, they closed the newspapers. And if there's one thing that raises our hackles it's closing a newspaper. We don't give a damn for the reasons. We don't close newspapers if we can do anything about it. It's axiomatic with us.

President Kirkland is by no means cut from the same mold as George Meany. Not nearly as doctrinaire, not nearly as rigid, not nearly as colorful, but a hell of a guy I think. I think you couldn't have picked a . . . well, as effective a guy to crank into the atmosphere in which he's functioning. Obviously when Meany was president he was operating in the heyday of the labor movement— . . . not only because he was George Meany, but because he spoke for 18–20 million organized workers in this country, in industries that didn't have 1 percent free riders, and had control of the steel delivery system of the world, the automobile industry of the world, the electrical industry of the world. That ain't today's ball game, and Kirkland's effectiveness is influenced accordingly.

Looking Back

American labor is in good stead until the pendulum swings back. But it's in a survival mode until we have the next great economic crisis. I don't think anybody should close the door to recession and even perhaps a depression. I have some very stark memories of those years. I was ten, eleven, at that time and I'll carry to my grave the expression on my mother's face—she was a domestic—the day she came home from work with the news that their bank had closed. The expression, the gray, drawn look on her face, I will never lose til the day I die. You know how much she and my father had in that bank account? $100. Today, that's only a decent night out. It may not have been a lifetime of savings, but it's all they had,

I had an economics professor once who told me, "If the American people had a choice to make between a world war and another depression, I have absolutely no doubt they would choose another world war." I can buy that. You know, I was in the service during the war, but I was a young kid, twenty, twenty-one, a second lieutenant, and I walked around like the "cock of the walk." I didn't get overseas until after all the shooting was over, so the war never touched me. And except for those families, of course, who had somebody get killed or injured, for the rest of the country, the war was a picnic. All the overtime you wanted. The bars were open, the beer flowed, the booze flowed, the women were free, it was something. But a depression—nobody escaped. You can't compare rationed butter, rationed gasoline, going weeks and months without a paycheck to what we had during the war. I can remember as a young kid during the Depression, men coming to our door and saying, "Can you spare something to eat? I'll do a little work for you." My parents always brought whoever it was in and gave him a meal. I don't think they ever put him to work, there wasn't much for him to do. But I can remember those things and it was nothing like that during the war, nothing. And that's what is going to put labor back in good stead.

The things that I'm most proud of in my tenure with the Guild are two: one seminegative, and the other, I think is quite positive. The seminegative one is holding our own. The size of most labor unions in terms of the number of members has deteriorated drastically in the last five to ten years. That's not been our situation. While we haven't grown, we've held our own with 32–33,000 members—despite the fact that we probably lost 9,000–to 10,000 jobs in newspaper closures, mergers, suspensions, what have you at the *Washington Star,* the *Philadelphia Bulletin,* the *Buffalo Courier Express,* the *Chicago Daily News,* and for all intents and purposes the *St. Louis Globe Democrat.* It's just been one hammerhead hit one after the other. When those things happen, and if we're fully organized, we lose 400 to 500 members overnight. So, to keep even in those circumstances over the past twenty years has been commendable I think, although it's nothing you'd rant and rave about.

The one positive achievement in the last dozen or fifteen years is that we've opened the eyes of our membership to concerns beyond those that hit us right in the navel. We have become much more responsive to the problems of journalists elsewhere in the world and to societal problems generally. It's been a slow gradual process, but our membership, by and large, has followed on that path and given, for our size, a fair amount of financial support. We've broadened our whole response to the professional issues that confront this organization and confront this membership—press freedom concerns, First Amendment concerns, and to a larger extent the economic concerns that affect women as well as journalists. When I go out of this job if I'm able to say, "We have a contract which guarantees, as a minimum salary to a fully experienced newsperson, $50,000 a year," I will consider this a career well earned.

There are some things though that I wish I had a second chance on. For example, we pay a big price for our democratic posture of having an annual convention. Although I don't hang my hat on it, there are substantial benefits from having an annual convention, but on balance you pay a big price for having to go to war with each other every year, even though I enjoy the process. While I am unopposed myself, I do participate very actively in the election of officers who serve on the board. Obviously, to be able to claim any success at all, I have to have allies. I have to have a board that will support me at least 51 percent of the time. I've been fortunate—most of the time it's been substantially more than that.

I believe now that I'm at this age of sixty-two that people do become more conservative as they get older. It's almost inevitable it seems to me, particularly in this kind of job where you keep getting pounded by conservative attitudes. Some of it's going to rub off. Also, your experience begins to add up in different terms and you begin to look at the "on-the-other-hand" positions. I can remember those nights when I'd sit up at weekend conferences and council meetings and argue like a son-of-a-bitch for a point of view for a position. I no longer have the stamina for that and frankly, no longer have quite the same interest.

I'm looking forward to retirement. I think I've paid my dues, and done a reasonably good job for this organization. I've earned my money. So I'm looking forward to some things that my wife and I want to do, like spending some time with the grandkids. They're all young now and it's a great opportunity to impart to them a lot of things I've learned and done here.

22. Once a Union Member, Always a Union Member

Robert G. Porter

There are times in this job when you have the feeling that you've worked like hell, and it has made no difference at all. What happens mostly though, is that you get a sense of some small successes, and they're not always on overwhelming issues.

Robert G. Porter has served as secretary-treasurer of the American Federation of Teachers (AFT) since his appointment by the organization's executive council in 1963. Previous to this appointment he served as administrative aide to Carl Megel, former AFT president.

Before achieving full-time union employment, he taught civics in the East St. Louis, Illinois, public schools. Mr. Porter was active in the early stages of the establishment of the East St. Louis Teachers Union, served as its treasurer, and helped to win one of the first collective bargaining elections for teachers in the United States.

Mr. Porter holds a bachelor's degree from Washington University and also studied labor education at Oxford University.

Mr. Porter is a member of the operating committee on political education, AFL-CIO, and has been an elected delegate to a number of AFL-CIO conventions. He is also a member of the AFT defense committee, established to protect the rights of teachers, particularly that of academic freedom.

For more than the first half of the twentieth century, teachers' efforts to organize unions often resulted in job dismissal. However, in 1916 eight local teachers unions from across the United States merged to become the American Federation of Teachers, and immediately affiliated with the AFL. Soon afterwards the AFT lost nearly 80 percent of its 3,000 members when the members of the Chicago Local were forced to accept a "yellow dog" contract[1] by city officials.

Since its inception the AFT has been a major force in the fight for civil and human rights. In the 1920s, for example, it adopted a policy of not holding an annual convention in any city or hotel that denied equal treatment between black and white delegates. In 1950, it filed an amicus curiae brief with the U.S. Supreme Court opposing racially segregated schools. AFT locals have successfully negotiated for equal pay rights between female and male teachers and to protect the tenure and pension rights of married women teachers.

Today, the AFT represents nearly 665,000 members, most of whom are elementary and secondary school teachers, college and university professors, paraprofessional, and other related personnel in the field of education. The AFT also counts among its members, physicians, nurses, and other health care professionals, as well as blue and white collar civil service employees at the state and county levels.

---

* * *

M Y local in East St. Louis made some history in the AFT in that it was the first local in which there was a representation election between the National Education Association [NEA] and the AFT. And despite all the predictions that we were going to lose—and logically we should have lost—we didn't, and that probably explains better than anything else how I got started on the path to this position.

But we had to work around the clock to win that election. We were teaching in the daytime, and working on the election every afternoon and long into the evening. I wasn't necessarily away from home, yet when eight or ten other people are in your home, planning strategy and using the phones, home is not really home. Often it was just a boiler room for the phones. But fortunately my wife was committed to our election efforts, and even my children, who were young at the time, were involved. My family's support was a great help to me then, so much so that I feel that any union officer or staff person who excludes their family from their work will eventually have problems. But if they are included the same way they are in some religions, then it's a different story. Dad is not elsewhere doing something they don't understand, but is somewhere doing something they do understand. I'm not saying that it will work for everyone, but it certainly worked for me.

Collective Bargaining

Collective bargaining for us is in some ways easier today than it was in the past. When I started, there were very few locals in the country that had collective bargaining, and so everything added to a contract was new. Now that doesn't mean that those clauses were necessarily complex or that other unions hadn't been doing them for a hundred years, but in the teachers' unions, they were new. Really, collective bargaining for teachers dates from the winning of contracts in New York City in the early 1950s. Once they were won there, bargaining for teachers swept the big cities, and then the suburbs and then, finally went into the rural areas. But there are still states today where collective bargaining for teachers is illegal, like in Virginia, Texas, and some other southern states.

Contracts have grown in size, though, since I first started. They used to be a couple of pages. Now it wouldn't be unusual to have a contract of 100 pages or more. So, in that sense, collective bargaining has become more complex. But as far as each item being new and a trauma, that's not true anymore. If you're negotiating a contract this year, you're really just concentrating on eight or ten sections from the previous year.

My Work

Each of my work days is different to a certain extent, and each day has some similarities. I'm responsible for the collection of per capita [dues] from our locals. Members do not pay the AFT individually. They pay their local, and the local pays us. So most days I spend some time reviewing the incoming per capita, and if a local is getting behind, I'll have to make some calls and find out where the trouble is. Rather than yelling "You owe us $200!" I'm more interested in whether the failure to pay is causing a serious problem in the local. In some cases, I'd rather not get the $200 if it's going to cause some problems for the local. As well, I'll also spend some time on—well, for example today, I was looking over a report on the Blue Cross-Blue Shield costs for our staff. Our premium is going up 30 percent, which means that we will have a budget problem in meeting that increase, so I've called for a meeting with the Blue Cross people to see if we can negotiate that increase downward.

I try to get out to see the members at least two or three times a month. I find that if I stay at this desk all the time, I lose contact with them and that's something I never want to do. And when I do go I usually conduct treasurers' workshops or other information meetings. We tend to have more meetings than most unions, and that's probably what you'd expect with teachers.

I've been spending a good deal of time in recent years working with the professional employees department of the AFL-CIO. As a professional union we're trying to convince the entire union movement that union membership can be increased if we do more organizing among professionals. The AFT is organizing all the professionals that we can, but we have to convince the AFL-CIO and the member unions that they should concentrate on organizing professional people, those who are dropping out of the Steelworkers and maybe being trained for professional jobs, and their children.

Part of my responsibility is also to supervise our staff here in the office. They're organized, and negotiating with them is one of the most difficult jobs I've ever undertaken. Really, it's the one thing I'd rather not do. We recognized our staff's union years ago, well before most other unions recognized their own staffs'. And while it's been difficult, there are definite advantages to having a staff that's organized. For example, there is uniform pay. We don't hide what so-and-so makes as some unions and many corporations do. In our union, everybody knows what everybody makes, even the management staff's salaries—they're all published in our minutes. Bargaining is tough though, and they've come close to a strike three or four times. It's their right, but if they struck, it wouldn't be any catastrophe.

There are times in this job when you have the feeling that you've worked like hell, and it has made no difference at all. What happens mostly though, is that you get a sense of some small successes, and they're not always on overwhelming items. You might add a few members to the organization, and that makes it stronger, but it's a small step. You might get people to pay a better per capita, and with that you can do a better job—that's another step. And if you can convince them that what they've paid for is worthwhile, maybe that's an even bigger one.

The Spirit of Unionism

The spirit of unionism is very much alive in our union. Others might not have it, but if you'd been at our convention, you'd see it alive and well. We had the largest convention ever with 2,700 delegates who either paid their own way or their locals paid it—they were not paid out of the national's treasury. The spirit was just great throughout the meeting. There was enthusiasm for almost all the issues before the convention, and especially for our support of the *Carnegie Report,* which will really change education in this country if it's implemented. Naturally, there was also a great deal of disagreement on some issues too, but that also [creates] spirit too.

I really did enjoy the convention though, despite the fact that it involves an enormous amount of work for me, almost beyond belief. Twenty-seven hundred delegates showed up, and nearly 4,000 people in all had to be checked out and certified, and all sorts of little nitty gritty details had to be seen to. While my staff takes care of most of that work, it's still my responsibility, and so I have to make sure that things are going right with the program, with the arrangements at the hotels, and all of that kind of work. That's not really fun work—that's just work.

Building up to the convention is something I can do without, but the convention itself, with everybody there, talking with friends that I haven't seen for a year, talking over political issues before the convention, convincing people to support our position on some issue, and getting their ideas about our ideas is really fun and I enjoy it. Once the convention is over there are letters to write, phone calls to make, and there are visits to people to shore up issues and to work the contacts that you've made. If I ever lose track of where our members are on a position, then this job will become rather meaningless.

Now then, the response you get at the convention is very different from what happens at a local union meeting. Getting people to those meetings has always been difficult. Regular attendance at a union meeting takes a good deal of work. It takes innovative leadership and sometimes in spite of it all it still doesn't succeed. If you've got a big enough issue, though, you'll get them there. I believe the real work of every union, of every organization—churches, the Boy Scouts, or schools—is usually done by 10 percent or less of the members, and that's true of our union and every union.

The Members

What concerns our members depends on the local that you're meeting with, because locals have different personalities. You'll find one might be more concerned about South Africa, another about salaries, and still another will focus more on the professional aspects of teaching. Accordingly, our convention takes positions on social issues as well as professional, economic, and union issues. Most surveys of teachers, though, indicate that they are more concerned about professional issues than anything else.

What those surveys don't measure though is the intensity felt towards those issues. For example, textbooks in class, how big an issue is that? Almost all teachers will voice it, but how many will actually strike over textbooks? Probably not many, if any at all. But of course they will strike over money.

By the way, our ability to stop a local from going out on strike is very limited, much less than other unions. We don't have a procedure for taking a local into trusteeship like other unions, nor do we have any control over our locals' finances, so we can't control them that way either.

Whatever influence we do have rests on what we have achieved through our relationships with the members or through professional contacts. There's no authority on the part of anybody in our organization, me or Al Shanker, the AFT's president, to go into a local and say, "Now this is what you must do." We can't prevent a strike from headquarters; we can only advise. However, there are times when I wish we had more control, but we just don't have it. And in the long run that's probably for the best, because if you're organizing teachers, it's an advantage to be able to tell them that they are in control of themselves, that we don't have trusteeship.

Looking Back

I don't know of any time that I ever felt that my work with the union was something that I didn't want to do. There were times though when I felt the union was in great difficulty. We went through a period in the sixties when we had a large number of strikes in which the union was in real danger of losing, and I spent a lot of sleepless nights over what in the world can we do to get over those crises. But at no time did I feel that I would like to dump it all, and go do something else.

Now some of our delegates one of these days might decide that it's time for me to do something else and that's their right, but I haven't got the feeling that I should quit. I don't want to stay around too long however and have people say, "Porter's too old." So I don't have plans to stay on forever; in fact I don't plan to stay past sixty-five years of age.

I know it's not going to be easy to leave, and I'll probably never leave in the sense that I'd be unconcerned, or don't keep up my friendships and contacts, or wouldn't attend the convention. Maybe there will be something for me to do with our retiree chapters when that time comes, and not for income or as a job, but as a matter of commitment to what I believe. I talked several years ago with an AFT retiree, and he said, "Well, I'm out of the AFT now, but the AFT is like a snake, you can't stop watching it."

23. Managing a Blueprint for the Year 2000

John S. Rogers

In order to be functional today, a union has to be large. They can no longer be that little fraternal organization where people came together once or twice a month to say "Let's go get em."

John S. Rogers is the general secretary of the United Brotherhood of Carpenters and Joiners of America. Prior to this position, which he assumed in 1978, Mr. Rogers served as general executive board member for the first district (New York-New England) from 1974–1978; assistant to the general president (1966–1974); international representative (1958–1965); and secretary-treasurer, Suffolk County District Council of Carpenters (1957–1958). Mr. Rogers was born in 1930, holds a bachelor of arts degree, and attended the Harvard University Trade Union Program. He was also a candidate for the New York State Assembly in 1960.

While unions of carpenters existed in colonial America, a national organization was not founded until 1881, when the brotherhood was established. Today the brotherhood represents 600,000 members, including carpenters, millwrights, cabinet makers, and allied industrial trades; among its other members are commercial divers and nurses. Because of the urbanization of the country, many smaller locals of the brotherhood are merging to gain economies of scale.

—————————————————— * * *——————————————————

O UR role as a trade union movement is to serve as a lobby for the people. When it comes to workers—the little guy, the only spokesman he has is really a labor organization. Sometimes unions go their separate ways, but we're all attempting to accomplish the same thing—change, reform, justice. As one of the bigger organizations in the AFL-CIO—there's only about ten of us that go over that half-million mark—we have a great responsibility on the behalf of workers. The little guys rely upon us.

We're the only labor movement in the world that embraces the social, political, and economic system of its country. Every other labor union or labor movement in the world fights to change the system. We only struggle here to humanize the system. Oh, there are a lot of good people out in our society who help also, from the churches to these young, ideological guys who come to congress starry eyed, and see their mission as a crusade. Their crusades don't last long after they get up on the Hill. You see, they come well intentioned, but they're not there too long before they become very quickly educated to the realities of life. That usually happens very, very quickly on Capitol Hill. If they're going to perpetuate their careers, they soon learn to pull up on the reins.

Getting Started

I've been an officer for thirty years and never lost an election; I haven't missed a paycheck in thirty years. There's been an element of luck in it all, being the right person, at the right time, and under the right circumstances. I think that plays a role in life, but I also had thought about what I wanted to achieve in the union.

In my first full-time position I served as recording secretary in my local. It's an excellent position to serve in because you're up in front of the body, and politically, you have the kind of exposure that's necessary to get identification with the membership. But it was still pretty unusual for me to get elected to the post because I was only out of my apprenticeship about three years.

In 1957, I was elected secretary-treasurer of the then Suffolk County District Council on Long Island. The council had about 3,000 members in thirteen or fourteen locals, of which mine was the largest, so that helped me get elected. But I ran against an incumbent who had been in the job for many years, and was a very casual type of guy who had little or no initiative, the kind of guy who sat back and felt, "Well, I have the job, I'm entitled to keep it." I beat him badly.

I had a lot of people who were very supportive of me because of my work in my home local. I had also been very active while in my apprenticeship program, where I met a lot of the young people in the other locals. As a result everybody knew "Whitey Rogers." Membership identification is necessary in this business; people only vote for those they know, or can identify with. In order to be successful, you have to be identified as a public type of person, a person that feels at ease with people and not afraid to communicate.

Old and New

This organization has changed considerably since the Hutchesons led it. Here we are an organization in our 106th year as an international union and for fifty-five of those years a Hutcheson was at the helm—that's fifty-five consecutive years with William L., and then Maurice. Our membership is middle class, conservative by nature, and very conservative by trade union standards. But let me say that we have always been out front on social and justice matters. Our organization was out in the forefront, maybe not ideologically, but out there nevertheless, of the civil rights movement. Old man Hutcheson was the general president then, and he sent the word out, "We're not going to have black locals anymore, we're not going to have white locals anymore, we're going to have locals." And back in the thirties we said, "We don't go for this commie business," and we purged the commies. Others came to us and said, "How'd you do it?" Hutcheson said, "I just threw the bastards out!" And women, there was a definite resistance on letting them into the brotherhood, not at the national, but at the local levels because a construction guy looks at this thing with a macho line. But that's changed. We have about 40,000 gals in our membership of 600,000. Women run locals and they do a good job.

During the period of the Hutchesons there was also a great deal of fraternal discipline because of their patriarchal type of leadership. But all that changed in 1971, when Maurice retired and Bill Sidell became the general president. He was younger, more with the times, more politically oriented, a doer. Bill was in for about ten years, a workaholic, a good leader, and well respected. After Bill retired, Bill Konyha came in as general president for about two years, and now Pat Campbell is at the top. So all of a sudden after fifty-five years of the Hutcheson dynasty, we had a revolving door kind of leadership. Once the general president goes, a whole lot of other chairs move on our executive board. So here we go through three or four general conventions, and each time there is a different guy standing at the helm. That has got to have a traumatic effect on an organization, because everybody wants to leave their footprints in the snow. A leader comes in, his priorities are different, so things change. In one way it's good, and in one way it's not so good.

Unfortunately all these changes came at a very difficult time for our union. We've had economic problems; we've had the wrath of our adversaries in the legislative, the judicial, and executive branches of government to contend with. We've been backed up against the wall, and all these leadership changes haven't helped.

Two of the most traumatic events for us, and all of labor, were the defeat in the labor law reform battle and the reversals of the NLRB and the courts of most things that have been accepted as traditional trade union activity. The loss of the reform battle was a turning point for the trade union movement because then employers began to say, "Well, maybe these guys are paper tigers." We couldn't even get the issue debated—we lost on the cloture vote. But it really isn't any one thing . . . ; we find ourselves operating in a very difficult atmosphere today. The whole public perception has changed.

People now have the sense that they are nothing but a commodity, nothing but a cog in the wheel, and because of that their whole perception is one of selfishness. They're out there to get what they can get. They buy this whole laissez-faire attitude. Look at the subterranean economy—people cheating the government by not paying taxes, while the country's struggling over the national debt. We could solve the debt problem in one year if we just focused on the subterranean economy. But that's the psychology that's out there. The IRS is fair game—let's beat them. The insurance companies are fair game—let's beat them. Everybody is playing a "let's beat the system" kind of a thing. We didn't have that forty or fifty years ago, but we have it today.

I would say World War II and the period thereafter right up to the Korean Conflict caused these changes in American society and our unions. Prior to that period, America was a nation where everything was black and white. It was either good or bad, there was no middle ground, and there was no social compromise. You either did something or you didn't do it. People were tied more closely to their community. They were raised in the community, they married, and they did live out their lives in the shadow of the place where they grew up. But with the advent of the electronic media, people no longer had those ties.

That fifteen-year period between World War II and the Korean Conflict changed America. Time and distance became insignificant. We took 6 million boys during the war, put them in uniform, and scattered them all over the globe. Women left the house and went to work. We were coming out of the Depression, and people started to build better lives for themselves. We became more oriented to the good things in life. We no longer belonged to the American Legion, the Eagles, and all of those fraternal and holy name societies. People began to travel. You got on a plane and went from Pittsburgh, to the Bahamas. If you go back a generation, a trip fifty miles from home was a vacation. In fact, if you went out and took a Sunday drive in the car, you fixed flat tires twice.

Now people have become tempered to recessions. In fact, it's really unbelievable that they've come to not only live through them, but to accept them. And because we've got safety nets in place, people don't feel the shock as soon, or traumatically. But these safety nets are being pulled away one at a time. The first people that had to feel it were the mentally ill, the retarded, and the dispossessed, and now we're trading good steelworker and automobile jobs for jobs at McDonalds.

The [Reagan] administration paints a picture of growing service and technological industries and their contribution to this country, but people are learning that yeah, that's growth, but they're not $8, $9, $10, $11, $12-an-hour jobs. They're $3 and $4-an-hour jobs. You can't have that house in the suburbs or that second car on those salaries, but society is only recognizing this very slowly. Groups of people are feeling it, and they're disenfranchised. It's going to cut across a larger segment of society all at one time, and that jolt will be cataclysmic.

Despite these changes I still believe that the aspirations and needs of people, whether blue collar or white collar, are no different today than they were in the Depression era. They're just taking different shapes. You know, in the thirties it was for recognition; now it's for job security.

Strategies

In order to be functional today, a union has to be large. They can no longer be that little fraternal organization where people came together once or twice a month to say, "Let's go get 'em." It has to have the financial resources to have a staff, offer legal advice—all the things that you need in a complex society. And maybe because of this, the trade union movement has become more businesslike, and to a degree more of an impersonal institution so as to keep up with the demands of society.

I think those unions which are failing today are tradition bound. They have not kept an open mind, or been flexible enough to change. It's tough—we've got some of that in our own organization. I'm not saying to discard all tradition, but you have to be able to change. If you were to look at a list of unions in the AFL a century ago you'd find that there were probably eighty or ninety international unions. Of those eighty or ninety international unions, probably half of them don't exist anymore as a result of amalgamation or merger, or because their area of activity doesn't exist anymore—the wheelwrights, people like that.

You still see mergers of smaller organizations going on today for similar reasons. For example, the Upholsterers' Union merged three or four months ago with the Steelworkers. Now their natural home should've been with us, but because of guarantees that they got for identity, something they considered to be important, they went and merged with the Steelworkers. Their leadership felt that a merge with the big Carpenters would've just gotten them swallowed up—they'd be just one of the boys. But if they went with the Steelworkers, they'd get a seat on the board, etcetera. The Furniture Workers are a small organization too, maybe 25,000 or 30,000 members now, and they're in dire straits. They don't have the economic wherewithal to carry on, and again their natural home is with us, but they're talking a merge with the International Union of Electrical Workers.

And we're concerned about ourselves, certainly. We're down from almost 900,000 members to just over 600,000 in a decade. Our strategy now is aimed at strengthening our internal structure through consolidations and mergers at the local level. And we've developed a blueprint for the year 2000 so we can stay ahead of problems.

Let me give you some illustrations. We've created new departments here at headquarters, one of which is called Special Projects. One of its tasks is to advise our 2,000 local unions and district councils regarding the investment of their welfare pension funds. We don't have any control over those funds from headquarters—it's all controlled through trust agreements locally between management and labor, but we've developed a data base to know how much money is out there and where it's invested. We want to be able to help our friends, and hurt our enemies, with our money, and Special Projects is handling that. Those monies ought to be invested in areas which will do its contributors the most good, or at the very least, it shouldn't be used against us.

Another one of our new departments is working in the area of health and safety, which the federal government has given up on. They talk about health and safety, and they write all kinds of laws and regulations, but the enforcement, the most important part, isn't there. Our department has a staff, a hygienist, and we do education programs for our membership. The government should be doing this work, but they don't, so we have to do it.

And we're constantly updating and strengthening our apprenticeship mechanism because that's our membership and leadership of the future. Young people have to learn the skills to meet the demands of the industry. We're one of the few international unions, and I implemented this program over fifteen years ago, which has mandatory leadership training. All of our full-time people must come in and go to school.

We've also expanded our legislative activities. When I first came to work in the general office, political activity was little or nil, and so we put on lobbyists then. Today, we have a full-fledged legislative staff, and we monitor every piece of legislation that's in the hopper over in Congress. We're constantly in contact with the policy makers so that we can have our say. You know, for too long our adversaries have had the upper hand in this whole area. Unfortunately, labor unions have always been depicted as these powerful entities which control the political process in this country. Nothing is farther from the truth, but convincing people of that is something else. From my window I can see the Capitol of the United States—it doesn't mean anything that we're so close to them. Nobody can influence them. The only thing we can hope to do is to educate them on the issues, what they're doing, telling them, "You realize that if you vote this way on this bill, this is the real world implication."

And in respect to education, we've even begun to go down into the school systems to see if we can begin to open up people's minds about labor while they're still young. There's a program at the AFL-CIO right now, Trade Unionism in the Schools, aimed at getting 5,000 remedial reading books entitled *What is a Union?* into elementary schools. We are getting it out to our affiliates and saying to them, "Hey, take a look at this thing, find a way to get it into your school system." It's very much like the strategy that Apple Computer has used donating a lot of their Apples to elementary schools and high schools in order to get students familiar with their system. They assume that as those students become business executives and store owners and such they'll go back to Apple Computers, as purchasers. We've got to do something about people's perceptions regarding unions, because what goes out in the media is not helping us.

My Work

Our people aren't bashful in telling me, or us, how we're doing. True, 99 percent of my face-to-face contact is with our field representatives or officers of local unions and councils, but we do get mail from the membership. We handle maybe 500 or 600 pieces of correspondence in a day—that's about 3,000 pieces of mail a week. Despite the fact that I have a big staff here, I do insist that any complaint letter, regardless of how minute the problem may appear in it, I want to see it because it gives me an idea of what we might be doing wrong in other areas.

I also edit our magazine and that gives me a great deal of visibility. I go into every member's home with that magazine, and when we do something in it they don't like, we get our hate mail. We got a lot during the last election, when I was anti-Reagan and very heavy for Walter Mondale for ideological reasons. But that's the role of the publication—ours is a propaganda organ. It's something that goes into the home and we've got to enunciate and articulate what labor's issues are and what our position is on these issues. A lot of our membership didn't like that material. They're home, mowing their lawns in front of their little house out in the suburbs and they're enrolled Republicans. They say Ronald [Reagan] is doing a good job, but they don't go beyond the big issues and look at the other things. Our leadership guys don't hesitate either to pick up the phone when they see something that they don't like.

One of the more difficult tasks I have is being a "manager" to our office staff here at headquarters. Our staff has its own union, the Office Employees International Local 2; and having been in collective bargaining all my life and sitting on the workers' side of the table, playing the role of "manager" in collective bargaining with them is a very difficult transition.

But I don't take the role lightly. As an officer of this organization I'm very concerned with its efficiencies, budgets, and all the other problems facing it. A couple of times over the past ten years we had to become real hard-nosed at the table. Their union's role is to get, and I have no quarrel with that. That's my mission when I negotiate for our people. But there came a time though when we had to say, "Hey, it's not here now." Our people in the field were tightening their belts, letting go staff, taking wage cuts, and those things had to be mirrored here at headquarters. The staff had to make the same kinds of sacrifices that our people were making.

I enjoy the challenges of my work. It's a distress oriented business and I enjoy getting the adrenalin up. This is one business you have no trouble keeping busy. Some people delegate too much and they lose a feel for what's really happening around them, but I like to keep involved in everything, never overinvolved though in anything, because then it detracts from something else. You've got to develop that second sense to know when enough is enough, and to move onto the next thing.

It's not easy to do all the time. You have to discipline yourself and do everything in their order, not pick the apples from the bottom of the tree and leave all the hard stuff for later. You've got to keep it moving, keep it flowing, and that takes discipline. Once you get used to doing it, it becomes second nature.

There is a downside though—my family grew up, and I wasn't there. My kids are all grown and married. It's the same in any form of public life, your family suffers because of your commitment. And I don't have any personal relationships outside of the trade union movement. All of my friends, and all of my time whether business or social, are all connected with the same people. You move in a community, and my community is the trade union movement, and those management types that we deal with.

On Management

People on the management side and I have an excellent relationship. I have always maintained the greatest type of nonadversarial relationship with them that I could. I've always just felt that you could do better by keeping the lines open than shutting them down. In fact, for many years I was liaison with all of the management groups that we deal with around the country. I know them all, the Iacoccas, the General Motors people, the big utilities, the big construction corporations, and while we may not agree all the time, at least we sit down and listen. If we don't agree with one another, we'll tell the other fellow.

The scales though are definitely tipped in management's favor now. They have gotten real tough since the Reagan administration came in. We've got three major impasses right now on the West Coast with the three biggest guys in the lumber industry, Louisiana Pacific, Weyerhauser, and Georgia-Pacific. Our relationships with employers in the construction industry though [are] very different; it's more of a partnership relationship. They're out competing in the marketplace, and oh, we have problems, but by and large, we're in a sinking ship together. If they don't get the jobs, our members don't work. So we work very closely with them.

Looking Back

For me, leaving footprints in the snow means doing your job and making your contribution. I have input though in this organization from the point of view of carrying out its missions. I can mold perceptions on what should be our role, and how we should go about doing something. So I guess it goes like anything else—if the job gets done people will remember, but if it doesn't they'll also say, "If it hadn't been for that horse's ass Rogers, we would've done it right."

24. A People's Person

John H. Serembus

Can you see this country, or the world, without trade unions? Only in dictatorships do you ever find a union movement being destroyed.

John H. Serembus left school at age sixteen to work at the James A. Kenney Company, a casket and funeral supplies manufacturer in Philadelphia. He became a member of Upholsterers' International Union (UIU) Local No. 37 in 1943, and was promptly elected department steward, serving in that capacity until he entered the armed forces in 1945. In 1952, he was elected chief steward and trustee on the local union executive board. In addition, he was elected to the UIU casket industry department advisory board.

In 1963, Mr. Serembus was designated to represent the UIU as an organizer with the newly formed coordinated organizing program of the industrial union department, and in 1964, he was appointed business representative of UIU Local No. 37.

The general executive board appointed John Serembus a vice-president representing the casket workers industry department in 1970; he was reelected to that post twice. In 1981, Mr. Serembus was appointed first international vice-president and in 1982 was elected president of the UIU.

Founded in 1882, the UIU became an affiliate of the American Federation of Labor in 1900. The UIU's membership consists of workers employed in the home and office furniture industries and in the casket and bedding industries. In a fall, 1985, referendum 83 percent of UIU members voted to approve the merger of their union with the United Steelworkers of America. At that time, the UIU officially became the Upholstery and Allied Industries Division of the United Steelworkers of America, and John Serembus, the director of that division. In 1985, the UIU's membership was approximately 34,000 and was located in twenty states and several Canadian provinces.

———————————————————————※ ※ ※————————————————————————

I MADE it a policy after being elected to visit our members out in the plants as often as possible. On one of those occasions, at our bedding plant in Columbus, Ohio, one of the plant managers started showing me around, really giving me a bum's rush through the place. I said, "Look, I know how mattresses are made—that's not the purpose of my visit. My visit is to check on my members." My wife happened to be along with me and was able to distract him while I took off and made my rounds. While I was making my rounds some people said to me, "It's the first time we've ever seen an international president except from a picture in the paper." And I remember one woman in particular, who said to me, "This is my machine, my Bertha. I've been working with Bertha for thirty-five years." Bertha was a big spring press, and I just couldn't imagine thirty-five years at it. This thing was just pounding "bam, bam, bam . . ." You know that people have to do these jobs, and you just have to ask yourself, "What more can I do to help this soul?"

Our employers talk about establishing quality of work life programs, productivity improvement, and gain-sharing plans, but when we actually sit down at the table to discuss these things, they never make any offers. So I'm afraid that jobs like operating Bertha will be around for quite a while. Basically, things haven't really changed much in our industry over the years. Take technological changes for example, they just don't occur. I mean, the staple gun was probably the biggest innovation in the furniture industry in years, as opposed to, say, using dowels, and tongue and grooves.

It really does sicken me though to see how furniture is put together today. It's put together "boom, boom, boom" with the staple. People see the end product and think it looks beautiful. Fifty years ago, you bought furniture and could have it reupholstered and reupholstered. Now, what people don't realize is that the fabric on the furniture will probably outlast the frame. But the workers who used to have the skill and know-how to build furniture from the bare frame all the way up are retiring, and no young people are coming into it because they don't want to spend thirty-five years doing a trade that's going to wind up paying them maybe $10 an hour.

Old and New

Our industry is only 15 percent organized, but the potential for increased organization is there if you could only get the National Labor Relations Board to enforce the laws they were meant to enforce. I believe that the pendulum has to swing back in favor of unions, I really do. Can you see this country, or the world, without trade unions? Only in dictatorships do you ever find a union movement being destroyed.

But I think we're fast approaching a return to the era of the 1920s and 1930s, when people desperately fought for their right to have unions. What's unfortunate though is that people today just don't express themselves the same way as they did back then. Although the problems for workers are much the same, the people in the earlier years felt they had a common cause, and they banded together, which is the opposite of today. There's no cohesiveness now, there's no sense they belong. It's a sad commentary when you ask "Do you belong to a local? and which one?" and the responses are, "Yeah," and "I don't know."

What's happened? Well, we now have a president [Reagan] in the White House who is antilabor, and with your right-to-work groups we're fast getting back to that era. In fact, it's the first time in my lifetime I've seen police dogs, security guards with clubs and guns and surveillance equipment out at picket lines, and I've been active as a member for forty-three years. I've seen these things in only the last three or four years. When Ronald Reagan was elected in 1980, I thought that was the best thing that could happen to the union movement. I said, "This can't be happening. He'll be out of there in four years, and he'll make people realize why they need unions." Well, he got a second term and just decimated our ranks.

Maybe it's too much for me to comprehend, I don't know. All I know is I'm in the people business and if somebody's got a problem, and I can help them, I do my best.

Getting Started

I guess what everybody who joins a union wants to know is, "What can it do for me?" Well, I started working in a plant when I was sixteen years old for $.40 an hour, $16 a week. I had my mother and a younger brother to support, and no father. But somewhere about a year or so into the job, the paymaster came to me and gave me my regular pay in one envelope and another envelope. I asked him what was in the second envelope, and he said my job classification had received a $.17 an hour increase because of the union contract and that it contained my retroactive pay. Apparently, the increase had been held up because of the war.

Well, I opened the envelope, and there was a check for $269.00. I went home, and in those days you turned over your money to your parents, which I did, but when I gave the extra money to my mother she smacked me in the face because she thought I'd robbed a bank.

That increase though got me active in the union. And I later served as a committeeman, department steward, chief shop steward and then was elected to my local's executive board. All through that time, I never had any aspirations of going full time into union work. I had a nice job in the factory, one which I enjoyed.

I guess the reason I didn't run for a full-time union position back then was the impression that the head of our local made on me. I just was uncomfortable with the way he handled himself in negotiations and things. He would yell and scream and I knew that was not in my nature, so I kind of decided that I would never be able to do union work full time. If that's what you had to be in order to be a leader, it just wasn't for me.

However, in 1963 I had a chance to go outside of my local union and work on a pilot program of the industrial union department. Its aim was to coordinate and organize all the union's manpower and finances and to set targets for them to work together. It was during this time that I realized not all labor people were like the head of my local. These people were really concerned about the workers in the shop, and they didn't have the abrasive style of my local's president. And from that point on, my attitude about working full time for the union changed. I wanted to help people, and so I decided that every move I could make up the union ladder just increased the possibilities of what I could do for them.

I guess the best illustration I can give you is from when I was working in a shop and serving as a member of my local's executive board. I said to our president, "You know, it's a shame that our people in our pension program never get any increase in their pensions." Well, those kinds of things really bugged me, but I couldn't do much about them back then. Can you believe that when I became president there were still people living who went onto pension back in 1953, and still only collecting $21, $22 a month in benefits. It's true.

So when I became president I did do something about it. However, it was not without a fight with our employers. When I bargained with them for an increase in pensions, they said "Let's take the $20 million you want to give those people and give it to the present employees in wage increases." I said, "Wait a minute. Our retirees helped build this fund, they made the sacrifice, they gave up the wage increases, they should get their pensions raised," and we prevailed. I wanted to be able to get them $40 more a month, but I had to settle for a lousy $20 increase.

But I'll tell you, the three months after we got that increase was the proudest time of my entire adult life. Every day I came into my office there were letters here you couldn't believe, like: "Please excuse my handwriting, I am arthritic. I had to take the time though to thank you for that increase, now I can buy something for my personal needs. It's good to know that there's somebody who hasn't forgotten, who still believes in people." I tell you I cried over many of those letters. What I didn't realize was that $20 for most people represented a 50 percent increase in benefits, and for some others, it was nearly a 100 percent increase. I wanted to do that for people twenty years ago, but I just wasn't in the position where I could influence it.

Another thing that used to break my heart was the fact that if you died before the earliest retirement age of sixty-two years . . . , your beneficiaries got nothing from the pension plan. I've seen people in our organization, good people, die at sixty-one years old and some months—everything they put in was gone. I'm happy to say that we turned that all around. Now, the named beneficiary receives every penny, 100 percent of paid-in pension, whether it was ten or twenty years of contribution.

There's nothing like the satisfaction you can get when you're able to correct a wrong. To go in and right the wrong—there's no better feeling, no better reward than that. To be able to do things without looking for an instant return is what working for a union is all about. I can recall times when somebody said to me, "Don't you remember five years ago when you took the time to . . ." That's kind of gratifying, very gratifying.

My Work

I really do love my work. For the seventeen years I was the business agent for my local, you couldn't count the hours I devoted to the membership. I served about a 180-mile radius, with shops all over Allentown, Boyertown, Pennsylvania, in Hackensack, New Jersey, and the base here in Philadelphia. My wife put up with a lot. Her favorite line for our children was, "See that man? That's the one who comes home to have his laundry done." Certainly the money wasn't the attraction for being the business agent, because with all those responsibilities I was making a grand total of $416 a week when I left the job in 1982—that's it. All honest money—I emphasize that.

People can make it very easy for you to be dishonest, though, and that's always bothered me. My first experience with this problem came about two months after I became business agent in 1964. About that time I began to visit all my shops and shake every member's hand and wish him a Merry Christmas and a Happy New Year. And on one of these visits, in one of the larger shops, one of the employers got me outside and said, "What can I do for you for Christmas?" That was my first indication that these things happen—I was very naive. I said "Well, what do you mean?" and he offered me a color television. I told him no thanks, that everyone in my family was color blind, but I hoped he would make the same offer to my members.

I never had any problems after that. Once the word gets around and the employers get to know who you are and what you stand for, they don't dare approach you with that kind of thing. Once you get that out of the way and you, yourself, can live with the fact that this is what you want to do for a living, make an honest living, the better you can get on with life.

I never enjoy Saturdays and Sundays. I'm always thinking of what's happening here in the office, but I know there's nothing I can do about it, and so I get frustrated. I have no hobbies whatsoever. I'm thinking about retiring at age sixty-two, and hope by that time I am able to support somebody who can step into the organization and provide strong, honest leadership. That's what I have in mind. I think you can get—and I hate to use the expression—burned out, but I don't want to find myself telling young people, "Yeah forty years ago I did this . . .." That is the most boring thing. I don't want to reach that stage where I start telling those stories. The previous president stayed in office for forty-four years, and died in office. I don't want to do that; it's not fair to the membership.

Leadership Style

What makes for an effective labor leader? You show leadership by giving direction and involving people in decision and policy making. You guide them in the right direction. When I took over the union, I had three or four people put on the board who were a coalition of so-called radicals. All the old-timers said, "John, how can you deal with two boards?" I said, "I don't ever want to hear that expression again. I don't have two boards—I have one board." And people are still amazed to this day. "How did you convert those people? How could you solidify that board in three months?" The answer was that on whatever level, you have to bring people in and make them part of decision and policy making. I never, in making reports, say I have done this or that. I always say, "If it wasn't for your team working along with me. . . ."

Understand that I'm running the show inside here—somebody has to—but still, if the board doesn't give me support, they could put a monkey wrench in everything I do and that would impact the membership. They would be the ones to get hurt. So whatever you do, at whatever level, you try to make sure it's done as smoothly as possible so it does not hurt the people in the shop.

I don't really like the politics involved in being a leader of an organization. I just want to do my job and let people know where I stand without having to go through the power brokers and say, "Hey, here's a pat on the back." The only time I can put my arm around anybody is if I mean it. If you come across to me as being a phony, I just can't relate to you.

And when John Serembus says something, you don't have to look in the shadows; it's there with the sun shining brightly on it. There it is. You don't have to start saying why did he say that? What did he mean? I don't want to confuse people because I don't want to be confused. I want to say what's on my mind and there it is. Straightforward. When you start to be devious, you have to have a hell of a good memory. I think that's why people get very comfortable with me real fast.

I've never scratched anybody's back. I got elected president on the hundredth anniversary of our union in 1982 without doing any of that. Our president had died and everybody had thrown their hats into the ring at the convention. But I prevailed. I didn't do any politicking. People knew me, and even though they said the person who is going to be our executive is going to have to do a lot of bickering in caucuses, etcetera, they elected me unanimously.

I just didn't get involved in the back room stuff. I don't like it—I hate it, it disgusts me. I know it's a necessary evil, and I can play politics with the best of them when I have to, but I stay away from it as much as possible. If you want to elect somebody who's going to buy you a few drinks, tell a couple of jokes, and win you over that way, fine, that's who you vote for. But if you want somebody who's got some integrity and really has your concerns in mind, then you vote accordingly.

Concession Bargaining

Sure I've made concessions in bargaining, but only when I felt in my heart and mind that it was the right thing to do. Since 1982 we've negotiated with three of our large chains and not one concession was made in any of them. They were looking for 10 percent reduction in base wages, vacation bonus givebacks, a giveback on an additional vacation week, and a reduction in the incentive program from twenty-one minutes down to fifteen minutes. And right from the beginning, even my negotiating committees, who had never dealt with me before, said that if we got away with a three-year wage freeze and got all these concessions off the table, we'd be in good shape.

Well, I got all the concessions off the table; we took a one-year wage freeze, got an improvement in the dental program and wage increases in the second and third years of the contracts. I've said right out that I do not negotiate concessionary agreements. You have to stonewall these companies while they're making their pitch, and then just ask them to show you their books. When you do that, they usually come back with, "Well, we have other interests and can't carve out the contents that cover this agreement." Don't give me that. I don't negotiate concessionary contracts.

If you have to give up something, give up a potential wage increase, because if you get a 25-cent wage increase, less the taxes, how much are you really talking about in take home pay? But if you give in on health benefits, a week or two in the hospital can wipe you out.

Looking Back

Our international union has always been on the small side, but we've always been a quality organization. No matter where I go, whatever local union, I can always speak proudly about our international union. And this union has a lot of "firsts." For example, despite what you might read about the autoworkers having the first sit-in strike, it really was by the Upholsterers' International Union. We've been a people organization and we always seemed to have the right ideas for the right times. Yes, I'm proud of our organization, really proud of our organization.

But because of the loss in membership, and our inability to educate the young people to what unionism was all about, getting them interested and building future leaders among them, we merged with the Steelworkers. It would have been easy for me not to go with the merger. I had reached the pinnacle in my union, and could've served as president until my retirement, but I just could not sleep at night over what was happening to the UIU. As a division of the Steelworkers, though, the membership is getting things like a union educational program, legal services—all the things that the Steelworkers can provide.

I looked at other unions, and I looked at their history and I looked at their brushes with the authorities. I considered every AFL-CIO union. The Steelworkers were honest; they were an awful lot like our people, both the officers and the members, and we were especially impressed with President Lynn Williams. In my opinion, I think he's great. He gets right to the point, issues decisions, and I think the stands he's taken with the steel companies has shown leadership. Where are our Meanys, our Murrays, and our Gompers? The next twenty years will show that they were here, and one of them was Williams.

25. Educating America

Albert Shanker

Public schools now are almost like the traditional automobile factories, . . . they both are on the way out.

Albert Shanker, a frequent guest on nationally broadcast news and public affairs programs and author of a weekly column ("Where We Stand") in the *New York Times,* has been president of the American Federation of Teachers (AFT) since 1974. Mr. Shanker first became involved in the union movement while teaching mathematics in New York City schools during the early 1950s. At that time, he played a significant role in the formation of the United Federation of Teachers (a local union of teachers in New York City), whose contracts would serve as a model for teacher contracts around the country. He was involved as well in its strikes and served time in jail for violating New York's collective bargaining statutes.

Mr. Shanker is a prominent voice in urging teachers to critically appraise the American educational system and initiate reforms in the classroom and in the teaching profession. Among his awards are honorary doctorates from Rhode Island College, University of Rochester, and the City University of New York. Since 1981, he has been president of the International Federation of Free Teachers' Union (IFFTU), an organization of teacher unions in the democratic countries.

For a description of the American Federation of Teachers, see chapter 22.

———————————————— ＊ ＊ ＊ ————————————————

THE labor movement is very rapidly declining in the percentage of the workforce it represents. In fact, the major reason we have a sizable unionized sector now in this country is because of the increase in the number of government employees who have joined unions. Normally, I like the idea of public sector people having a major voice and place in the union movement, but it means that an awful lot of others in the private sector have lost their jobs. Even the autoworkers' union is organizing public employees in Michigan and elsewhere.

The fact is we're getting dangerously close to the point where the labor movement will not be a significant political, social, or economic force within the country. And if you ask yourself what does that mean for us as a nation, the answer is frightening. What other force could possibly emerge which could have the same impact on social policy as the labor movement has had over the last century? One just cannot find such a movement.

There are a couple of things though that could help the labor movement turn itself around. First, there has to be a change in the law to give unions a fair chance at organizing new members. Right now they have almost no chance against a determined employer. For example, back in the late seventies, the AFT went into Denver and successfully organized a bunch of private hospitals. What was the employers' response? Well, they refused to bargain with us, harassed and fired some of our most active people, brought in a lot of antilabor consultants, and went to the NLRB claiming that the bargaining unit was inappropriate, that some people shouldn't have voted, etcetera. It took us seven years with all the employers' appeals and delays, but we won all those cases.

In the meantime, we had no union, we couldn't bargain, we couldn't produce anything for our members, and we couldn't do anything for the people who got fired. And not because the employees didn't want a union; remember, they voted us in. Ultimately, those people who were fired got reinstated with back pay, but that was the only price the employer had to pay. So if you are willing to commit some unfair labor practices which don't have any significant penalties attached to them, you can keep a union out for quite a while. That's unfair competition.

On the other hand, the Canadian labor movement is growing very rapidly, both in numbers and as a percentage of the workforce. It's not because their people are overwhelmingly pro-union, and ours are antiunion. The major difference is that in Canada if you sign up 51 percent of the people in a bargaining unit you have representation, and if the boss refuses to negotiate a first contract, there is binding arbitration, which at least gets the membership a grievance procedure, some benefits, and some other things. Their law, unlike ours, protects those who want a union.

The second thing that would help the labor movement is if the movement itself changes considerably. I believe its image, slogans, and everything else are geared toward a workforce that is more akin to garment workers and miners than those in the growing sectors of the workforce. This new group is educated, mobile, and it has salable skills, and while it may be treated badly in some ways, they're not starving and exploited in the same sense that, say, miners were.

This new group is also very likely to view unions as an outside force that's going to be yet another boss and inflict work rules on them that will restrict them from moving upward in the organization, and even increase some costs in their industry and thus make their jobs less secure. The fact is they don't want to be a part of an adversarial relationship; they value collegial relationships, and they want flexibility in their work rather than rules. So the labor movement has to recognize that it cannot organize them only around the same issues that we've traditionally used. While that's easy to recognize, and it is outlined in the AFL-CIO's report on the future of work, it is very difficult to change an institution that has policies and traditions in place.

The Industry

We certainly have our share of traditional thinking and policies in education. For example, there are a lot of teachers in the United States, England, Germany, France, and in every industrial country bemoaning the fact that there's a declining student population, which for them means that there will be fewer teachers needed and that sort of stuff. But actually, education is growing faster than any other industry in the world. Now it's not growth in elementary and secondary education, the traditional areas for teachers; it's community education, education in industry, reeducation and training, and it's people who are living a life of leisure, and who want to learn how to cook and fix their automobiles.

So there's an explosion of opportunities in the teaching field, and if teaching organizations were really entrepreneurial, they'd do something about it. But most fail to include in their jurisdiction anything but elementary and secondary schools.

Most important, our schools still continue to follow the orientation of schools of a hundred years ago. Back then, society only needed about 10 or 15 or 20 percent of its people to be educated, and the schools sorted them out. It sort of said that 80 percent of you are failures, and the rest of you will make it. Today, if we're not going to compete with the Koreans on their salary and working conditions, we've got to produce a new breed of worker who can work in new types of industry. Instead of weeding out people, we have to cultivate them. We have to produce not 10 or 20 percent, but we have to get 70 or 80 percent to know and be able to do what 10 or 20 percent used to achieve. The Japanese are very good at this. They've produced an educational system which took the education of the samurai and applied John Dewey's philosophy to it by way of Douglas MacArthur. So they have a system that gives to the masses what used to be given to a very small number of people.

But you have to understand that it's impossible to do anything to improve the productivity or effectiveness of schools in the short run. And a problem that we have in teaching is that our employers are basically elected boards of education, which have very high turnover and which are very political. We're often dealing with a totally different board every few years, and every four years a different superintendent. What we have then is a reluctance on the part of teachers to really go beyond the call of duty and try something new, because they've been through "innovation" before and they know, "Gee, we started something three years ago but the new board or superintendent has swept it out just because it wasn't theirs." Because our boards, community tax policies, and school personnel policies have such a short-term focus, it's almost impossible to protect any innovative programs long enough to find out whether they worked or not. One result is that students and teachers get jerked around a lot.

Similarly, if you really want to try and improve the product coming out of our schools, you can't start at the high school level. By the time kids are fifteen and sixteen, it's kind of late to change them. I'm not saying that it's absolutely impossible. Religion tells us that there are conversions at all times of life, and that there are miracles occasionally, but you can't always rely on those occurring with any great frequency. So if you have a certain theory that the best way to teach mathematics or reading to kids is such-and-such, you need to start with a group of kindergarten kids and then spend the next thirteen years to find out whether it works. Meanwhile, what's usually happening is that the management of the system is probably being ousted on the basis of a bunch of issues that have nothing to do with your program.

I believe a school should be treated as a place for inquiry, and not as a factory, the way it is today. You can't think of kids as products who are taken from one station to another on the assembly line and stamped out. The kid really is the worker in the school, and the job of the school is to motivate the worker. It's basically only what the kid does for himself that he actually gets. You can have all kinds of lessons, and you can have all kinds of wall charts, and you can have all sorts of technology, but it's all external. If the kid is not a worker and isn't engaged in his own education, he gets nothing out of it.

And right now we have a system that is failing because so many kids are not getting anything out of it. For instance, of all the children who remain in school until they graduate high school, only 20 percent can write an adequate letter that requires persuasive arguments. Or if you ask them to figure out something about a bus or railroad timetable that requires manipulating six pieces of simple information, it's only 4.9 percent who can do that.

Why is this? Well, the reason is that the school system is set up to do things that essentially destroy a kid's self-image and make him stop trying. It's inadvertent, but it's there.

One thing they do, for example, is to take a bunch of little kids, put them in seats in a room, and tell them to sit still and be quiet for six hours each day, which is something most adults can't do, let alone physically active, developing kids. But anyway, those kids are then taught their lessons by having someone talk to them 85 percent of the time, and, again, not very many adults can learn much by just listening to somebody for six hours a day.

What I'd like to see is a totally different institution, an institution in which teaching is not lecturing. In other words, the teacher's job is not to talk at kids, but is essentially to connect the kid with a learning experience, whether it be a book, a simulation game, a computer or video tape, an audio tape, a parent volunteer, a college student who is in there, or a group of kids working together trying to solve a problem.

Teachers now are required to do so much lecturing that they have no time to mark kids' papers, or to coach them on how to rewrite them, or how to organize their thoughts. They have little time for those who never raise their hands to answer a question. It's not their fault—they hate it—but the system forces it. In my system, the teacher engages each student in different ways in the study of some particular work. In my system, little Johnny and Mary are getting plenty of individual attention. It's not because I'd hire only geniuses. It's because changes in the school structure allow for such attention.

They can get that focused attention because what I want to see is for our schools to have a team of adults working with the kids. Each team would have a lead teacher who is certified by a national board of professional teaching standards which has been created. That person would be someone who is able, in a sense, to give prescriptions to the kids: "Mary, I think you can get this by reading a book. Johnny, I think you ought to do the video tape with Sally." That person would also be able to create such materials. The other adults who are part of the team would not necessarily be board-certified teachers and would not evaluate a kid's work, but they'd be licensed and could work along with the kids. These licensees might be college students who graduated and are trying to learn how to become certified teachers. They'd be used the same way interns and residents are in hospitals.

You could even use community volunteers in the classroom, the way a

Boy Scout troop might use them. Parents who help out with a Boy Scout troop might not be qualified to teach the whole array of material needed for merit badges, but there isn't the mother or father who can't help some kid with something.

By the way, one of the reasons why I like a school that would be more open and would encourage a lot of people to come in and volunteer is that people who now get all their information about teachers from the press could come in once, twice, three times a month and actually see what's happening in there. The press always reports bad news. They never say, "Hey, fifteen students got scholarships"; it's so and so was pushed out of a window, or a kid was raped, or a teacher was knifed or was found using drugs, or the achievement scores went down. If you get all of your news from the media and never have the opportunity to see actually what's going on, well, you probably are going to have a lousy image of teachers.

There's an interesting thing about the image of teachers. If you ask the general public, "What do you think of schools or teachers?" the marks are either failing, or more C's and D's than A's and B's. If you ask people who have no kids in school at all, "What do you think about the schools?" they think the worst. But if you ask the parents of children who are now in public schools, their opinions are better, and if you ask them what they think about their particular schools and teachers of their children, the marks are extremely high.

But people ought to be concerned about the quality of the teachers in our schools. In some places where prospective teachers were required to take a test, the test was at an elementary basic skills level with a passing score of about 65 percent. Nonetheless, between 35 and 40 percent of the applicants failed. In fact, nobody actually failed in many of those places because the officials realized that they had a teacher shortage and needed warm bodies. So what they did was to just lower the passing score on the test. Without a doubt, though, it was a miserable performance on the part of those wanting to be teachers.

The situation exists of course because we're trying to hire 2.2 million teachers. See, if everybody who worked in a hospital had to be a doctor— if you had no nurses, no paramedics, no pharmacists, no x-ray technicians— you'd have 7 million doctors and they'd all be earning teachers' salaries. And if you had to hire 7 million doctors, they would not be of the same caliber as the 500,000 you have right now. But unless we're going to pay top dollar to 2.2 million people, we're not likely to attract and retain our fair share of talent, and officials will continue to lower standards and hire unqualified people just to fill classrooms.

But if we were to differentiate responsibilities, roles, and salaries, which also means getting away from the traditional classroom approach, then we can pay top dollar to the most qualified teachers in the most responsible teaching roles and figure out the additional roles (and decent salaries) for the rest. No one would be unqualified but there would be a new recognition and set of responsibilities for the most qualified. That's the way just about every other profession or occupation is organized, and we ought to consider it in teaching. Now that's a strange thing for a union leader to be saying.

Now, my system also breaks from the traditional authority structure in a school system because it increases teacher power and decreases supervisory management power. Needless to say that changes the labor-management relationship in the school because it gets the faculty involved in directing the focus of their institution. For instance, our contract in Rochester, New York, used to rely on seniority as the basis for selecting which teacher could transfer to another school. Management said, "Well, who says that the senior person is the best person for that school?" We said, "Fine, but we're not about to let you decide who goes there. You're not going to pick the best person. You're going to pick some favorite to reward."

Well, Rochester, New York, just abolished the seniority system, but they didn't replace it with additional management power. The contract now stipulates that a faculty committee in each school will interview all the applicants for the transfer, engage in discussions regarding the strengths and weaknesses of their faculty, and based on that information make a judgment as to who comes into their school.

The public school of the future is going to be like the one that I'm talking about and nothing like the one we have now. Public schools now are almost like the traditional automobile factories, . . . they both are on the way out. We just can't continue with the school system as it is, because it only works for about 20 percent of the kids.

So our educational system is in very great danger, and I don't know if we are going to get people within the system to realize how great the danger really is. They say, "Look, we all went to the same kind of schools—the teachers spent most of their time lecturing to us and we passed, didn't we?" And so they have the feeling that if only the teachers would talk a little better and be a little more interesting, and if only we could push the kids a little bit harder, then somehow it would work. But nobody is going to convince me that we're going to go from a condition where only 4.9 percent can figure out an airline or bus timetable, which essentially means 95.1 percent can't understand a chart with words and numbers, to a point where the number is 65, 75, or 85 percent just by having slightly better teachers or increasing the length of the school day by an hour.

The effectiveness of our production process in schools is so startlingly poor that you have to come to the conclusion that there is something basically and systematically wrong in the process. You know, it's very similar to the automobile situation. It wasn't the worker or just the tail fin, or the stereo set, or some other minor thing that was wrong, it was the production of 500,000 complete lemons. You just can't modify a few things; you have to totally rethink and rebuild.

The problem exists throughout the country. When I gave that 4.9 percent figure, that's all of America, not just minorities. In fact, since a higher proportion of kids have dropped out in the big inner cities, that figure reflects how white America and middle class America are doing. Interestingly, there's more learning going on among blacks and Hispanics than among anybody else. Black and Hispanic 17 year olds used to be eight years behind whites; now they are only four years behind. So, in a period of something like fifteen years the gap has been narrowed by one half, and pretty soon we'll have blacks and Hispanics who are doing just as well as whites, which is progress, but they'll all be doing miserably.

I think it's unfortunate that there is this picture that the schools are doing all right with whites and with middle class people. The whole thing is a disaster, for everyone. If you pressed a button and tomorrow there would be no gap between whites and blacks and Hispanics in America, you would still have these horrendously low rates of achievement. And it's absolutely destructive for our standard of living. What those rates mean for us as a society and economy is that the only way we're going to be able to have full employment in this country is if Americans work for the same low salaries and the same number of hours as the Koreans and Taiwanese. That would put us back for generations, wipe out most of what we've accomplished as a nation.

But most people in public education just don't see the handwriting on the wall. They have had a monopoly for so long that they cannot imagine there will ever be any other system, just like the people in the auto and steel industries, who never, never could really imagine in the fifties or sixties that the Japanese would knock the hell out of us in producing cars or steel. And we're on the same suicidal course in education.

And already, about half the public is so dissatisfied with public schools that they now favor tuition tax credits and vouchers and other systems that would allow people to escape from the public school and go to nonpublic schools. Minnesota has a tuition tax deduction plan. Iowa has now enacted a tax deduction and credit plan. I don't know what it is going to take, but I'd say we are within less than a decade away from the public rebelling and saying, "Here we are, we're pouring huge sums of money in the schools, and yet a very small percentage of the kids are learning. Let's smash the bureaucracy and try something else. Let parents go out and buy what they want."

I wouldn't necessarily be against it either, except for the fact that our schools just don't teach kids arithmetic and English: they also teach Jews, Catholics, Protestants, atheists, blacks, whites, and browns, Irish and Cambodians to live with each other. See, it wouldn't make a difference if all the schools in Japan became private—they are all one tribe. But here, it's different. The schools have the function of creating an artificial tribe where one doesn't exist. So it would be rather destructive socially and politically if we just had private, sectarian schools. Ironically, it wouldn't even be educationally productive, because for the most part, private schools do just what the public schools do.

The only reason private schools look a little bit better is that they're like those hospitals that don't take really sick patients, only those with minor ailments. That's what Humana did when it first went into business. It only took those patients who require a short stay, and who weren't very critically ill, and so it looked like they were doing a real great job. Private schools, for the most part, do the same thing: they don't take any kids who are really in trouble. And if a youngster starts to develop serious problems or disrupts others' learning, the private school can easily kick him out.

Getting Started

I got drawn into the labor movement when I was a graduate student at Columbia University finishing my Ph.D. in philosophy. Although I had an assistantship, two assistantships actually, I sort of ran out of two things. One was patience, and the other was money. Patience because I was a very compulsive character, and every time I sat down to write I realized that I still had a hundred books that I needed to read. Because of that and my money situation, that is, the lack of it, I decided to teach for six months or a year, earn a little money, and get away from my compulsion for awhile.

So I went to work in a New York City elementary school. The pay was $36 a week, and I joined the AFT there. Although the AFT had been around since 1917, when I became a teacher in 1953, it had only organized 5 percent of the teachers in the City of New York. But there was a logical explanation for that. At the time, there were 106 different teacher organizations in the city, and the AFT was one of them. There was just about one union for each borough, one for each race, one for each level in the school system, one for each grievance, and all of them rather small. Most of them had very small dues, as well, something like 50 cents a year.

Anyway, I wrote for the union newspaper, which was all done by volunteers, and when the guy who was the editor moved, I was asked to take over the position. That meant I wrote the whole newspaper, went down to the printer, did the proofreading, did the headlines, pasted the whole thing up, came in after school and wrote flyers, and so forth. Well, there were also a number of us then who started thinking about the idea of collective bargaining for teachers, which naturally was pretty radical stuff for public emloyees. But by the early 1960s we had been able to merge those many smaller unions and win bargaining rights. Basically, I stayed in teaching for those years just because I wanted to build the union. Otherwise I would have gone back to graduate school.

Looking Back

Really, there hasn't been a year that's gone by when there wasn't a major crisis for the union, for me, internally, externally. But there are a lot of things that stand out in my mind about this union. There was the strike in Ocean Hill-Brownsville; there was our investing $3 billion of the teachers' pension fund in New York City when the city went bankrupt; there was our presenting Martin Luther King with a bunch of station wagons for his voter registration drives and being on the bridge with him in Selma, Alabama. I'm very proud that we organized paraprofessionals and brought them into a teachers' union. Do you know how difficult it was to get teachers to accept the idea that these welfare mothers and high school dropouts should be in the same union as they are? Now there isn't anybody who remembers that they were against it.

I was very close to George Meany, and had a few dealings with Dave Dubinsky and Walter Reuther. Meany was a person with a marvelously sharp mind. First of all, he had a photographic memory. He could say, "Well I'll tell you, the background of this is as follows. This all started back in 1924 in the Commodore Hotel on the fourth floor when so-and-so from these unions and that politician were in that room. Here is what was agreed to. And four years later . . ." And he would trace the whole thing. But not only was his memory terrific, he was also a great teacher with a very good sense of humor—as well as a sense for the jugular.

But what you see in the newsreel footage of him is not typical Meany. He was not loud or bombastic. I would sit through press conferences after every council meeting—we'd have a long press conference, sometimes we'd go for an hour—and he would joke with the press and they were always in stitches. They would go back and forth, and they would bait him, and somewhere during the thing he would shoot out something, and that's what would get in the news. I'm not saying what the media did was wrong. From their point of view they were right in picking the outburst. But it doesn't give you a good picture of what he was like.

I didn't know Reuther very well, but I was in his office along with our AFT national president as he was trying to convince us to leave the AFL-CIO and go with him.[1] He was a spectacular speaker. But where Meany would sometimes read a speech, Reuther not only read speeches, he had people with stopwatches timing different jokes to see which brought the house down. So he always had a polished speech, and he really was magnificent at it.

My Work

My work does keep me very busy. For example, today I woke up in Minneapolis at 5:00 A.M., and now it's 3:00 P.M. and I'm here in New York City. Last night I was the keynote speaker at a national conference on technology and education. Today, I have several meetings with people, a board meeting of the International Rescue Committee, of which I'm a member; then I go to a reception for the president of Hunter College, who's leaving to be the chancellor of the University of Wisconsin. Tomorrow morning I'm off to Washington, where I have a number of meetings at the AFL-CIO, including a meeting with the committee of the future.

Next morning I go up to Hartford, Connecticut, to speak to a convention; then I go back down to Washington for a number of meetings that afternoon. On Thursday, I'm addressing the convention of the Iowa School Board Association. Then the next day I'm speaking to a convention of something like 6,000 school board members and superintendents in Nebraska. Friday night I go to San Diego, where I have four speaking engagements with basically university people and administrators. Monday morning I will be in New Orleans to address the state convention of American Federation of Teachers affiliate in Louisiana. It fills up a week certainly.

I love it all, though, and don't have any idea when I might step down. I guess I'll do it when I feel I'm not doing a good job or I'm tired or exhausted or something like that.

But I've seen a lot of people who were vegetables holding onto their unions, and I know I won't do that. What I tried to do in my New York City local before I left to be full-time national president was to get a mandatory retirement age. I think it's better to lose some talent than to end up with long periods of time where the union isn't functioning. But I wasn't able to do it then, and now of course mandatory retirement is outlawed anyway.

But there are lots of other things I would like to do, and if somebody comes along who wants to be AFT president, and is good at it, he or she will have my blessings. I never wanted this in the first place. Every job I ever had in the AFT satisfied me, and I never looked to the next one. It just happened that somebody would leave, or do some really horrible things, and others turned toward me.

26. Attracting New Members to Labor

John J. Sweeney

. . . I don't think this country has lost basic industry jobs forever. In fact, we simply cannot afford to walk away from them.

John J. Sweeney was elected to a second four-year term as president of the Service Employees International Union (SEIU) in May 1984. Mr. Sweeney, past president of SEIU Local 32B–32J in New York City, was born in 1934 in the Bronx, New York. He attended Iona College and was graduated with a degree in economics. *Across the Board* has called Mr. Sweeney "one of labor's rising stars."[1]

While working his way through college, he was a laborer in a cemetery and a member of SEIU Local 365. Once out of school, his first job was with the International Ladies' Garment Workers' Union. Tom Donahue—then with SEIU Local 32B, now secretary-treasurer of the AFL-CIO—met Mr. Sweeney in 1960 and persuaded him to join 32B as contract director. In 1976 Mr. Sweeney was elected president of Local 32B. In 1977, his local merged with Local 32J in New York, creating one of the largest local unions in the AFL-CIO, with some 55,000 members. As president of Local 32B–32J, he led two city-wide strikes of apartment maintenance workers, including an eight-day landmark strike of 20,000 in 1979 against the New York Realty Advisory Board.

Among his many activities, Mr. Sweeney is an active member of the Coalition of Labor Union Women, and also a board member of the American Arbitration Association, the American Red Cross, and the Catholic Youth Organization.

The SEIU is one of the largest and most diversified of AFL-CIO affiliated unions. It represents approximately 850,000 members, including nurses and allied health care workers; federal, state, and local public sector employees; custodial and other building service workers (its original jurisdiction); industrial and allied industry workers; and clerical workers. The SEIU has in recent years conducted corporate campaigns against Beverly Enterprises and Equitable Life Assurance and has joined in an effort with nine other national unions to organize employees of Blue Cross and Blue Shield.

* * *

I DON'T think that America can survive as a strictly service economy. As Fritz Mondale used to say, "What good is it going to do us if the only jobs we have are sweeping up around the Japanese computers or Japanese electronics?" The fact of the matter is, though, that whatever we have or have not done as a country, we have a situation where we have lost jobs in basic industries and are replacing them with jobs that pay lower average hourly wages.

It is not going to do the labor movement any good to cry over this, or to be bitter about it. The fact of the matter is that regardless of who the workers are, or what industry they're in, we should be out there organizing workers to raise wages and improve benefits. And, if we're going to have the political power and the legislative power to do something about the industrial policy of this country, wages, and benefit standards, we've got to have the might of the rank and file. Unless we organize in the unorganized sectors of the economy, unions are just going to continue to decline and will not be a major force in setting policy or having an effect on policy.

But I don't think that we have lost those basic industry type jobs forever. In fact, we simply cannot afford to walk away from them. That would be disastrous for the economy of the country, and for the defense of the country. So what we need for our own sake is to find ways to bring back some of those industries. Then, I think we need to look at more labor-management cooperative efforts, like that between GM and the UAW on the Saturn project. Finally, we may have to provide industries with resources to get back on their feet. It doesn't matter if the jobs are in Michigan or South Carolina, what is going to make the difference is whether they're in the United States or not.

Organizing

The original jurisdiction of the SEIU was building service employees. In fact, our name was originally the Building Service Employees International Union until the mid-sixties, when the word *building* was eliminated, and we began to organize health care and public employees.

Interestingly, part of my program now is to reinvigorate our building service organizing program. For instance, we are organizing janitors in a number of cities where we once had them as members, but lost them as management began contracting out the work to nonunion firms—and as the downtown areas of cities began to decline, and the unorganized suburbs exploded. We're also aggressively organizing janitors in places like downtown Denver, Colorado, which has undergone tremendous expansion in recent years.

We're also organizing right here in Washington, D.C. You know, when I came to Washington seven years ago, I couldn't believe how a city, just a couple of hundred miles from New York, could be so "southern" in terms of having so many nonunion hotels, nonunion restaurants, and nonunion service workers. So we have a very ambitious organizing program going on here based on issues revolving around justice for janitors. We are using radio commercials, and we're working with the church leadership and other community organizations here in D.C. to take advantage of social-minded individuals who are interested in seeing workers achieve some dignity. In that respect our organizing program is similar to some of the methods used in the civil rights movement of the sixties.

Our success in organizing though is a result of our flexibility. We're not wedded to any one traditional jurisdiction, and we're not so firm in our organizing programs that we can't change them to meet the needs of new workers. For instance, we've been fortunate to build our organization through affiliations with independent unions, mostly in the public sector, like the New Hampshire State Employees Association.

There are just millions of clerical and health care workers in this country who are still unorganized. So there are more than enough workers out there who can use our assistance, and we've embarked on some ambitious organizing efforts. We and the UFCW [United Food and Commercial Workers International Union], for example, are organizing Beverly Nursing Homes, the largest chain of nursing homes in the private sector. That's a workforce of 55,000 employees, and only 10 percent are organized. And there's a coalition of nine major unions who are working together to organize Blue Cross-Blue Shield.

In our efforts to organize workers, we've seen initially some reluctance to "go union" completely. So, if workers aren't convinced that full membership in a labor union is the answer to their work situation, we will offer them an organization or a level of membership that they are comfortable with. We've done this with our clerical organizing and it has brought workers together on issues that are important to them, whether it's promotional opportunities, equal pay, or sexual harassment. What usually happens though is that those workers themselves eventually realize that full resolution of their concerns can only be done through collective bargaining, and we're there to help them achieve full membership in labor.

The Hostile Environment

Labor's biggest disappointment has been our inability to defeat Ronald Reagan. With this administration, we have seen the worst gutting of social programs and worker related programs in the past fifty years, and it is going to take years to reinstitute many of them. And there's no question about it, Ronald Reagan set an example with the PATCO situation. Corporate America, along with the public sector employers, got the message that it was now time to take on the labor movement.

Recently, however, I've been noticing a number of signs that indicate the pendulum is swinging back a little bit in our favor. Workers and middle class folks are saying, "Enough is enough" in regard to the number of jobs being exported overseas, about this whole plant-closing situation, mergers, acquisitions, takeovers, and givebacks.

There are other things happening, too, which indicate a shift away from the Reagan agenda. And while they may not have a direct relationship to the labor movement, they represent a move towards improving social conditions. For instance, there's a new interest in some social legislation, increasing the minimum wage, and providing parental leave and minimum employer health benefits. Even though there are some in the labor movement who would say that legislation on these issues is going to negate the issues that unions can organize people around, I don't look on it that way.

I believe legislation in these areas will be a tremendous advantage to millions of unorganized employees, and frankly, to organized employees and the country as a whole. For instance, a lot of organized workers will benefit from legislation increasing the minimum wage. And minimum benefits will help employers already providing health benefits because they won't have to carry the burden of health care costs of spouses and other family members who happen to work for employers that don't offer coverage.

And furthermore, if anyone was to say ten years ago that we would be looking at some form of national health insurance, we would have said they're out of their mind. Yet, I see a move within the next couple of years towards essentially having a national health program. I believe all of these initiatives are examples of the pendulum swinging back, and of some innovative ways to address our industrial transformation. We're just going to have to come up with new economic and social initiatives to resolve the issues of competition and trade, and the erosion of living standards in this country.

Looking Back

What am I most proud of? I'm proud of my family, and I'm really proud of this union. SEIU just hasn't established a good track record over the past seven or eight years—it has had an ongoing record of achievement, going back really to the sixties. It was then when it really started to move in terms of growth and expansion to new jurisdictions. And really, both of my immediate predecessors made major contributions to SEIU. David Sullivan, who was an Irish immigrant and our president in the sixties, started out as an elevator starter in the garment district. He got elected to a position in his local and from there rose up to international president.

George Hardy, who was our president in the seventies, had a completely different background. He was born in Canada but came to the United States as a youngster. George's real strength was in organizing. He worked at it himself and actually ran organizing conferences all across the country for our local unions.

What we have tried to do over the past years that I've been in office is to build on my predecessor's work. For example, we have managed to attract very dedicated, able young people from some of the best schools in the country to work as organizers in all parts of the country. These young people are committed to the labor movement and trying to help workers achieve some dignity, some improvement in their standard of living, and I'm very proud of them.

Management Style

I think that I have brought to this job a new openness to the management of this organization, as well as a focus for getting into a number of new areas in organizing, but done in a way that I think is adjusted to the new needs of workers. I knew and worked very closely with my two predecessors and I think that I learned an awful lot from both of them.

But I also grew up in a union family. My father was a New York City bus driver and a member of the Transport Workers Union. In fact, I sometimes tell my staff how my father would say, "Oh, God bless the union for this," when we were on vacation at Rockaway Beach in New York. And so I heard a lot of union talk as I was growing up, and it obviously had a strong influence on me. As a youngster I went to union meetings, walked picket lines, and just got a lot of satisfaction from helping somebody else do something.

27. Taking the Offense for the Fourth Arm of Defense

Shannon J. Wall

The demise of this nation's merchant fleet has been going on for a long time. Somebody has said it's our economic Pearl Harbor with Japan.

Shannon J. Wall became chairman of the unlicensed division and executive vice-president of the licensed division of District 1 National Marine Engineers' Beneficial Association/National Maritime Union (MEBA/NMU) upon the merger of the two organizations. Previously, he had been president of the NMU. Born in Seattle, Washington, in 1919, and educated in public schools there, he entered the University of Washington where he majored in sociology. He left the university in 1941, following the attack on Pearl Harbor, to take his first job aboard ship. He served on ships through World War II, mainly as able seaman (AB) and bosun on freighters and troop carriers.

When the war was over, Mr. Wall decided to make the sea his career. The son of pioneer trade unionists, he was active in union affairs aboard ship from the beginning. He was elected by his shipmates to be the NMU ship's chairman and department delegate on many of his vessels.

In 1966, Mr. Wall was elected national secretary-treasurer of the union and reelected for a four-year term in a special election held in 1969. When Joseph Curran, who had been president of the NMU continuously from its founding in 1937, retired for reasons of health in March of 1973, Shannon

Wall succeeded to the presidency in accordance with the NMU constitution. In June 1973, Mr. Wall was elected to his first full term of office.

Among his many activities, Shannon Wall is vice-chairman of the Seafarers Section of the International Transport Workers' Federation and titular head of the Joint Maritime Commission of the International Labor Organization in Geneva. He serves as cochairman of the Labor-Management Maritime Committee, an organization in which major steamship operators and unions seek to develop programs to promote the U.S. Merchant Marine.

On October 18, 1986, President Reagan named Mr. Wall as one of five members of the new Commission on the Merchant Marine and Defense. After confirmation by the U.S. Senate, the members of the commission began to examine the current relationship of the United States Merchant Marine and the shipyard industry to the national defense.

The National Maritime Union was established by East Coast seamen, within the International Seamen's Union of America, who were disenchanted with the lack of support of the union over their demand for wage parity with West Coast seamen. In the early 1960s membership in the union stood at 35,000; however, as a result of the decline in the number of U.S.-flagged passenger and merchant marine ships, the union's traditional membership has suffered a significant decline in the intervening years.

As of 1988, the NMU represents approximately 6,000 deep sea seamen and 15,000 shoreside members including employees on U.S. Army and Navy bases, in light industry, as well as bridge operators and allied workers in the Panama Canal Zone. At the time of the following interview, Mr. Wall was president of the NMU.

———————————————————* * *———————————————————

THE whole premise of the American Merchant Marine is that we're the fourth arm of defense. We lost more men in the Merchant Marine on a percentage basis than any of the armed forces in World War II. But we get no recognition for this. Some of our guys don't even want a GI benefit so they could go to school; all they want is the right to have the American flag on their coffin when they're buried. It's pretty simple, but we can't get it. Every veterans' organization is opposed to us on this, they claim we were "overpaid during World War II."[1] The facts are that we were not overpaid. I'm amazed—I found one of my vouchers from when I got paid off from a ship during the war, and it was for $500—for two months' work at sea—and with that I probably thought I was a millionaire!

Getting Started

As a seaman, I had some doubts as to the sanity of people who worked for the union. They had a thankless job and got a lot of abuse from most seamen. We'd always be saying, "We're paying your wages, why aren't you out here working for us, why aren't you doing this . . ." and so I didn't give any thought to becoming involved in union work until I came ashore in San Francisco back in 1951 and went into the marine hospital.

While I was in San Francisco, the business agent for our union asked a friend of mine if he could help him out with an assignment. It seems that a union patrolman had quit, just walked in and chucked it all. Well, my friend wasn't really interested, but said I might be. But it was probably the fact that I had a car that made me a likely candidate for the job. Anyhow, I took the job, which paid something like $20 for one day's work including bridge tolls. The agent gave me the union agreement, a constitution, and a dues book, and sent me off to pay off a ship's crew and to handle their grievances.

I had no intentions of doing the job for any length of time since I could make more money going to sea as a bosun, but after two per-diem assignments, I got interested in doing the work on a full-time basis. I found that there was a great deal of satisfaction in doing those per diems, and seeing that the guys responded to somebody who was conscientious and who stood up for their rights. Well, after a few more per-diem assignments, I was offered a full-time job as acting patrolman. And when the next election came around, I got elected as field patrolman for the port of San Pedro, California. Of course the secret of getting elected in the NMU is to be on the administration slate, which I've always been. I think there's only been two instances of individuals who have ever beaten us out. They were former officers of the union who were very popular, whereas the administration's candidates, who lost, were almost unknowns.

But anyway, in those days my wife and I had a social life that was completely tied up with the union—we couldn't go anywhere without the union. Even stopping off in a bar to have a drink on the way home, there would be somebody in there, "How's shipping, Shannon? How's so and so?" We really had no weekends we could count on. I might have had to open the hall on Saturdays or pay off a ship. Theoretically, headquarters said that if you had to work on the weekend, you could take a day off during the week. Impossible! Absolutely impossible! You were lucky if you could break away at 3 or 4 o'clock in the afternoon on your day off. So weekends were very unreliable, and vacations were one week a year. But if you want to make it to the top of this union, you have to pay your dues.

Making It to the Top

It was far easier for a Joe Curran to come off a ship and become president of the NMU back in 1936 than it would be for a rank and filer today to come off a ship and become a national officer. The reason is that very soon there's going to be far fewer elected jobs in our union. Right now, we have a president, secretary-treasurer, three vice-presidents, and business agents in some twenty ports. But because this nation is losing its maritime fleet, we're naturally going to have to tighten up. I can envision the constitution being changed to provide for a president, a secretary-treasurer, and an executive vice-president and cutting the branch agents from approximately twenty to nine or less.

You really have to be committed, though, to the cause if you want to have a career in a union. I have been told by all the old-timers in the NMU that there always were book carriers, even in the height of the biggest battles and struggles of the labor movement. These were people who had union books only because they had to be a part of the union. They would have been company stiffs right straight through if they thought they could get away with it. And I know that there still are card carriers or book carriers today in unions. What was my attitude before I was coerced or cajoled into taking the job in San Francisco? I thought they were crazy. They worked night and day; there was little reward, and often they got a bad time from the members—"You didn't collect my overtime, you didn't handle my grievances," etcetera.

The Members

The membership of the NMU has changed considerably since the union was first organized in 1937. You know, back in the thirties there were "workaways," guys who signed on for a penny a month just to have a job—they'd work for their room and board and keep their skills. So clearly the expectations of our membership have changed quite a lot since then. In fact, of all the thousands of members who have introduced me to their children for example, I can count probably on one hand at the most, two, those who have introduced their child as a steward or an AB or a mate or something. The rest are all colonels in the Air Force or Army, or they're doctors, or they're lawyers.

The membership itself has also changed. When this union was first organized in 1937, 90 percent of the American seamen were foreign born: Greek, Italian, Spanish, Scandinavian, and perhaps some British on the passenger ships. Today, we have a very large minority membership who came into the NMU, and not just working as wipers, messmen, or ordinary seamen. They move right on up into the skilled jobs and become bosuns, ABs, electricians, pumpmen in the engine room, all highly skilled and certified men, and a number of them go on up and get their licenses.

My Work

Since I became president in 1973, my work has become far more technical, and far more involved with our investments in the union's pension and welfare plan and the seaman's pension and welfare plan. We're over $300 million in the seamen's plan, and our biggest concern now is the protection of that capital. We're well diversified in fixed income, equities, bonds, long term, short term. Lawsuits are also a constant occurrence today, and I spend far more time with the attorneys today than in previous years. Since I took over thirteen years ago, the time I spend with lawyers has more than doubled.

I spend a great deal of time in meetings as well. Shipowners come in regularly to meet with me and our research department, or our contract enforcement staff. Our contracts cover a variety of ships. We've got a passenger ship on the Great Lakes; we have river boats; there's dry cargo, subsidized and nonsubsidized; we have tankers, both industrially owned—Texaco, Gulf Oil, Amoco, and independent tankers that carry cargo for the majors, Keystone, Marine Transport, Eastover Carriers, and Shell Oil.

But I really enjoy negotiating contracts more than anything else, and that's an ongoing task. Because the day I finish with a contract, I have a folder that has pretty much what the next demands are going to be, and you're always revising it.

I do enjoy the political side of being president, the campaign for office and the election, because that's all a part of communicating with the membership. There are many of them who are amazed that I don't have bodyguards, but I feel that I have to always keep my door open.

But staying in office can also have a downside. There was one officer of another maritime union—he's pretty much president of his own division—who called us up about six months ago and said, "I just quit." We asked him why and he said, "A guy came in here to the office with what is essentially the same grievance I handled thirty years ago, and I'm damned if I'm going to stay in a job where I do the same things as I did thirty years ago. So, to hell with it, I quit." But it's true, you do see the same things. The work rules in our contracts don't change that much, and yet 80 percent of the grievances are over contract language. But I enjoy the job, more than any other I've every had, no question; it's a good job, a lot of satisfaction.

The Industry

The demise of this nation's merchant fleet has been going on for a long time. Somebody has said it's our economic Pearl Harbor with Japan. I don't want to say it's the only hope for the American Flag Merchant Marine, but the strongest hope for saving the industry is bilateral trade agreements. But Congress is so slow, cumbersome, and uninformed about this industry that a big part of my time is spent just educating them to the issues.

For instance, somebody convinced Congress a long time ago that all American ships were 50 percent overmanned. This all started because the Coast Guard's Certificate on Manning of Vessels called for a certain number of crew—three watchstanders, an officer on watch, two ABs on watch, and in the engine room, a number of engineers and unlicensed.

But see, the Certificate of Manning was for navigational purposes only. It does not say a thing about the additional crew required to discharge cargo, or the need for a pumpman if it's a tanker. And it doesn't say a thing about maintenance. You just can't take a vessel that you've built for a twenty to twenty-five year life and let it rust out in five years—you have to have somebody on board to maintain it. The certificate doesn't say a thing about the people who are on board in the steward's department and who feed all the others on the ship. So that's how they came up with the idea that we were 50 percent overmanned. And it still crops up, despite all the time we spend explaining it. For example, we thought we had convinced Congressman Biaggi of New York a long time ago, but son of a gun if he doesnt' say, "You guys are overmanned." We told him, "Biaggi, don't you remember what the Coast Guard Certificate calls for, and why it calls for it?" He remembered, but only after we spent more time going over it with him.

And even President Reagan has let us down, despite the fact we supported him in both elections. His speech to our convention in October of 1980 outlined an eight-point maritime program, probably the finest maritime program enunciated by any president, including Roosevelt. But he's come through only on increasing the level of participation by civilians in naval support vessels. We even thought that the defense initiatives of his administration would've assured us of having a strong American Flag Merchant Marine, but that hasn't happened either. See, when you've got to get cargoes, men, and materials somewhere, you need a large fleet, but the U.S. Navy has too few troop ships to really do it. Robert McNamara, the former U.S. secretary of defense, tried to convince the country twenty-five years ago that he could fly everybody, all the troops that he needed anytime, anywhere. It's just not so. When Berlin was fogged in, planes were of no use.

So when I heard President Reagan's plans for a 600-ship Navy, I thought that we would be manning a lot of the support vessels, which would free up the larger ship Navy, but that hasn't occurred. It's essential that civilians, a merchant navy, does this work—the tankers, the supply vessels, the tugboats, and the rest of it—and let these young Navy guys go aboard the fighting vessels, which is what they're trained for. They should not be out there on a tanker that's picking up oil or gas products and taking them out to the fleet. The larger the Navy, the more critical it is to have civilians manning noncombat vessels.

Looking Back

After I've retired from the NMU I hope to be remembered as the president who led the NMU during its transition phase, picked it up as the industry was going down, negotiated good contracts, sound contracts, told the membership the facts, that there were no increases, and that we had to stand still. The pendulum has been swinging; it's swinging a long time against us, and we've just been surviving. So far, it hasn't made too much difference whether it's been a Republican or a Democratic administration. We go through the same problems, but the country can't escape the fact that it needs an American Flag Merchant Marine.

28. Commitment in a Declining Industry

Charles E. Wheeler

Our membership knows that no railroad management ever voluntarily has given them anything.

Charles E. Wheeler worked as a carman for the former Gulf, Mobile and Ohio Railroad from 1942 to 1946. He served as a local representative, general chairman and vice-president of the Brotherhood Railway Carmen of the United States and Canada prior to becoming the union's general president in 1984. Upon the merger of the brotherhood with the Transportation Communications International Union (TCU), he assumed the position of international vice-president of the TCU and general president of the Brotherhood Railway Carmen Division/TCU.

The Brotherhood Railway Carmen was founded as an organization of rail car repairmen in 1888. Within a few years it had merged with several other rail employee unions, and by 1899 it represented car inspectors, oilers, repairmen, and other carmen. Since the 1960s the brotherhood's membership has been declining as a result of technological improvements and the substantial decline in the usage of the U.S. railway system. Today the brotherhood represents approximately 25,000 working members employed in the railway industry, including repairmen, upholsterers, engine carpenters, pattern makers, and coach cleaners. The brotherhood is one of thirteen rail unions that negotiate a national labor management agreement with the National Railway Conference, the management bargaining arm for the major rail carriers.

—————————————————————— * * * ——————————————————————

THE Staggers Rail Act of 1980, which deregulated the railway industry, was the beginning of our downfall. And believe it or not, we even supported it. But once deregulation went through, the large lines began very quickly to sell off miles of track, and they did it without having to hold public hearings as they had to previously. And as those lines were sold, thousands of our members were laid off by the major lines. As you might imagine, those layoffs came as quite a shock to a lot of our members who had worked twenty or thirty years with those companies. In fact, many of our members didn't even know what a reduction in force was when they first heard about it.

Let's see, in the last seven or eight years there's been well over 300 short lines created through these sales, with a major portion of them, twenty-five, thirty, and forty miles long. And some of our members have gone to work for these Ma and Pa operations, but they work for much less in pay and benefits than what they got with the front line, or major, railroads. They also have to deal with the insecurity that the line may fold, because in most cases, the selling railroads had allowed the track to get in such terrible condition that it takes a fortune to rebuild the roadbed to where you can move the train at any speed. You can't haul freight at ten to fifteen miles an hour and expect to make a profit. You've got to move it across country pretty fast. And the short lines just don't have the money to rebuild the track.

The large companies claim that they've sold off the track because profits are marginal, or there are no profits at all on them. But you must understand that today the large railroads are usually owned by a parent company, a holding company, and they are so diversified that they're more concerned about the relative profit wrung from their interests than they are in keeping up a railroad.

They never say there's no profit off the railroad, just that they get more return from their other industries. In fact, they claim they're only making 6 to 8 percent return on their investment from the rail portion of their businesses, while they earn 10, 12, and 15 percent from their other holdings. Even the Interstate Commerce Commission [ICC], Mr. Reagan's union-busting appointees, have said that railroads should reasonably expect 11.25 percent return on their money to be a strong railroad. There's a lot of people who would like 11.25 return on their money, but they're not getting it. Maybe with a new administration and ICC that rate will come down, and not serve so much as an incentive as it does now for the railroads to get rid of any track that's not making 11.25 percent.

Collective Bargaining

I think management's attitude to us has always been the same. They tolerate us as a necessary evil, and put up with us as long as we don't exist too prosperously. There are a few, however, who'll admit they'd rather deal with us than to try to deal with 3,000 or 4,000 individuals.

What some railroads are now doing, though, really does have us very concerned. Many have let us know that they're going to negotiate with us on an individual basis in 1988, rather than on a national basis. Apparently, they must believe that they are in such a strong position individually that they really don't need to remain a member of the National Railway Carriers Committee. Burlington & Northern, for instance, has already submitted informally its proposals to us, and all of the organizations on that railroad, and they're ridiculous. Even though it's submitted informally, they've asked us to agree to start negotiating formally, which means that they can put the changes into effect right away.

It's never been like this. Normally, whenever we served notice on the railroads that we expected a pay raise, more holidays, greater improvements in vacations, or health and welfare benefits, well they usually countered them. Now, what they're trying to do is to hold everything at the level you're at, or even reduce some of our wages, holidays, and make it a little tougher to get vacation time. When you look at what the Burlington & Northern wants—well, they just want to roll back the clock about fifty years.

Negotiating with each railroad makes it a lot more costly for us as well. We're going to have more staff people involved and more representatives out negotiating with each individual railroad, instead of having one group in negotiations with their association. And of course, the greater expense is carried by the membership. Let's face it, that's the only place we can draw from to pay for these negotiations. In fact, we got a little per capita tax increase at our last convention, based on the fact that it's going to be more costly.

In addition to serving those notices on us, Burlington & Northern has been holding meetings with the employees throughout the country trying to sell them on the idea that "We're your savior, not your union." They deny they're trying to union bust but that's what they're doing. Our membership knows though that no railroad ever voluntarily has given them anything.

The Future of the Rail Industry

Beyond what the Staggers Act has done to us, it's also done a great disservice to America. Since its implementation, I just haven't seen any growth in the amount of tracks being laid. If the government keeps allowing the railroads to abandon marginal lines, that's got to be bad for the safety of the country. We never know when an emergency is going to occur, when you have to haul troops or freight, and we hope that never takes place, but if we had to get back into a situation like we were in the early 40s, we'd be in a pretty tough position.

Now we know we can't just tell any company, "You've just got to keep operating this thing whether it's going to bankrupt you or not." We're not talking about that. But these holding companies are skimming the profits off the railroads, and putting them into other portions of their holding company, rather than back into rebuilding the line. There is nothing wrong with making money, but if those dollars are at the expense of the country and the citizens, then that's bad. The government has to recognize that we cannot afford to ignore the rail system in this country. I don't want a return to government management of the railroads, but I do want a policy that would create a strong railroad industry. Look, the way the population is increasing, there's not going to be enough room on the highways for everyone's cars and all the trucks. We need a rail system.

In fact, that's what prompted the rail industry and the shippers to go with the top of freight car service (TOFC), and the road railers. And you're going to see more businesses using those services in the future, more and more. Unfortunately though, those services have a very adverse effect on the size of our membership. We build and repair freight cars and boxcars, whereas those services use flat cars, which require relatively little maintenance. So, we don't get much work out of those systems.

And already, the railroads have begun subcontracting out a great deal of that work anyway, along with work that our members normally performed. They're also contracting out the rebuilding of cars and even the operations of these intermodal facilities . . . all of these container and piggyback trains operate out of. We believe the subcontracting is in violation of our agreements with those companies, and have so contested it, but the railroads are probably going on the basis that it's just one more area where they can afford to ignore us.

My Work

I really don't know why I've had a successful union career. I don't have much formal education, just a high school diploma. However, when I became a union officer, I worked and studied hard to become as effective a representative that I could, and I think the people recognized that. They see what I've done, that I'm no magician or anything like that—I just stick to it and work hard.

When I became general president of this organization, many people asked me, "Why did you ever accept or even seek this position at a time when you know things are going to be terrible?" And I answered, "Well, I think I can do as much or more than anybody else." But it's been very tough. Membership has gone down considerably, the railroads have shrunk, and I can't say that I accomplished anything new or innovative for the members. We've just been struggling every day to try to get it back on track. And that may not happen until someone wakes up and stops the railroads from plundering the public good.

As an officer of this union, I'm really here to serve the members, who, for the most part, 95 percent of them, just want to be treated fairly, have a decent job, and go to heaven when it's all over. But we've got about 5 percent, I guess, who, if they got it all, it wouldn't be enough. Those are the people that make me climb the wall. When they call in, they say, "I thought I'd call you and give you a chance before I turn it over to my attorney." We usually just tell them, "Get in line."

In fact, I was just talking to one of our representatives on the L & M Railroad a few minutes ago about a fellow who wants his seniority adjusted. It seems he went to summer camp in the National Guard back in the mid-50s, and he wants the credit for it. I dealt with this fellow's problem eight years ago, and there was nothing we could do for him then—he just didn't have a fair complaint. But now he's brought it up again, and threatening to sue. If his seniority is adjusted, it'll put him above two others, so it's either him suing us or those two! I guess you'll always have a few greedy people who want it all, and it's things like that which get you upset.

29. Toughness and Idealism in Steel

Lynn Williams

With the privilege of living in a democracy goes the responsibility of using whatever push you have, strengths you have, or pressure points you command to improve society.

Lynn Williams, a lifelong advocate of trade unionism, is the fifth president of the United Steelworkers of America (USWA), one of North America's largest unions. Sworn in for his first full four-year term in March 1986, he has headed the USWA since November 1983, when he was elected temporary acting president by the international executive board following the death of President Lloyd McBride. He has been a member of the USWA since 1947, and in the intervening years has served as an organizer, staff representative, director of the 130,000-member district in Toronto, and international secretary (1977–1983). *Business Week* described him as ". . . tough minded but flexible negotiator and a shrewd strategist."[1] Mr. Williams was born in 1924 in Springfield, Ontario.

The USWA is one of the great early success stories in the cause of industrial unionism. Founded in 1936 as Steel Workers Organizing Committee (SWOC), and financed by the CIO, it claimed a membership of over 300,000 by 1937. While the membership of the USWA generally increased over the years, hitting a peak in the late 1970s at approximately 1.2 million members, the downturn in the American basic metal industries, caused in great part by increased foreign competition, cost the USWA hundreds of thousands of members.

At the same time, however, the Steelworkers have reached beyond their traditional jurisdictions. For example, the current membership of the Steelworkers includes employees of nursing homes and other health care facilities, social workers, airport guards, and public sector employees. Today, membership in the USWA totals 700,000.

---

* * *

I SUPPOSE my interest in working for the labor movement may stem from the fact that my dad was a minister of the United Church of Canada. During the Depression years, his church was located in the working class section of Sarnia, Ontario, just across the river from Port Huron, Michigan. It was a railway and oil industry town in those days, and it was very hard hit by the Depression. So in our home you sort of grew up with a preoccupation of what was happening to the people in my dad's church, who of course were experiencing a lot of personal and family distress during those years.

After a while, though, we moved to Hamilton, Ontario, and to a middle class church in a sort of university section of town. Hamilton, of course, is a town with a long and deep labor tradition. And while we were there I became friendly with some of the people in the Steelworkers, who, at the time, were struggling to get established at Stelco, which is Canada's equivalent to U.S. Steel. Well, I had finished my degree in economics at McMaster University by '44, put in a year with the Canadian Navy, and was beginning grad school when I sort of got involved on the periphery of the '46 Stelco strike.

It seems Canadian employers decided after the war to kind of go after the labor movement, and there were key struggles in all industries—auto, electrical, rubber, steel, among others. As it turned out, the Stelco strike proved to be the definitive strike for steelworkers in Canada, and working with them really clinched my decision to get into the labor movement.

So at the end of the spring term of school in 1947, I got a job at the John Inglis Plant in Toronto, Ontario, which was a Steelworker organized plant, and there I joined the union. That summer I went to the first summer school offered by the Canadian Congress of Labor [CCL], which was the CIO of Canada. While I was there, the CCL began a major organizing campaign at the T. Eaton Company's retail store in Toronto and I was asked if I was interested in going to work on the campaign as an organizer. I leapt at the opportunity.

The campaign itself was financed by a variety of people including the Retail and Wholesale Department Store Union, which was the union directly involved; the CCL, whom I worked for during the campaign; the Amalgamated Clothing Workers Union; and the Steelworkers. In fact, the Steelworkers provided a great deal of support throughout the campaign, and it was one of their employees, a woman, who actually headed it up. They were also the biggest union in Canada by then and were always the leader in all these kinds of efforts. They were the standard for the progressive wing of the labor movement, always a social union, in contrast to a business union.

The Eaton campaign, though, was a magnificent strategy, but an organizing failure. It was a wonderful campaign and did everything right, but succeed. Well, after organizing some other stores in Windsor, Ontario, and an unsuccessful attempt at organizing the Simpsons Sears mail order house in Regina, Saskatchewan, I was offered the opportunity to go with the Steelworkers full time, and I've been with them ever since.

Organizing

I believe the union idea is a valid idea for people in all types of jobs, whether they're service sector jobs, public sector jobs, private sector jobs, or manufacturing jobs. Workers need to be represented, need to have an opportunity to present their concerns, and they need to have the right to bargain. I think the evidence of that is just overwhelming—it's all around us. Look at the inadequacies of service jobs in terms of income and security; look at the exploitation of part-time workers, the feminization of poverty, and the decline in living standards of workers in America. All of that is evidence of a great, enormous need for a strong and effective labor movement.

There's just all kinds of plants out there waiting to be organized, despite what you may have heard me and others say about the deindustrialization of America. This country is still 80 percent unorganized. And the Steelworkers aren't too shy about reaching out to nontraditional sectors, like the service economy. We're not trying to turn ourselves into sort of a service union, but where you have a single industry town, and the Steelworkers have lots of those, it often makes more sense for the union that's established in that community to represent the public employees, and the hospital workers, and everybody else.

Our organizers have absolutely no problem finding all kinds of workers who want to have a union. I've always said you can start walking in a straight line from any of our offices, in any direction, and in half a day find umpteen workers who need unions and want a union. However, the process of organizing a union in America is neither simple nor easy and oftentimes mitigates people's desire for a union. If we had the labor laws of Quebec, for example, in America, I think workers would be flooding to the labor movement by the hundreds of thousands. All you have to do there to get recognition is to have 51 percent of the employees sign up—that's it.

Our guiding light in organizing, though, is to try to focus on people who want to be organized and who want to have a union. In my view, there's always been a great tendency by the labor movement, and which I was a part of myself back in the old days, for the movement to decide who ought to be organized and to develop these great schemes and strategies to get them a union. That approach very often utilizes enormous amounts of energy, resources, and money in trying to persuade people to come into a union. I think the effort should go the other way. We should be looking for the workers who want to have a union, because they're the ones that organize it—we don't.

But in any event, whenever you are successful in organizing, you also create difficulties for yourself. There's no question that as unions push things forward, employers become more considerate and watch more closely the human resource relationships, and naturally that inhibits future organizing efforts on our part.

For example, we haven't yet been able to persuade workers in major banks that they need unions. And we've never been able to organize Dofasco, the second largest, and probably the most profitable steel company in Canada. Dofasco even sits on Hamilton Harbor right next to Stelco, which is organized. In fact, if you fly over the place, you can't tell one from the other. But the fact is that Dofasco has matched everything we've achieved at Stelco, and we've just never found a way to get in there. Maybe one day something might happen, but I don't imagine it. It's funny, but every new wave of leaders that come along in the Steelworkers, and wants to criticize the existing leadership, always takes a shot at "you guys who can't organize Dofasco."

I think what really may have happened there was that Stelco was organized first, and Dofasco just became a little more careful and judicious in managing their employees. There were a number of other places like that—Weirton Steel, a couple of Armco plants, Middletown—where one way or another the company avoided that initial surge for organization, and then got very careful in their human relations, and paid people a little extra.

But as I said there are plenty of people out there who need unions. And the issues for them are much the same as they were when I first started organizing. Not much has changed in that regard. It comes down to some security, some voice, some better income, and a better shot at life. The specifics change certainly, like with day care and part-time work, but essentially the issues are the same. I often say to our own folks that there will always be a labor movement so long as there are employees and employers.

Lost Jobs

Now, I don't deny that the labor movement itself has fallen on tough times. But it's not because people have all turned their backs on the movement and decided it's irrelevant. It's because their jobs have gone overseas. And that certainly hasn't happened because of what unions have achieved for their members. Only a narrow-minded person who is completely unaware of what's going on in the world could advance that thesis. Why didn't Europe collapse? They've had unions bargaining and improving things enormously, and they're very progressive and social democratic. Why hasn't Japan collapsed? Their unions have pushed hard to improve living standards over the years.

We've lost jobs to overseas because of the changing world scene. It has to do with multinationals going out to see if they couldn't make any more money by exploiting cheap labor overseas. It has to do with the fact that for their economic development, Third World countries were encouraged by bankers and international investment companies to build a bunch of steel mills, and then invite the multinationals to come in and use their cheap labor. We have a global economy now, it's certainly not American unions and our collective bargaining efforts that have sent jobs overseas.

True, we've done pretty well in the Steelworkers, but it really isn't all that much. All this business of a union guy with a summer cottage and boat is greatly exaggerated. In the Steelworkers, average income is about $12, $13 an hour, so you're talking about $25,000 a year. That's an income a young professional walking out of school would consider to be inadequate. And there is a mass of workers out there as well who are making $6 and $7 an hour in the high-tech and service industries, and those people are in despair. There are plenty of others too who used to make $13 an hour, and now are making half that. So $13 an hour isn't a lot by my standards, and I don't think by the standards of this society.

So there still is an enormous need for unions. Just look at what's happening with those unions that are organizing in the public sector, they're growing tremendously. And every time a new state passes a law that permits collective bargaining, there's no hesitancy by public employees to join it. It doesn't become an issue of whether they have a union or not—it's an issue of "which union?" So I think it's pretty difficult to describe a movement in which this is going on, as not relevant, or dead, or about to disappear.

Collective bargaining is no sin for a country. In fact, I would argue the reverse, that things would be much, much worse in America if free traders had their way, and there wasn't any labor movement around.

What we've had in this country, though, is a succession of very negative political administrations, negative to the labor movement and working people. And yes, they were popularly elected, but I would argue not around issues related to labor or work. They were not elected to bash unions. When Reagan was first elected, I don't think people perceived that the American union movement was particularlay vulnerable, that this guy might do some union bashing along the way. That wasn't why he was elected. But now we see the labor movement is struggling in part because of him.

The Hostile Environment

The labor movement obviously doesn't have the influence with this [Reagan] administration that we had with the Carter administration, or with any democratic administration. But I think it's also wrong to perceive the American labor movement as having been totally impotent in this period. The Steelworkers, along with Bethlehem Steel, for example, were instrumental in establishing the Voluntary Restraint Agreement (VRA) on steel trade. While the VRA never accomplished what it was intended to do, if we didn't have it, the devastation in the steel industry would have been much worse. And I've always looked at President Reagan's announcement of it in 1984 with some amusement, because he started out by stating his support for the principles of free trade, which would never be abandoned, and then went on to announce a program of voluntary restraint.

So even in the most hostile atmosphere possible, if we push, and prod, and politic, and involve your members in the process, the labor movement can contain the excesses of those who are not altogether supportive of us. With the privilege of living in a democracy goes the responsibility of using whatever push you have, strengths you have, or pressure points you command to improve society. The American labor movement has always tried to do that and will continue to do just that.

But the worst that can happen to us now . . . is something like another Reagan administration is elected again, the free traders carry the day, and America continues to deindustrialize by shipping away its ability to produce things. This country cannot be prosperous with some kind of service economy that produces nothing to service. I think that would be absolutely disastrous for America and for the world.

Beyond what's going on politically, though, we're also experiencing an increased amount of hostility towards unions by employers. Their reliance on these antiunion consultants is doing great harm to America. It's the worst thing going on, there's no question about it. At the very least, it's inhibiting the development of a more united approach by unions and companies in confronting the major industrial problems of America. Look, if the labor movement was accepted as a part of this society in a real and secure way, then we'd have a lot more creative energy put towards solving America's problems. But as long as the employers insist on retaining warfare, there's no option but to deal with it, and the labor movement will.

Even with those pressures, though, labor has been very creative and constructive in saving a great deal for people and the country. Look, we just won back the Senate, and we've done very well in the congressional races. Sure, we didn't win the presidency, but we have a shot at it every election. We are still very much a part of what is going on in this country politically. In fact, if you take out the labor movement's support for progressive ideas and politicians, you would weaken the democratic process of this country fatally, and permanently.

And we've taken the depression in the steel industry and dealt with the problem of massive shutdowns, and enormous pressures to reduce wages, and so on. We've sacrificed a bit in the downturn, but by golly, we got something in return for it, like workers having something to say about what goes on in the workplace, having some input in terms of a company's strategic plans, and what's going to happen to them. So we view our sacrifices as only investments.

The Members

Through it all the spirit of our members has been terrific. Our members are by and large very progressive politically, and are deeply concerned about where the American economy and society is going. Whenever we've turned to our members for their support in some critical struggle, they've been there with us. Our USX people took a six-months' lockout in 1986, and there was no sign of weakness among them. And a bit earlier, the same occurred for our members at Wheeling-Pittsburgh. Given the depths of the crisis in our industry and all the reasons to be concerned and to feel insecure, I think the members are handling it all remarkably well.

Of course, you might not be able to tell anything about their spirit from the low attendance at union meetings. But that's not really a good indicant anyway. I've worked in the labor movement for forty years and never was in one of those places where everybody rushed off to their union's meeting. You have to recognize that the average union meeting is not a very exciting affair to begin with, and as the world gets more exciting and there are other forms of entertainment, it puts more pressure on the union meeting.

Looking Back

There are several things in my life of which I am extremely proud. I consider it an honor and a privilege to be president of the United Steelworkers—it's something I never expected. Working for this organization has been my life—it's been vocation, avocation, and recreation; it's been the whole thing pretty much.

My wife and I have raised a wonderful family, but she certainly assumed over the years more than her share of the responsibility for that. In our family, we had a division of labor all the way, I worked at the labor movement, and she looked after the other aspects of our life.

I am also proud of the fact that I was a founding member of the New

Democratic Party in Canada. There's a great difference between being an NDPer in Canada, where you're a viable part of the election process, and the various socialist, social democratic, democratic socialist groups in the United States who are just very sectarian and disputatious and far removed from the mainstream. We really win elections and have to assume power and responsibility. And if you follow what's happening in Canada politically today, the NDP might even have to do that nationally.

But I don't think I've made a major imprint on the Steelworkers as of yet. I think if I have a hope of doing that, it would be to try to turn it into much more of a properly administered organization, rather than just one that's running on. For example, we're just in the process of moving to a budgeting system in terms of our time, our objectives, and our money. In a way, maybe it's going back to our roots. We've just finished issuing a statement that really sets out our three fundamental objectives: (1) to look after our existing membership, and what that implies; (2) to reach out to the unorganized; and (3) to play our full role in the service, social, and political issues of the day. There is no priority among the objectives; we'll pursue each with all of our diligence, effort, imagination, and resources. We believe you are not a full-scale, complete union if you don't have all three. Within that framework, hopefully, we'll leave an imprint on the members and the organization.

30. A Machinist and a Left-of-Center Progressive

William W. Winpisinger

But this whole laissez-faire idea, an unbridled marketplace, is absolute anathema to the American ideal, to the American dream!

William W. Winpisinger was born in 1924, in Cleveland, Ohio, where his father was a trade union journeyman printer. Upon reaching enlistment age during World War II, Mr. Winpisinger dropped out of high school to join the U.S. Navy, where he became a rated diesel mechanic. After honorable discharge, he went to work as an auto mechanic and became a member of the International Association of Machinists and Aerospace Workers (IAM) Automotive Lodge 1363 in Cleveland. He quickly became shop steward and within two years was elected local lodge president by his coworkers.

In 1951, he was appointed to the IAM's national field staff—one of the youngest members ever so appointed. He organized auto mechanics in and around Cleveland for a time, then served as an all-around trouble-shooter for the union throughout the Great Lakes territory. Within a few years, he was assigned to IAM headquarters in Washington, D.C., where he served as automotive and truck mechanic organizer; and in 1965, he was appointed IAM national automotive coordinator, representing some 120,000 members in that sector of the union. In 1967, he was elected IAM general vice-president, and his jurisdictional authority was expanded to include the airline and rail industries.

In the 1970s, he became resident vice-president, the IAM chief of operations and staff officer at headquarters.

In 1977, Mr. Winpisinger was elected international president, and marked his inaugural by calling a staff meeting promptly at one minute after midnight, on July 1, 1977, when he assumed the duties of his office.

A left-of-center progressive, Mr. Winpisinger believes Western European-style democratic socialism offers viable and necessary alternatives to chronic economic stagflation and corporate dominance in the current U.S. political economy.

He is a member of the executive committee of the International Metal-workers Federation, a Geneva trade union secretariat serving members around the globe in free world industrialized countries and in the Third and Fourth Worlds. Mr. Winpisinger is founder and president of the Citizen/Labor Energy Coalition, which actively promotes and seeks to protect the interests of energy consumers in the current energy crunch, cochair of the U.S. Democratic Socialist Organizing Committee, and a frequent guest on radio/TV news programs. In addition, he serves on the executive council of the AFL-CIO, where he often expresses the dissenting opinion on federation policy. Mr. Winpisinger was awarded an honorary Doctorate of Laws by Wilmington College.

The IAM, which began as a union of railroaders one hundred years ago, today represents 800,000 members in manufacturing and nonmanufacturing industries as well as local, state, and federal employees. The union represents members in all fifty states, the District of Columbia, Puerto Rico and ten provinces of Canada; IAM members work for over 8,700 employers.

Beyond its collective bargaining initiatives on behalf of its members, the IAM sponsors a "Guiding Eyes" program that provides trained guide dogs to the blind; and a disabled workers program, which, along with private industry and the federal government, trains and places handicapped individuals in jobs. It has also recently presented a comprehensive legislative program to the U.S. Congress (called the Rebuilding America Act) that offers various initiatives to restructure America's infrastructure, investment strategy, labor policy, energy industry, foreign trade policy, and other policy areas.

✳ ✳ ✳

I REJECT the idea of a laissez-faire economy, and I always have, from the earliest time I can remember. I used to rail, with my meager knowledge of economics, against the notion that there could be such plenty in this country, and yet we still could have people starving right under our very noses. I just reject that out of hand as a denial of what America is all about. First of all, nothing that I know of ever ordained laissez-faire as the way to go, that it's part and parcel of the American democracy. That's bullshit! But nobody bothers to point that out anymore. You can't even get a good economics professor who's anti-Reagan to really take that on foursquare.

You know, I got so sick in the early days of the Reagan administration over the fact that every time I turned around, every time I turned on a radio or television, I heard, "There is no alternative, supply side economics is the New Deal. There simply isn't any alternative. Yackety yak." I know that's bullshit. I know it as a matter of experience. And I know it as a matter of looking at a great piece of real estate called the United States of America, which at the dawn of the industrial revolution was the richest remaining piece of real estate on the face of this globe, and in 200 short years—well hell, in less than that, in literally a hundred years of the industrial revolution, we've plundered it to near impotence.

President Johnson is the only one who ever made any kind of an ordained attack on the disparity between the poor and rich, but everybody tuned him out because not all his initiatives succeeded. So they threw the baby out with the bath water, and just gave up on the idea that every American who needs a job and is willing to work ought to have one. Now we're just taxing the needy and giving it to the greedy.

Franklin Roosevelt made a big thrust in the right direction, too, but he was probably prodded into it by his wife, because he was an aristocrat in every sense of the term. She seemed though to have a pretty fine sense of what America might have the capacity to be.

But this whole laissez-faire idea, an unbridled marketplace, is absolute anathema to the American ideal, to the American dream! And this whole thing has built up in a way so that everyone says, "That's the way it is." Well bullshit. Look, the market left to its own devices will run amok. The collapse on Wall Street in October [1987] sent that message. Hell, corporations have been adjusting the marketplace to suit themselves for years— there's no free market operating in this country despite what this idiot [Reagan] babbles about it.

Does management have the right to take up capital, which by and large was created by the purchases of hard-working Americans, and then say it belongs exclusively to them, and it can be spent in ways even to negate the best interests of those who created it in the first place? Or, does management have the right to go dump that capital in some dictator country because they think that our environmental laws, occupational safety and health are cumbersome? I think not. And I think there's nothing wrong with legislating against that kind of bullshit. Who is it that said capital has worldwide mobility unfettered? Nobody, for Christ's sake!

What we need to do right away is to abolish all the tax laws that make it more attractive to go overseas and invest your money. We have to establish a development bank with funds derived from taxation sources so that potential entrepreneurs can get a few bucks to get something going here in the United States, and thereby create some real competition.

If I was a democratic candidate for president right now, man, I'd be on the drawing board and I'd be out there hustling something that is the antithesis of the pablum that this outfit's [Reagan's] been feeding us. I'd be showing people how you can intervene in the market, and how every American will be better off when you do. Now is the time for the democrats to be acting like democrats, get back into their economic activism, the activism of the Roosevelts, the Kennedys, Johnson, and be true to the underlying precepts of the Democratic party.

Jesse Jackson is like that. He's the first politician in the modern era, the era of Reaganomics if you will, who can rally 2,000 farmers, a thousand workers, not a black face in the whole goddamned crowd out in the cornfields of Iowa, because he's saying what they want to hear, and what he's saying is not illogical. He's talking about a different approach to these problems. He's talking moral life, a Roosevelt of the modern times, just more so than any of the other presidential candidates. And that's why he's getting the attention he's getting. That's why he's going to wind up with a slew of delegates to this convention, and that's why he's going to be the power broker there. And that's why I'm on the Rainbow Coalition's board of directors, because I want to be at the banquet, not on the outside looking in.

But the conventional wisdom is that it's still too early for a black candidate to be elected to that office, irrespective of how well qualified the runner is. And it's out of that fear that he won't be nominated in my opinion. But he understands that too, I mean, Jesse is a pretty bright guy, goddamned bright guy. Mario Cuomo could also bring it off [if] he throws in.

On Reagan

Ronald Reagan has been almost miraculously fortuitous in being able to survive as long as he has, riding this wave of popularity with the American people brought on by God knows what. I've never found him personally magnetic or dynamic. He's an ideologue, and he runs his mouth with his three-by five-inch cards. You take the cards away from him, he's a nothing, he's a genuinely dumb man. If this man gets his just reward, he's going to be turned out in near disgrace before it's over, because he's certainly planted all the seeds. And he's been hoping as he's been planting them that the democrat that replaces him, if that should be the case, is going to reap the harvest and appear to be inept and almost as bad as hapless Jimmy Carter. Then you'll get eight more years of Republicans again.

But Americans invited it and got it. Reagan has created an economy that forces two breadwinners in every family to provide an income that was once achieved by one. I don't view that as progress, that's retrogressive in my humble judgment. Here's a guy who stands there and shouts at Congress, "It's your fault we got all these deficits!" And that's crap. He's doubled the national debt in the years he's been there by his own demands on military spending. And he and the Congress have scrapped domestic programs.

If he would stop savaging the national budget to the tune of a couple hundred million dollars here and there on these crazy star wars projects, and all the other things that don't work, and that we really don't need to defend ourselves, it might be all right. All we've bought for all that money is more insecurity, not less! And I think that's one place the kids see through him, more so than union members by the way, who tend to be red, white, and blue.

Workplace Democracy

Reagan can talk about the 12 million new jobs he's created, but every one of them pays at the marginal edge of poverty. Well, shit, jobs aren't the deal—slaves had jobs! It's how much they pay in this country that means anything. And with all the destruction of union jobs, and companies going offshore, the consumers really haven't benefited.

And you know, there's a certain amount of violence in all of it. We did a study in Washington, D.C., a few years ago on the cost of shoes. It seems that all the shoes being sold around here were being made in Italy, Spain, and Portugal, and the stores were merchandising these imports along with the few remaining American made shoes. By the way, the price of the imports was the same as the price of the indigenous shoes, they just had bigger markups.

So of course the merchants hustled the foreign shoes because they could make more money. And that's symptomatic of this laissez-faire stuff, and how much heart our businesses have when it comes to giving the consumer a break. They've got a heart like a hunk of goddamned granite. The economic power of the boss in the workplace is absolute, absent a union. And even a union has only been able to erode that marginally, create a little bit of democracy in the workplace, and that's what I find ironic over my forty years.

Christ, you get up every morning, if you're up early enough you hear the national anthem on the TV, and it rises up in you, you know, that's my country, you dress your kids and send them to school where they learn to recite the pledge of allegiance, and you leave for work knowing that Old Glory is going to be flying over all the public buildings in the state capitols— that's great, everything is secure. But then you walk in probably the single most important institution in your life, certainly the most important one of a political economy, and what do you walk into? Absolutely no democracy unless you got a union! Now what the hell makes it so hard for young people to understand that? Don't they care about democracy? Is the right of management so absolute they can ride roughshod over your democratic rights eight hours every day of your life?

Getting Started

Well, first of all, I was raised in a union family and therefore had some modicum of union appreciation as I was growing up. My father was a union printer and he had a good job all through the Depression, and so our family never really wanted for anything. But he never let us forget that it was because of his union paycheck, his union-sponsored, union-acquired, union-driven paycheck.

After I quit high school I went into the military, and I guess if there were any lingering vestiges of doubt in my mind about the wisdom of having a spokesman for employees on the job, the autocratic rule of the United States Navy eliminated it. I have a tendency to run my mouth when I'm displeased, and I paid a heavy price for that in the Navy. In fact, I was denied quite a few rating advancements because I was so outspoken.

When I got discharged, a large oil company out in my native Ohio was recruiting a small cadre of people to conduct an outreach into engine tune-up and engine service in their service stations as opposed to just selling gas, oil, lubes, and so on, and so I joined up with them. The only drawback was they had a company union, and I mean it was a company union in the most negative sense of the term. And I wound up being discharged for literally no reason at all. One employee alleged that I attempted to steal something. I don't know how you *attempt* to steal something, either you do or you don't, it's like being half pregnant!

As I understood the story later on, the cashier claimed I attempted to steal two dollars. But even then I had sense enough that if I was going to steal something, not to mess around with two dollars! Because two dollars, even in this days, wouldn't buy a whole hell of a lot for a newly married couple with a brand new youngster.

So, I raised a little hell over it, including picking up a district manager right off his feet and shaking him a little bit. He was just a puny little fellow, and I was a pretty brawny kid in those days, and I told him "I didn't fight a war for this, you son of a bitch." Anyway, I decided that departing the company would probably be mutually productive, but I made it a point then and there not to go to work anyplace that didn't have a legitimate bona fide union. So then I went to work for an auto dealership, and joined the IAM there, and it's been a long association.

My Career

I never had an election that I lost. But you have to understand that that's not really saying a whole hell of a lot in the normal context of things. There were a lot of opportunities back then, and the early elections, well, I just sort of moved into the jobs. For example, the shop steward at one of the dealerships that I worked at wasn't quite aggressive enough to suit most of the guys, including me. And I used to sound off about it a lot—he worked right next to me, so it was easy to wrangle with him, you know. I guess he got disgusted finally with me wrangling with him all the time, so he said, "O.K. cannon mouth, we'll have an election." So we had an election, and I got in as steward. Within a year the recording secretary's job was vacated and nobody wanted it, so I volunteered for it and got the position.

And then again the fellow who was president of the local was an elderly fellow who was just kind of automatically reelected all the time. Well, the old chap said to me, "You know, you're the likeliest looking young guy that's come by in quite a while. You've got a lot of promise and I'd like to get somebody installed as president so that I can retire." So I told him, "Hell, yeah, I'll take it on," and so he bowed out at the end of the term, and I ran unopposed.

See, nobody really wanted those jobs because they didn't pay anything, they were just extra work. When you were a steward you lost time in the shop, and you had to work your tail off to make up for that so you didn't punish your income. In fact, you lost money by being a steward because there was no way you could ever really make it all up. When you're a steward, they don't tend to channel you any of the easy "gravy" jobs, you know?

So at least back then moving up in a union required being in the right place at the right time, and a lot of fortuitous circumstances. It didn't necessarily track to qualifications or ability or anything like that.

And it certainly wasn't the kind of thing where a lot of cut-throat tactics had to be used, like you find being used in businesses by some people to get ahead. First of all, a labor organization, particularly in those years, simply can't afford the luxury of divisiveness that's normally created by "brown nosers." It takes every bit of substance that you've got to keep everybody together—witness the football players' recent experience[1]—and it requires a large measure of loyalty. If you're going to work for a union, loyalty is the ultimate test, flat out.

Look, everyone has an opinion on everything, and who's to say that mine is necessarily better than the guy who's my boss? He's older, wiser, more experienced, and didn't kill anybody to get the job. And that doesn't say that we always get the best people, but in this union, the constitution says the president has the last word, and even if I disagreed with him, if you're gonna respect the constitution at all, you've got to respect his right to make a judgment. And then you've got to follow it through—that's your job. And I've never really had difficulty with that.

The Military Budget and the IAM

I've watched for well over thirty years the roller coaster boom-and-bust cycle of defense spending. Feast and famine, feast and famine. And all the while that's been going on, the defense companies have successfully negotiated with the procurement people of the Pentagon that if there's a premature wind-down on any of their contracts for any reason, they get paid off as though it runs to full term. So they take care of themselves. But what do the members get? You get an honored place at the end of the unemployment compensation line if you've been with the company long enough, and the contempt of all your neighbors because you're on the dole! But the company gets taken care of—by the taxpayers—and so I think, by God, our members ought to be entitled to be taken care of too. After all, nearly 25 percent of our members work on that weaponry.

The fact is I did have dialogue going with the Pentagon during President Carter's years. And we were working towards getting transition benefits for people displaced by these cycles, just as the companies got 'em. So that you could spare the members some of the shocks of immediate dismissal or layoff by getting them some retraining or having alternative production arrangements. Well, from the moment Reagan was sworn in, all conversation stopped. I mean, the iron curtain came down.

But we still think that there ought to be in every defense contract between the government and a company, mandatory, an alternative production feature. So if the military thing goes down the tube, you've got something for the workers to go to immediately. By doing so, you can maintain the skills and capabilities of that workforce and also save their families from going down the drain, and in effect, whole communities from going down the drain. So we think economic conversion is the answer.

And we've been trying to do that through collective bargaining, but it's very slow. But really, the only place to get it is through legislation. We first introduced this to Congress in the 1970s, and while it hasn't gone through yet, it keeps gaining additional cosponsors every Congress. And that's suggestive that one day we'll have enough, and it'll be a reality.

Rallying Cries

One of the standing jokes among our airline membership is that if they strike they'd show up for their strike benefits in their campers and towing their boats. Oh, it's true to some extent. Obviously, union wages by and large have permitted people to enjoy what have become the emoluments of the American life style, and has permitted them at the same time to stash away a few bucks too. They're able to withstand periods of discomfort to a far greater degree than say the workers of fifty years ago. And with the insulation of federal statutes that have come along over the years, they have the ability to withstand a lot of unpleasantness, including strikes and the loss of income, to a much higher degree than their predecessors, a much higher degree.

Of course, the danger to that is that it can breed the syndrome of "I might be a capitalist because I'm living among a bunch of Republicans who have it and so do I." But that really hasn't happened, because just look at how managements behave. What about the football team owners right now? That was some demonstration of benevolence. Not only am I going to kick the shit out of you, I'm going to rub your nose in it.

Two-Tier Wage Systems

Two-tier wage systems are ticking time bombs, and I said that from day one. We've repealed most of ours because they were getting ready to go up in the employers' faces. One good thing that unions have always done is keep a relative level of peace through the contract, but with these things there was not going to be a chance of that. When you have a two-tier wage system, there ain't nothin' that's gonna preserve the peace. 'Cuz every time I look over at you and you're making two bucks an hour more for doing exactly what I'm doing, I say to myself, "this rotten, goddamn company," and that resentment is there every day and it'll boil over sooner or later.

Women in Leadership Roles

We've had a good bit of distress over the fact that we haven't gotten too many women into leadership positions. I made one attempt to elect a woman to our executive council, appoint her actually on an interim basis, and it would have set her up for the next ensuing election, but I couldn't bring it off. The board wouldn't go for it because it would've been a marginal appointment, and I'd be the first to concede that. Machinists and mechanics are a tough breed to raise women through, so my only other option has been to try a grass roots deal to get human rights programs in the shops, the locals, and districts to encourage the women to get active in leadership positions.

The AFL-CIO, on the other hand, is doing pretty well in getting women on to the executive council. Joyce Miller first, then Barbara Hutchinson, now Lenore Miller. So we cracked that line, you know.

On Retirement

All of the unions, well nearly all of them, have taken steps to stop these lifetime tenures. Even the federation, at the end of Meany's term, took action to make sure that you don't have that work-till-you-die syndrome. We always observed a sixty-five age rule here in the IAM, but now because of Congressman Claude Pepper's statute, to which we couldn't get an exemption, it no longer is in our constitution. But we still abide by a gentlemen's agreement among ourselves to quit at age sixty-five. And so I'm in my last term right now, even though I don't consider myself to be an old man philosophically or any other way. But a year and a half from now I'll be gone on the thesis that the IAM is entitled to some new leadership and new ideas.

The AFL-CIO

I was a critic of the federation when it was under Meany's control. Because it didn't seem to me that you had to be Methuselah to recognize that we were headed for some pretty difficult goddamn times with his attitudes towards things. His approach to things was, "We'll live with what we got. We're fine like we are, we're big and tough, we're the biggest, meanest son-of-a-bitch on the block, we'll take care of ourselves. We don't need any new members." It wasn't quite that crass, but that was the thrust of it. A lot of reporters ask me now, "You used to bust Meany's chops—how come you're not on Kirkland's case?" Well, all I was ever screaming for was action and to the extent that Kirkland's created some, he bought my silence and my cooperation. He's trying, he's doing some new things, a great number of them.

But at the same time I would like a little bit more, to use the going terms on the street, a little bit more liberalism in the foreign policy stance of the federation. I think Kirkland still buys in too much on the side of any presidential administration, but particularly this one [President Reagan], and that's always made me uncomfortable. I just don't know why we always have to be where the CIA is—it's out of step with the realities of our existence.

I'd also like to see the federation get a bit more of an aggressive approach to the notion that there are alternatives to this outsourcing bullshit. We need alternatives that are constructive and augur well for all Americans, particularly those who have to work for a living for somebody else. We rail a good bit about what is, but we don't do too much proposing in terms of what ought to be, and I'd like to see more of that.

The Image of Labor

After an unrelenting thirty-year campaign in the media to paint all of the union leaders of the country as thieves, thugs, gangsters, and mobsters, it's no surprise that the average guy comes to the conclusion, "They're a bunch of thieves and thugs so why the hell should I pay any attention to them?"

And it doesn't matter that I've never been a thug or a thief, that's the perception. Sure, I fight, somebody smacks me in the mouth, I'll smack 'em back, and maybe when I take enough verbal abuse, I'd smack 'em first! But I view that to be kind of the American way—that's not being a thug, especially when it's in isolated circumstances, or when I was a hell of a lot younger. Back then, I always tried to get a sandwich in even when the other guy had a meal. But the whole cold hard fact of it is organized labor has never ever been accepted as an integral part of American life.

31. Building on Diversity

William H. Wynn

Look, I'm a strong supporter of the free enterprise system. But, what I don't support is the greed that is entwined in it.

Wiiliam H. Wynn's career in the labor movement has spanned five decades. He was born in South Bend, Indiana, in 1931. In 1948 he became a member of the Retail Clerks International Union (RCIU) Local 37 and six years later became an organizer, and then chief executive officer of RCIU's District Council 12. Subsequently, he became international representative for the southeastern division headquartered in Cincinnati, and was elected international vice-president in 1972. Mr. Wynn was elected RCIU's international secretary-treasurer in 1976 and international president in 1977. He became the United Food and Commercial Workers' (UFCW) international president in 1979, and was reelected in 1983.

In addition to his UFCW position, Mr. Wynn serves as a vice-president of the AFL-CIO and is an advocate of efforts to restrain the military budget and to freeze production and deployment of nuclear arms.

Among his numerous activities, he is a member of the Democratic National Committee's labor council, the board of the Center for National Policy, the Joint Council on Economic Education, and the Labor Institute of Public Affairs.

The United Food and Commercial Workers International Union, currently the largest union affiliated with the AFL-CIO, was created in 1979 with the merger of the RCIU and the Amalgamated Meat Cutters and Butcher Workmen. Since then, the Barbers, Beauticians and Allied Industries International Association, United Retail Workers, and the Insurance Workers International Union have joined the UFCW. The UFCW represents 1 million men and women in the United States and Canada working in the commercial, retail, and service sectors. Among UFCW members are employees of supermarkets, department stores, packinghouses, manufacturing and processing plants, health care institutions, nursing homes, insurance companies, and banks. The UFCW represents over 18,000 collectively bargained agreements.

--------------------------------- * * * ---------------------------------

LABOR unions are one of the last institutions in this country which are truly democratic. Although it's true that they are also great bureaucracies, decisions are ultimately made by the membership. I have great authority as president, but everything, including the election of the president, is decided by the members. They elect all their own officers, determine the wages of those people, establish the organizational structures of their locals, and decide for themselves whether to strike or accept a company's wage offer.

Getting Started

My whole family was CIO, my father, mother, sisters, brothers, brother-in-law, all my cousins, almost without exception. So as I was growing up the debate in my family was never union or nonunion. In fact, the only debate I can recall was over the merits of the AFL and the CIO.

I joined the Retail Clerks International Association in 1948 while I was still in high school. Unfortunately, my introduction to the union wasn't especially impressive. I had gotten a job working after school for an A&P, a grocery store, and the local's business agent really just turned me off. He just had an offensive manner, and as I look back at that time, it was a terrible thing for him to take a young boy, who was prounion to begin with, and tell him he had to join the union, or get the hell out of the store.

I also recall that on my first payday he demanded that I pay my $5.00 initiation fee and dues that day. Well, my pay was something like $11, and he wouldn't even consider letting me pay the monies over a couple of weeks. When I became business agent for the local, I made sure that this sort of nonsense didn't continue.

I certainly never had any ambition to become a union officer. In fact, when I was a young man, I thought about staying with A&P until I could open a grocery business of my own. But I have loved every minute of working for the UFCW, and I've worked hard for my union. Like I tell my people, "I've never backed up to the pay window."

I recognize that I'm just not an office worker, and so I don't enjoy sitting here in headquarters. In fact, when I came to headquarters in '69, I couldn't get over it—the work day ended here at 4:30 P.M. I didn't know what to do with myself. Of course, you have to understand that when I worked in the A&P, and had a day off, I used to wash cars, deliver milk, anything, just to keep busy. As a matter of fact, I even organized the workers in some of those stores in which I delivered milk.

Organizing

Organizing is not easy in today's climate. Employers are as vicious and greedy as they've ever been, maybe even more so. And the NLRB is of no help at all. In fact, when I became president, I challenged our attorneys to find ways to circumvent the board as much as possible. Look, an employer can say just about anything it wants to employees, even threaten them with a plant closing if they try to organize; and yet, the board will say that's all a part of free speech.

Let me give another example of how difficult it is to organize. We organized SeaFirst, the big bank, out in San Francisco, in 1977. And despite all the court decisions, including one at the Supreme Court, and board decisions in our favor, SeaFirst, through delays and court actions, has not engaged in any sort of bargaining with us to this day. So, if an employer is willing to spend some dollars in legal fees, and break a few labor laws, which, by the way, have no financial penalties attached, they can keep a union out.

Look, I'm a strong supporter of the free enterprise system. But, what I don't support is the greed that is entwined in it. It seems like there is such a demand for these corporate people to look at only the short run, for possible takeovers, or sales of their businesses that they really don't think too much about either the human costs in what they do or making a business into a viable institution.

I don't want to run a company, but because they only understand economic pressure, we're developing programs so that we can speak out for our members in those terms. For instance, if we can get 6 million shares of a company, then we're going to speak for 6 million shares. And because corporate takeovers have taken more people nonunion than anything else, we're going to insure that whoever takes over a company will keep our contract and our members in place.[1]

Appendix A

PARENT BODY UNIONS: RECENTLY REPORTED FINANCIAL DATA, NUMBER OF REPORTING AFFILIATES, AND CHARTER STATES

Name of Parent Body Union: Short Title	Headquarters: City and State
Actors & Artistes, AFL-CIO	New York, NY
Aeronautical Examiners, Natl. Assn., ind.	Chula Vista, CA
AFL-CIO^c	Washington, DC
Agriculture Employees, ind.	Charleston, SC
Air Line Employees Assn., ALPA, AFL-CIO	Chicago, IL
Air Line Pilots Assn., AFL-CIO	Washington, DC
Air Traffic Controllers, US, ind.^d	Washington, DC
Air Transport Employees, ind.	Los Angeles, CA
Aircraft Mechanics Assn., ind.	Saint Ann, MO
Allied Workers, ind.	Hammond, IN
Aluminum Brick Glass Workers, AFL-CIO	Bridgeton, MO
Asbestos Workers, AFL-CIO	Washington, DC
Atlantic Independent Union, ind.	Philadelphia, PA
Auto Workers, AFL-CIO	Detroit, MI
Bakery & Tobacco Workers, AFL-CIO	Kensington, MD
Bakery Employees, ind.^e	Alexandria, LA
Barbers State Assn., ind.	Alma, MI
Berkshire Transportation Assn., ind.	Pittsfield, MA
Building & Construction Trades Dept., AFL-CIO	Washington, DC
Boilermakers, AFL-CIO	Kansas City, KS
Bricklayers, AFL-CIO	Washington, DC
Broadcast Employees, AFL-CIO	Bethesda, MD
Carpenters, AFL-CIO	Washington, DC
Catholic School Teachers Assn., ind.	Philadelphia, PA
Cement Workers, AFL-CIO^f	Elk Grove Village, IL
Chemical Workers, AFL-CIO	Akron, OH
Christian Labor Union, ind.	Zeeland, MI
Civilian Technicians Assn., ind.	Rockville, MD
Clothing & Textile Workers, AFL-CIO	New York, NY
Communications Workers, AFL-CIO	Washington, DC
Congreso Uniones Industriales, ind.	Catano, PR
Coopers, AFL-CIO	Louisville, KY
Craftsmen & Allied Trades, ind.	Brentwood, NY
Die Sinkers, ind.	Independence, OH
Distillery Workers, AFL-CIO	Englewood, NJ
Dupont Workers, Intl. Brotherhood, ind.	Martinsville, VA
Electrical Workers, IBEW, AFL-CIO^g	Washington, DC
Electrical Workers, IUE, AFL-CIO	Washington, DC
Electrical Workers, UE, ind.	New York, NY
Elevator Constructors, AFL-CIO	Columbia, MD
Engineering Assn., Southern CA, ind.	Westminster, CA
Engineers & Architects Assn., ind.	San Diego, CA
Engineers, Flight, AFL-CIO	Washington, DC

	Union Financial Data from Most Recent Annual Report Filed with OLMS (all amounts in dollars)					Parent Body Unions and Their Reporting Affiliates as of April 30, 1986	
				Fiscal Year			
			Disburse-	Year		Active	Charter
Assets	Liabilities	Receipts	ments	Mo.	Yr.	Filers[a]	States[b]
381,485	908	461,779	406,196	04	85	6	3
5,600	0	4,709	6,660	12	85	6	2
49,033,816	2,002,488	238,765,188	238,539,182	12	85	71	21
22,577	0	53,073	30,495	12	85	15	12
4,697,425	449,992	2,305,892	2,833,448	12	85	32	1
29,174,018	25,465,965	120,418,093	119,861,566	12	84	159	3
62,731	6,098	289,411	247,570	06	84	2	2
463,599	7,228	964,976	912,389	12	85	11	8
19,679	13,803	109,800	109,435	12	85	2	1
0	0	0	0	12	84	8	5
4,922,404	1,182,233	7,853,526	7,686,752	03	85	351	33
3,005,551	54,020	3,756,300	3,552,910	12	84	108	43
62,081	2,798	296,462	311,318	10	85	1	1
793,684,503	4,468,361	422,762,985	420,727,473	12	85	1,374	40
22,601,341	3,903,740	19,581,563	18,309,424	12	85	151	39
7,432	5,877	6,425	2,785	12	81	0	0
8,850	0	12,541	10,058	05	85	8	1
250	75	1,085	1,010	12	81	3	1
5,602,012	711,114	5,191,940	5,462,509	06	85	341	50
46,375,572	4,188,804	46,713,167	43,143,724	06	85	539	48
15,210,446	973,828	16,722,186	17,341,505	12	85	571	51
2,151,576	56,055	6,425,381	5,959,961	06	85	44	17
171,057,160	1,414,326	574,207,284	571,243,967	12	84	1,551	52
68,625	1,338	126,651	165,636	12	85	5	3
4,543,054	196,260	4,092,595	4,054,471	03	84	0	0
7,053,634	1,844,314	7,261,106	6,681,663	06	85	290	40
166,299	19,500	271,372	259,952	03	85	11	4
258,936	1,739	520,000	515,547	12	85	45	16
16,606,079	1,780,600	47,932,244	48,085,212	12	84	1,101	44
59,257,790	21,225,689	153,402,867	151,746,477	12	84	769	46
56,213	522,037	553,269	527,319	12	84	4	1
39,712	1,036	101,576	114,633	02	85	5	4
4,632	12,067	45,285	45,393	12	79	4	2
674,674	854	358,886	423,939	12	85	27	11
3,010,157	3,062	1,131,322	985,934	03	85	52	13
1,114	0	9,850	14,456	06	85	4	2
96,687,401	421,748	230,889,705	232,931,833	06	85	1,281	53
36,172,294	889,854	20,440,287	22,598,711	12	84	493	38
17,355,381	151,748	8,816,463	8,582,437	07	85	125	20
3,070,626	0	5,182,393	4,877,213	06	85	100	41
136,873	716	148,209	132,187	01	86	4	2
787	0	13,480	12,982	06	85	4	1
131,776	100,742	206,926	233,638	12	85	5	4

Name of Parent Body Union: Short Title	Headquarters: City and State
Engineers, Operating, AFL-CIO	Washington, DC
Engineers, Prof. & Tech., AFL-CIO	Silver Spring, MD
Farm Workers, United, AFL-CIO	Keene, CA
Federal Employees, Natl. Fed., ind.	Washington, DC
Fire Fighters, AFL-CIO	Washington, DC
Firemen & Oilers, AFL-CIO	Washington, DC
Flight Attendants Assn., AFL-CIO	Washington, DC
Food Allied Svc. Trades Dept., AFL-CIO	Washington, DC
Food & Commercial Workers, AFL-CIO	Washington, DC
Food Handlers Union, NFIU	Brookville, PA
Furniture Workers, AFL-CIO	Nashville, TN
Garment Workers, AFL-CIO	Hermitage, TN
Garment Workers, Ladies, AFL-CIO	New York, NY
General Workers, Intl. Brotherhood, ind.	Mount Prospect, IL
Glass Pottery Plastics, AFL-CIO	Media, PA
Glass Workers, Flint, AFL-CIO	Toledo, OH
Government Employees, AFGE, AFL-CIO	Washington, DC
Government Employees, NAGE SEIU, AFL-CIO	South Boston, MA
Government Inspectors, ind.[h]	Norfolk, VA
Grain Millers, AFL-CIO	Minneapolis, MN
Graphic Arts Union, AFL-CIO[i]	Washington, DC
Graphic Communications, AFL-CIO	Washington, DC
Guard Workers, Plant, ind.	Roseville, MI
Guards, ind.	Denver, CO
Health Care Assoc., Connecticut, ind.[j]	Wallingford, CT
Hollywood Stuntmens Union, ind.[k]	Los Angeles, CA
Horseshoers, AFL-CIO	Fort Lauderdale, FL
Hospital & Health Care Employees, AFL-CIO	New York, NY
Hotel Employees, Restaurant Employees, AFL-CIO	Washington, DC
Independent Group Assn., ind.	Philadelphia, PA
Independent Unions, Congress of	Alton, IL
Industrial Police & Firemen, ind.	Cypress, CA
Industrial Production Employees, ind.	Babylon, NY
Industrial Trade Unions, ind.	Jamaica, NY
Industrial Union Dept., AFL-CIO	Washington, DC
Industrial Workers United, SIUNA, AFL-CIO	Camp Springs, MD
Industrial Workers Union, NFIU	Lima, OH
Industrial Workers, Allied, AFL-CIO	Milwaukee, WI
Inlandboatmen, ILWU, ind.	Seattle, WA
Insurance Agents, ind.	Milwaukee, WI
Insurance Workers, AFL-CIO[l]	Washington, DC
Iron Workers, AFL-CIO	Washington, DC
Joint Board 1115, ind.	Westbury, NY
Laborers, AFL-CIO	Washington, DC
Laborista de PR, Confederaçion, ind.	Mayaguez, PR
Lace Operatives, ind.	Cumberland, RI
Laundry & Dry Cleaning, AFL-CIO	Pittsburgh, PA

Union Financial Data from Most Recent Annual Report Filed with OLMS (all amounts in dollars)						Parent Body Unions and Their Reporting Affiliates as of April 30, 1986	
Assets	*Liabilities*	*Receipts*	*Disburse-ments*	*Mo.*	*Yr.*	*Active Filers*[a]	*Charter States*[b]
38,014,919	1,156,554	37,864,995	36,596,695	12	85	172	41
813,317	110,995	1,254,388	1,249,768	03	85	63	20
4,640,543	502,345	3,417,756	4,379,438	12	84	1	1
3,081,778	733,551	4,025,812	4,144,985	06	85	441	45
3,648,265	1,786,058	8,229,913	8,090,044	09	84	82	37
658,237	114,710	2,020,616	1,974,260	12	85	263	45
						1	1
776,532	119,334	1,058,273	1,100,340	09	85	13	11
66,991,026	13,507,389	283,860,672	283,724,527	04	85	599	49
223,249	0	328,563	290,322	12	83	1	1
937,810	135,856	1,983,545	1,911,137	12	85	87	23
2,536,938	76,131	1,549,151	1,682,624	06	85	102	30
150,437,814	2,117,913	294,695,807	296,677,405	12	85	381	34
0	0	0	0	12	84	9	3
30,393,278	204,862	13,428,656	13,440,201	10	85	283	32
10,130,321	40,344	4,932,448	4,310,020	03	85	196	28
17,957,470	18,157,358	19,510,806	19,661,617	12	84	1,271	54
4,920,401	1,459,466	7,464,280	7,999,910	08	85	138	31
4,979	0	8,863	10,945	06	84	0	0
1,680,456	65,161	4,747,355	4,085,273	12	85	196	34
22,744,182	1,150,033	24,976,119	25,805,600	05	83	0	0
55,425,742	1,315,798	49,718,087	49,500,643	06	85	592	50
6,228,644	146,878	2,499,523	1,875,673	03	85	131	34
212,394	0	59,759	22,639	04	85	58	21
50,205	133,992	337,634	381,114	08	84	0	0
18	3,789	100	100	05	84	0	0
81,802	0	52,136	40,718	12	85	21	14
6,771,968	1,874,634	17,798,089	20,240,628	12	84	25	9
15,192,320	903,589	21,247,538	23,449,154	04	85	194	46
57,227	0	135,211	128,018	12	85	13	2
590,783	17,099	492,598	505,264	10	85	9	3
12,160	0	17,529	19,635	12	80	5	1
3,881	19,545	126,286	127,805	06	84	5	1
801,949	2,520	607,859	451,499	03	85	8	2
1,742,485	132,951	4,148,402	4,117,019	06	85	3	3
1,123,954	6,657,392	4,741,803	4,967,037	12	84	34	14
2,704	0	30,575	30,941	12	85	11	6
11,234,537	6,603,749	17,071,199	16,899,148	12	85	345	23
298,885	105	1,973,783	1,945,193	12	85	1	1
78,732	4,000	183,897	216,827	12	85	36	3
365,852	1,344	1,014,631	1,179,150	09	83	0	0
38,274,232	0	41,381,397	39,011,375	06	85	304	50
15,551,217	24,921	5,184,509	4,246,709	12	85	4	2
93,267,229	1,144,944	43,117,403	40,170,065	12	85	734	51
21,594	3,697	60,586	50,706	12	83	2	1
26,862	0	10,766	14,119	02	85	8	3
608,448	49,937	451,684	357,109	03	85	27	17

Name of Parent Body Union: Short Title	Headquarters: City and State
Leather Goods Workers, AFL-CIO	New York, NY
Leather Workers, AFL-CIO	Peabody, MA
Letter Carriers, Natl. Assn., AFL-CIO	Washington, DC
Letter Carriers, Rural, ind.	Alexandria, VA
Locomotive Engineers, ind.	Cleveland, OH
Log Scalers, ind.	Aberdeen, WA
Longshoremen & Warehousemen, ind.	San Francisco, CA
Longshoremens Assn., AFL-CIO	New York, NY
Machinists, AFL-CIO	Washington, DC
Maintenance of Way Employees, AFL-CIO	Detroit, MI
Marble & Granite, AFL-CIO	Alexandria, VA
Marine & Shipbuilding Workers, AFL-CIO	Bethesda, MD
Marine Engineers, AFL-CIO	Washington, DC
Maritime Trades Dept., AFL-CIO	Washington, DC
Maritime Union, AFL-CIO	New York, NY
Masters Mates & Pilots ILA, AFL-CIO	Linthicum Heights, MD
Mechanics, AFL-CIO	Detroit, MI
Metal Polishers, AFL-CIO	Cincinnati, OH
Metal Trades Dept., AFL-CIO	Washington, DC
Mine Workers, Progressive, ind.	Springfield, IL
Mine Workers, United, ind.	Washington, DC
Molders, AFL-CIO	Cincinnati, OH
Motor Expressmen's Union, NFIU	Oklahoma City, OK
Musical Artists, AAAA, AFL-CIO	New York, NY
Musicians, AFL-CIO	New York, NY
National Education, Assn., ind.	Washington, DC
National Fed. of Independent Unions	Philadelphia, PA
National Industrial Union, ind.	Corona, CA
National Production Workers Union, ind.	Chicago, IL
National Staff Organization, ind.	Trenton, NJ
Newspaper Guild, AFL-CIO	Washington, DC
NLRB Union, ind.	Phoenix, AZ
Novelty & Production Workers, AFL-CIO	New York, NY
Nurses Assn., of CA, United, ind.	Claremont, CA
Nurses Assn., American, ind.	Kansas City, MO
Nurses, Michigan Licensed Prac., ind.ᵐ	Lansing, MI
Nurses, PA State Licensed Prac., ind.	Harrisburg, PA
Nurses, Practical, ind.	Durham, NC
Obreros Unidos del Sur de PR, ind.	Salinas, PR
Office & Professional Employees, AFL-CIO	Washington, DC
Office Sales & Technical Employees, ind.	Milwaukee, WI
Oil Chemical Atomic Workers, AFL-CIO	Lakewood, CO
Omnis International, ind.	Seattle, WA
Packinghouse & Industrial Workers, NFIU	Hurst, TX
Painters, AFL-CIO	Washington, DC
Paperworkers Union, United, AFL-CIO	Nashville, TN

	Union Financial Data from Most Recent Annual Report Filed with OLMS (all amounts in dollars)					Parent Body Unions and Their Reporting Affiliates as of April 30, 1986	
Assets	Liabilities	Receipts	Disburse-ments	Fiscal Year Mo.	Yr.	Active Filers[a]	Charter States[b]
939,195	61,373	1,688,949	1,578,124	12	85	75	21
6,966	830	59,356	65,238	12	85	9	4
22,312,711	6,142,527	41,566,370	41,542,976	03	85	4,172	54
5,253,957	2,541,055	7,033,342	6,534,776	06	85	1,103	48
8,956,913	1,279,565	14,108,918	13,518,428	12	85	678	49
0	0	6,618	10,069	12	79	3	2
977,834	52,512	2,269,047	2,274,193	12	85	179	5
32,410,810	0	54,579,083	36,506,657	12	84	276	29
192,510,810	11,830,699	177,346,493	183,220,553	12	84	1,568	52
39,502,530	11,231,871	43,478,441	42,271,181	03	85	797	49
519,140	173,898	768,547	697,709	12	85	96	35
1,932,223	3,112	1,385,523	1,570,714	07	85	35	11
38,229	31,201	1,108,220	1,088,333	12	85	11	5
29,034	19,531	347,249	343,949	12	85	23	18
4,403,140	318,482	8,984,926	8,834,385	06	85	2	1
7,307,453	62,867	9,467,187	10,867,926	12	84	3	3
1,800,870	0	523,621	448,367	12	85	27	3
129,678	0	364,799	332,243	12	85	42	14
645,265	0	857,584	722,599	07	85	55	30
5,449	22,013	321,181	318,788	12	84	16	5
153,074,861	11,636,415	125,577,218	66,406,846	12	85	767	22
13,622,080	2,659	9,777,046	9,012,474	12	84	186	35
146,775	3,759	384,388	395,655	12	85	21	1
392,396	214,885	743,921	899,508	09	85	1	1
9,216,928	1,720,066	14,064,029	13,683,110	12	84	514	53
41,894,247	13,736,936	105,029,739	102,860,214	08	85	33	19
12,002	530	76,095	74,634	12	85	33	11
3,428	0	3,308	1,282	03	82	1	1
9,158	767	183,461	184,090	12	85	5	3
9,367	0	196,633	203,279	08	85	23	20
6,019,469	237,299	5,379,462	5,288,614	03	85	73	29
68,821	0	108,902	67,941	01	85	33	25
3,723,920	1,270,321	1,239,610	1,510,339	12	85	16	5
251,258	62,160	999,451	1,034,620	08	85	15	1
7,928,370	1,994,602	14,575,069	14,111,333	12	85	51	45
0	0	146,528	193,979	12	82	0	0
30,329	1,357	67,119	57,123	12	85	3	1
60,748	44,373	279,660	273,641	06	84	15	8
550,746	61	350,010	209,065	07	85	15	1
3,209,060	125,657	4,726,462	4,264,566	02	85	163	44
17,004	2,898	182,582	170,476	12	85	3	1
10,893,081	1,906,733	15,746,960	17,543,286	03	85	460	43
72	870	2,025	1,847	07	84	1	1
57,654	1,210	106,776	95,432	04	85	8	4
20,344,273	295,480	21,600,946	21,184,851	12	84	693	49
31,420,124	9,325,771	26,799,585	24,523,288	12	85	1,134	44

Name of Parent Body Union: Short Title	Headquarters: City and State
Pattern Makers, AFL-CIO	Moline, IL
Petroleum Workers, SIUNA, AFL-CIO	Paramount, CA
Physicians & Dentists Union, ind.	Oakland, CA
Physicians & Dentists, Am. Fed., ind.	Springfield, MO
Planner-Estimators, ind.	Vallejo, CA
Plant Protection Employees, ind.	Lynn, MA
Plant Protection, ind.	Lorain, OH
Plasterers & Cement Masons, AFL-CIO	Washington, DC
Plate Printers, AFL-CIO	Bronx, NY
Plumbers, AFL-CIO	Washington, DC
Police Associations, Intl., AFL-CIO	Washington, DC
Police Security Officers Union, ind.[n]	Washington, DC
Post Office Mail Handlers, LIUNA	Washington, DC
Postal & Fed. Employees Alliance, ind.	Washington, DC
Postal Police, Natl. Assn., ind.	San Francisco, CA
Postal Security Police, ind.	Pittsburgh, PA
Postal Workers, American, AFL-CIO	Washington, DC
Printing & Graphic Comm., AFL-CIO[o]	Washington, DC
Prof. Airways Systems Spec., MEBA	Washington, DC
Professional Athletes, Fed., AFL-CIO[p]	Washington, DC
Public Employee Dept., AFL-CIO	Washington, DC
Pulp & Paper Workers, ind.	Portland, OR
Railroad Signalmen, AFL-CIO	Mount Prospect, IL
Railroad Yardmasters, UTU, ind.[q]	Park Ridge, IL
Railway Airline Clerks, AFL-CIO	Rockville, MD
Railway Carmen, AFL-CIO	Kansas City, MO
Railway Technical Employees, Assn., ind.	San Francisco, CA
Retail Wholesale, AFL-CIO	New York, NY
Roofers, AFL-CIO	Washington, DC
Rubber Workers, AFL-CIO	Akron, OH
Screen Actors, AAAA, AFL-CIO	Hollywood, CA
Seafarers, AFL-CIO	Camp Springs, MD
Security Officers, ind.	San Leandro, CA
Security Police & Guards Union, ind.	Brooklyn, NY
Service Employees, AFL-CIO	Washington, DC
Service Station Employees, ind.	San Francisco, CA
Sheet Metal Workers, AFL-CIO	Washington, DC
Shield of Labor Alliances, Intl., ind.	Ridgewood, NY
Shoe Craftsmen, ind.	Brockton, MA
Siderographers, AFL-CIO	Manassas, VA
Southern Labor Union, ind.	Cumberland, KY
Special Police, ind.[r]	Great Neck, NY
Stage & Picture Operators, AFL-CIO	New York, NY
State County & Municipal Employees, AFL-CIO	Washington, DC
Steelworkers, AFL-CIO	Pittsburgh, PA
Stove Workers, AFL-CIO	Saint Louis, MO
Teachers, AFL-CIO	Washington, DC

	Union Financial Data from Most Recent Annual Report Filed with OLMS (all amounts in dollars)			Fiscal Year		Parent Body Unions and Their Reporting Affiliates as of April 30, 1986	
Assets	Liabilities	Receipts	Disburse-ments	Mo.	Yr.	Active Filers[a]	Charter States[b]
828,170	4,035	843,036	651,272	03	85	66	24
689,753	111,959	923,544	985,040	12	84	10	2
3,616	0	111,288					
297	20,731	2,125	2,977	12	84	14	
17,528	0	12,704	5,497	12	85	11	6
2,021	0	2,420	4,290	03	85	11	3
25,730	1,361	68,256	60,346	03	85	13	2
4,113,788	49,992	9,352,829	9,094,412	12	85	311	46
40,814	395	20,946	20,086	04	85	9	3
80,992,271	1,993,660	108,624,001	109,311,107	06	85	479	52
19,509	100,765	814,356	817,721	03	85	2	2
0	15,810	0	8,081	12	78	0	0
2,492,861	1,210,568	23,355,529	22,570,599	12	85	37	32
5,146,435	1,566,485	81,893,799	82,242,689	06	85	99	32
11,938	0	7,494	5,055	12	83	3	1
112,613	1,317	196,767	204,678	06	85	25	19
15,554,048	3,268,038	60,833,617	59,426,477	12	85	3,447	54
29,770,745	116,233	17,961,456	18,737,618	06	83	0	0
127,701	1,746,118	922,063	932,435	12	85	118	44
xxx	xxx	xxx	xxx	xx	xx	4	1
233,910	15,594	1,140,895	1,072,189	12	84	1	1
1,139,274	0	2,703,101	3,586,356	12	85	57	4
4,583,570	181,542	7,188,367	8,485,929	06	85	173	39
832,746	158,805	1,260,455	1,304,322	03	85	46	25
9,663,375	84,468	17,687,531	17,223,821	12	85	589	48
1,214,029	54,474	5,596,456	5,488,938	03	85	437	46
1	2,295	23,947	23,896	08	84	10	3
14,870,397	121,174	27,673,703	29,067,715	12	85	172	27
15,913,767	730,847	5,013,283	4,316,747	06	85	147	44
12,931,066	223,609	15,929,280	13,773,495	03	85	401	37
13,838,181	8,202,266	16,523,140	15,008,077	09	85	12	1
3,334,017	799,342	3,623,852	3,629,376	12	84	18	8
326,982	14,662	650,567	636,191	12	84	2	2
52,899	293	49,903	45,758	12	85	12	6
23,935,162	28,266	37,430,605	37,041,163	12	85	205	36
1,795	1,000	5,663	6,528	08	85	1	1
12,531,385	2,662,657	18,954,613	19,237,584	12	85	269	48
1,009	2,905	70,195	77,337	12	82	6	2
223,647	0	128,351	75,526	06	85	16	1
3,208	0	305	103	06	85	2	2
267,719	137	182,408	221,388	09	85	21	5
0	0	252,923	249,460	05	84	2	1
5,458,319	49,042	4,853,495	4,775,877	05	85	644	49
19,088,639	7,307,246	104,069,361	100,839,635	12	85	161	28
250,009,132	13,038,554	713,391,801	705,522,840	12	85	3,514	50
469,734	1,936	543,691	385,258	06	85	36	7
17,842,381	7,157,643	46,785,481	49,365,623	06	85	116	28

Name of Parent Body Union: Short Title	Headquarters: City and State
Teamsters, ind.	Washington, DC
Telecommunications Intl. Union, ind.ˢ	DePew, NY
Telegraphers, AFL-CIO	Rockville, MD
Telephone Employees Accounting Dept., ind.	Brooklyn, NY
Telephone Guild, Pennsylvania, ind.	Fort Washington, PA
Telephone Workers Pennsylvania, ind.ᵗ	Philadelphia, PA
Texas Unions, Federated, ind.	Arlington, TX
Textile Processors, IBT, ind.	Chicago, IL
Textile Workers, UTWA, AFL-CIO	Lawrence, MA
Tool Craftsmen, NFIU	Bettendorf, IA
Trabajadores de PR, Confed., ind.	Santurce, PR
Trabajadores de PR, Libre Flt., ind.	San Juan, PR
Trabajadores Industriales de PR, ind.	Rio Piedras, PR
Train Dispatchers, AFL-CIO	Berwyn, IL
Transit Union, AFL-CIO	Washington, DC
Transport Workers, AFL-CIO	New York, NY
Transportation Union, ind.ᵘ	Cleveland, OH
Treasury Employees Union, ind.	Washington, DC
TV & Radio Artists, AAAA, AFL-CIO	New York, NY
Typographical Union, AFL-CIO	Colorado Springs, CO
Unidad General de Trabajadores, ind.	Santurce, PR
Union Employees, American Fed., ind.	Auburn, MA
Union Label Svc. Trades, Dept., AFL-CIO	Washington, DC
United Labor Unions, ind.ᵛ	New Orleans, LA
United Security Intl. Union, ind.	North Adams, MA
University Professors, Am Assn., ind.	Washington, DC
Upholsterers, USWA, AFL-CIOʷ	Philadelphia, PA
Utility Co-workers Assn., ind.	Bloomfield, NJ
Utility Employees Assn., ind.	Richmond, VA
Utility Workers, AFL-CIO	Washington, DC
Utility Workers of New England, ind.	Providence, RI
Variety Artists, AAAA, AFL-CIO	New York, NY
Weather Service Employees, MEBA, AFL-CIO	Washington, DC
Western Railway Supervisors, ind.ˣ	El Paso, TX
Westinghouse Engineers, ind.	Bloomfield, NJ
Westinghouse Salaried Unions, ind.	Monroeville, PA
Woodworkers, AFL-CIO	Portland, OR
Writers Guild East, ind.	New York, NY
Writers Guild West, ind.	Los Angeles, CA

Subtotals:
   Parent body unions and their reporting affiliates
   Reporting affiliates of affiliations not listed aboveʸ
   Unaffiliated unions not listed above

	Union Financial Data from Most Recent Annual Report Filed with OLMS (all amounts in dollars)					Parent Body Unions and Their Reporting Affiliates as of April 30, 1986	
				Fiscal Year			
Assets	Liabilities	Receipts	Disburse-ments	Mo.	Yr.	Active Filers[a]	Charter States[b]
201,501,094	2,905,806	445,041,885	438,854,908	12	85	674	52
65,435	2,070	446,160	441,160	12	85	6	4
368,710	6,585	992,406	927,664	06	85	55	28
294,933	3,557	284,298	265,761	03	85	4	1
196,652	0	586,820	510,490	02	85	5	1
2,798,965	323,679	3,894,708	2,610,811	03	85	9	1
5,819	0	3,381	4,228	08	85	3	1
414,100	798	733,990	677,428	03	85	34	17
3,430,708	92,524	2,362,730	2,480,154	03	86	146	24
36,658	0	23,115	20,535	12	85	7	5
41,860	0	1,919	1,837	12	85	7	1
59,196	28,024	260	3,540	12	85	4	1
147,320	33,148	102,179	104,032	12	85	1	1
742,059	230,251	1,239,844	1,115,362	06	85	49	26
40,079,552	90,806	15,863,512	17,628,934	06	85	186	44
3,876,698	370	12,185,932	12,063,682	08	85	62	19
35,044,609	10,700,915	134,468,103	132,244,778	12	85	952	50
3,188,589	857,856	10,159,877	9,665,779	09	85	190	53
1,157,800	574,755	3,453,359	3,362,280	04	85	31	21
8,585,048	819,783	13,831,297	14,867,961	12	85	446	50
9,976	0	4	447	10	85	4	1
8,929	0	966	116	06	85	3	2
829,555	11,047	1,157,911	1,020,044	07	85	2	2
0	0	0	101	09	84	0	0
801	30	500	0	12	85	3	2
1,498,036	955,306	3,650,431	4,159,288	12	85	17	7
262,646	188,789	1,782,369	1,849,911	12	85	110	29
155,414	2,517	269,049	268,667	12	85	16	1
7,149	0	251	8,122	12	84	3	3
3,798,644	8,660	4,192,633	3,281,602	06	85	213	21
64,401	14,582	161,166	148,076	04	85	14	3
628,662	770,246	465,576	513,094	01	85	1	1
134,484	40,394	354,739	362,278	06	85	268	54
33,246	0	57,778	72,459	12	83	4	1
24,611	0	7,576	9,324	12	84	4	3
75,803	4,509	177,262	178,978	12	85	15	8
613,835	244,699	2,126,171	2,149,484	06	85	122	28
607,737	152,552	1,704,603	1,537,767	03	85	1	1
6,410,975	440,268	4,305,121	3,556,247	03	85	1	1
						45,395	
						75	
						1,638	
						47,108	

Total reporting unions

Source: *Registry of Reporting Labor Organizations 1986*, Department of Labor, Office of Labor—Management Standards.

[a]The number of active filers includes the parent body union.

[b]The charter States include the 50 States, 7 territories or possessions of the United States (American Samoa, the Canal Zone (now the Republic of Panama), the District of Columbia, Guam, Puerto Rico, the Virgin Islands, and Wake Island), and 12 foreign countries (Bahrain, Bermuda, Canada, England, West Germany, Italy, Japan, Korea, the Netherlands, the Philippines, Spain, and Turkey).

[c]The AFL-CIO total of active filers includes its directly affiliated local unions; the financial data applies solely to the AFL-CIO, however, and does not include its directly affiliated local unions.

[d]The Air Traffic Controllers, U.S. (ind.) terminated Nov. 30, 1984.

[e]The Bakery Employees, ind. terminated in 1982.

[f]The Cement Workers AFL-CIO merged into the Boilermakers AFL-CIO (000074) Apr. 1, 1984, as its Cement, Lime, Gypsum, and Allied Workers Division.

[g]The liabilities figure for the Electrical Workers, IBEW, AFL-CIO does not include $15,194,623 set aside in special reserves.

[h]The Government Inspectors (ind.) merged into the Government Employees AFGE AFL-CIO (500002) as National Council 257 in 1984.

[i]The Graphic Arts Union AFL-CIO and the Printing & Graphic Comm. AFL-CIO (000059) merged July 1, 1983, to form Graphic Communications AFL-CIO (000373).

[j]The Health Care Assoc., Connecticut, ind. merged into the National Hospital & Health Care Division (069680) of the RWDSU Sept. 11, 1981. The AFL-CIO issued a charter to the division in 1984, making it a new parent body union; file number 069680 was cancelled and file number 000375 was assigned to the Hospital & Health Care Employees, AFL-CIO. The Connecticut Health Care Associates subsequently became D 1199 of NUHHCE and was reassigned file number 516769 in Sept. 1984.

[k]The Hollywood Stuntmens Union, ind. terminated Oct. 31, 1984.

[l]The Insurance Workers AFL-CIO merged into the Food & Commercial Workers AFL-CIO (000056) Oct. 1, 1983 as its Professional, Insurance and Finance Division.

[m]The Nurses, Michigan Licensed Prac., ind. merged into D-1199-M, Michigan Health Care Employees, RWDSU (070781), as an intermediate body Sept. 1, 1981; in 1984 it changed its affiliation and became LU 1199-M, National Union of Hospital Nursing (070781), an affiliate of the Hospital & Health Care Employees, AFL-CIO (000375).

[n]The Police Security Officers Union, ind. terminated in 1983.

[o]The Printing & Graphic Comm. AFL-CIO and the Graphic Arts Union AFL-CIO (000219) merged July 1, 1983, to form Graphic Communications AFL-CIO (000373).

[p]The Professional Athletes, Fed., AFL-CIO has not filed a financial report.

[q]The Railroad Yardmasters AFL-CIO merged into the Transportation Union AFL-CIO (000314) as a division Oct. 1, 1985, and is now an intermediate body; the Transportation Union AFL-CIO disaffiliated from the AFL-CIO Apr. 1, 1986.

[r]Special Police, ind. merged into the Allied International Union of Security Guards (067022) in 1984.

[s]This annual financial report filed by the Telecommunications Intl. Union, ind. advised that the organization would terminate or dissolve March 31, 1986.

[t]The Telephone Workers Pennsylvania, ind. terminated in Aug. 1984 by merging into the Communications Workers, AFL-CIO (000188) as its LU 13000; the annual financial report for the fiscal year ending in Mar. 31, 1985, was filed by LU 13000, which was assigned a new file number (516822).

[u]The Transportation Union, ind. disaffiliated from the AFL-CIO Apr. 1, 1986.

[v]The United Labor Unions, ind. terminated Sept. 30, 1984.

[w]The Upholsterers, USWA, AFL-CIO merged into the Steelworkers AFL-CIO (000094) Oct. 21, 1985, as its Upholstery and Allied Industries Division.

[x]The Western Railway Supervisors, ind. merged into the Railway Airline Clerks, AFL-CIO (000196) Aug. 1, 1983, as its System Board of Adjustment 555, and was assigned a new file number (515983).

[y]These other affiliations include the following: Confederacion Obrera y Campesina; Operations Analysis Assn., ind.: Other Councils & Committees, AFL-CIO; Police, Fraternal Order, ind.; Public Workers, United, AFSCME; and Sindicato Trab. Puertorriquenos.

Appendix B

General President

A Section 10. The General President shall issue and sign all charters, may grant dispensations in extraordinary cases and shall fill any vacancies among the General Officers by consent of a majority of the General Executive Board. The General President shall have the authority to appoint any member as a Representative to assist in carrying on the affairs of the United Brotherhood. Such representative shall have the same qualifications as those required by General Officers. When directed by the General President, the Representative shall assist and advise the officers and Business Representatives of Local Unions and District Councils. They shall also perform such other duties as directed by the General President. The compensation for Representatives shall be fixed by the General President.

B The General President may personally, or by deputy, take possession for examinations of all books, papers and other records, including all financial records, of any Local Union, District Council, State Council or Provincial Council, summarily when necessary, and the same shall remain in possession of the General President within the jurisdiction of the Local Union, District Council, State Council or Provincial Council until a complete report has been made and filed. During said examination a representative of the Local Union, District Council, State Council or Provincial Council may be present.

C The General President may issue charters to Ladies Auxiliary Unions composed of the mothers, wives, daughters and sisters of members of the United Brotherhood.

D The General President may authorize the formation of Retiree Clubs composed of retired members of the United Brotherhood no longer working at the trade.

E The General President shall appoint a committee to compile the laws of the United Brotherhood, and all other committees unless otherwise provided. The compensation of all members of committees shall be regulated by the General Executive Board.

F The General President shall have the authority to decide all points of law, grievances and election appeals, under Section 57-G, except death and disability donations. All other appeals shall be decided by the Appeals Committee established in Section 57, except as otherwise provided. The General President shall have the power to suspend any Local Union, District Council, State Council or Provincial Council for violation of the Constitution and Laws of the United Brotherhood, or for wilfully or directly violating the Constitution and Laws or principles of this United Brotherhood, or acting in such a manner as to undermine its welfare, after due notice and hearing and subject to an appeal to the General Executive Board by the subordinate body involved.

G The General President shall supervise the entire interest of the United Brotherhood, and perform such other duties as the Constitution and Laws of the United Brotherhood may require, and shall by virtue of the office be a delegate to the Conventions of the AFL-CIO and the Building and Construction Trades Department, and such other Departments with which the United Brotherhood is affiliated, and shall submit a quarterly report to the General Executive Board and shall also submit monthly, to the General Secretary an itemized account of all moneys expended by the General President on behalf of the United Brotherhood.

H Whenever it appears to the satisfaction of the General President that any Local Union or member thereof, or any District, State or Provincial Council is acting contrary to the welfare of the United Brotherhood of Carpenters and Joiners of America, or that supervision should be established over the conduct of the affairs of any subordinate body as set forth in Section 6-D, the General President may appoint a committee to hold a hearing, after due notice to such subordinate body or member. Upon completion of the hearing, the committee shall report its findings and recommendations to the General Executive Board and to the member or subordinate body involved. The General Executive Board is empowered to take such action as is necessary and proper for the welfare of the United Brotherhood of Carpenters and Joiners of America, subject, however, to the right of appeal to the next General Convention, to the extent permitted by Section 57-G. If the General President determines that an emergency situation exists, the General President may appoint a representative to assume supervision over any Local

Union or Council pending the holding of a hearing and the completion of the proceedings as provided for in this Section.

I Where an Auxiliary, Local Union, or District Council, State Council or Provincial Council has asked the assistance of the General Office, the General President may, with the consent of the General Executive Board, make settlement with employers, and the said Auxiliary, Local Union, or District Council, State Council, or Provincial Council must accept the same.

J Whenever, in the judgment of the General President, subordinate bodies or the members thereof are working against the best interests of the United Brotherhood, or are not in harmony with the Constitution and Laws of the United Brotherhood, the General President shall have power to order said body to disband under penalty of suspension.

K The General President shall have the power to grant dispensation on all matters which will be beneficial to the United Brotherhood.

L No two subordinate bodies of the Brotherhood shall negotiate for the same contract with the same employer but if two subordinate bodies do open negotiations, the General President shall designate the proper bargaining unit of the Brotherhood which shall complete negotiations for said contract.

First General Vice-President

A Section 11. The First General Vice-President, under the supervision of the General President, shall render such assistance to the General President as may be required and by virtue of the office shall be a delegate to the Convention of the Union Label and Service Trades Department, AFL-CIO. In case of a vacancy in the office of the General President, the First General Vice-President shall become General President and perform the duties of that office.

B The First General Vice-President shall maintain headquarters at the General Office. The duties of the office shall be to examine and approve or disapprove all Local Union, District Council, State Council or Provincial Council Laws. The First General Vice-President shall have charge of and issue the Label and keep a record of same in accordance with the Constitution and Laws of the United Brotherhood, also keep a record of all union and non-union shops, mills and factories, their wages, hours, and conditions for the General Office. This information shall be made available to Local Unions, District Councils, State Councils, Provincial Councils, Representatives, Deputies and Business Representatives. The First General Vice-President shall perform such other duties as may be assigned by the General President.

Second General Vice-President

A Section 12. The Second General Vice-President shall render such assistance to the General President as may be required and in case of a vacancy in the office of the First General Vice-President, shall assume that office and perform the duties of same.

B The Second General Vice-President shall assist the General President in the discharge of the duties of that office. In the absence of the General President and the First General Vice-President from the General Office, the Second General Vice-President shall perform the duties of the General President and when not engaged at the General Office shall devote full time to the interest of the United Brotherhood under the direction of the General President.

General Secretary

A Section 13. The General Secretary shall preserve all important documents, papers and letters and retain copies of all important letters sent on business of the United Brotherhood, and shall conduct all official correspondence pertaining to the office and sign all charters, if in proper order, also have charge of the seal of the United Brotherhood, and shall affix it to all important official documents; keep a record of all contributing members of the United Brotherhood, also those owing three months' dues, dropped, deceased, resigned, expelled and the cause of expulsion.

B The General Secretary shall publish the Official Journal on the 15th of each month, and mail a copy of same to the home address of each member who is entitled to donations, and shall also issue the General Password quarterly, and a General Password to the Ladies' Auxiliary semi-annually, and publish a monthly Financial Statement in pamphlet form of all moneys received and expended and the sources from which they have been received, same to be forwarded to the Secretary of each Local Union.

C The General Secretary shall print the Constitution and Laws of the United Brotherhood in English and any other appropriate language as approved by the General Executive Board, and the interpretation of the Constitution and Laws in the English language shall be the only one by which the United Brotherhood shall be governed.

D The General Secretary shall receive all moneys due from Local Unions and other sources, and credit for same will appear on the Monthly Statement, and shall keep a correct financial account between Local Unions and the United Brotherhood and draw an order on the General Treasurer for all bills legally due by the United Brotherhood, and also those authorized by the General Executive Board and shall notify the Local Unions by registered letter when two months in arrears, before the fifteenth day of the third month.

E   The General Secretary shall compile statistics as to the hours of labor, rate of wages, meetings, place of meetings and holidays of all Local Unions and District Councils, and make same available to each Local Union, District, State and Provincial Council. The General Secretary shall make an annual report, and shall perform such other duties as are required by the Constitution and Laws of the United Brotherhood.

F   The General Secretary shall daily turn over to the General Treasurer all moneys received, taking a receipt therefor.

G   The General Secretary shall employ clerical assistance in the office of the General Secretary at reasonable salaries payable from the General Fund, and shall by virtue of the office be a delegate to the Conventions of the AFL-CIO and Building and Construction Trades Department.

General Treasurer

A   Section 14. The General Treasurer shall receive from the General Secretary all funds and deposit same in the name of the United Brotherhood of Carpenters and Joiners of America in such banks as may be designated by the General Executive Board, and shall make no disbursements except on order of the General Secretary and signed by the General President, and in case of drawing money from the bank(s), all checks must be signed by the General Treasurer and counter-signed by the General President or General Secretary or those designated by the General President and approved by the General Executive Board.

B   The General Treasurer shall submit an itemized statement of all monies received and expended by the United Brotherhood to the General Executive Board at the quarterly meeting for the preceding three months, and submit to them all books and vouchers pertaining to the office of the General Treasurer for inspection and shall deliver to the General Executive Board all such books and vouchers when called on to do so.

C   The General Treasurer shall examine and pay all legal claims in accordance with the Laws of the United Brotherhood; order Local Unions to furnish such evidence and information as may be required to render decisions in death and disability claims, and may retain such evidence and papers on file as the case may warrant, but upon the request of the Local Union must furnish it with a copy of the same. The General Treasurer shall perform such other duties as the General Executive Board may require.

From *Constitution and Laws of the United Brotherhood of Carpenters and Joiners and America,* January, 1, 1987. Reproduced with permission.

Appendix C

AFL-CIO SCHEDULE OF CONTRIBUTIONS,
YEARS ENDED DECEMBER 31, 1986 AND 1985

	1986	1985
Support Groups, institutes and impact projects		
Support groups		
A. Philip Randolph Institute		
Administrative budget	$ 373,626	$ 361,758
Coalition of Labor Union Women	99,998	70,075
Concerned Seniors for Better Government		
Administrative budget		71,668
Supplemental budget		41,659
Frontlash		
Administrative budget	312,122	169,344
Supplemental budget	28,525	
Labor Council for Latin American Advancement		
Administrative budget	310,868	194,333
Supplemental budget	5,000	103,602
National Council for Senior Citizens		
Administrative budget	229,884	229,884
Supplemental budget	15,000	
	1,375,023	1,242,323
Institutes		
African American Labor Center	166,500	
Supplemental budget	1,500	166,500
American Institute for Free Labor Development	200,000	250,000
Asian American Free Labor Institute	80,000	120,000
	448,000	536,000
Impact projects		
African American Labor Center	50,000	16,667
American Institute for Free Labor Development	30,000	37,500
Asian American Free Labor Institute	50,000	25,000
	130,000	79,167
	$1,953,023	$1,857,990
Other contributions		
A. Philip Randolph Educational Fund	$	$ 4,000

	1986	1985
African Drought Relief Fund		2,500
African-American Institute		1,000
American Federation of State, County and Municipal Workers		3,000
American Irish Historical Society	1,000	
American Jewish Committee	1,000	1,000
American Labor Salutes American Athletes	2,500	
American Merchant Marinesmen Memorial	10,000	
Americans for Energy Independence	3,000	
Andrei Sakharov Institute	2,500	2,500
Aurora High School FBLA	2,000	
Belfast Summer Child Program	1,500	
Blair House	10,000	
Boy Scouts of America		1,500
Center for National Policy	7,500	5,000
Center for Study of Social Policy	4,500	4,500
Charles H. Pillard Committee	1,000	
Citizens Committee for Immigration Reform	2,000	
Citizens Network	5,000	
Citizen for Labor Energy Coalition	4,500	4,500
Citizens for Tax Justice	20,000	13,500
City of Hope—Robal Chapter	1,500	
Coalition Against Double Taxation	7,500	50,000
Coalition to Protect Social Security	7,500	7,500
Committee for Voter Participation	2,000	
Committee for the Study of the American Electorate	5,000	
Conference on Economic Progress	7,500	10,000
Congressional Black Caucus Foundation	3,000	
Congressional Hispanic Caucus		1,500
Consumer Energy Council of America	4,500	4,000
Consumer Federation of America	4,500	5,500
Crowley Institute—Fordham University School of Law	1,500	
Diabetes Research Institute		10,000
Dole Foundation		1,500
Duke Law School	1,000	
Economic Education for Clergy Inc.	3,000	3,000
Economic Policy Council UNA—USA	5,000	
Economic Policy Institute		10,000
Foreman Co.		2,500
Free South Africa		1,000
Freedom House		2,000
Full Employment Action Council	10,000	10,000
Fund for an Open Society	3,000	3,000
George P. Schultz Professorship	5,000	
Girls Club of America	1,000	1,500
Health Security Action Council	30,000	30,000
Human Resource and Development Institute	3,500	3,500
Industry Labor Council	2,250	2,250
Institute for Civil Justice	2,000	
International Brotherhood of Boilermakers	1,000	
International Confederation of Free Trade Unions	200,000	257,000
International Federation of Plantation, Agriculture and Allied Workers		1,000
International Rescue Committee	2,500	2,000

	1986	1985
Ireland Fund	5,000	5,000
Israel Histadrut	2,000	
Jewish Labor Committee	11,500	16,500
JLC National Trade Union Council	1,500	
John T. Dunlop Award	25,000	
Joint Council on Economic Education	13,500	13,500
Joint Center for Political Studies	2,000	
Kids, Inc.	1,000	
La Prensa Workers Aid Fund	10,000	
LCCR Civil Rights Award Dinner		1,500
Leadership Conference on Civil Rights	16,500	15,000
League of Industrial Democracy	13,500	13,500
Metro Baltimore Council AFL-CIO Unions		3,000
National Academy of Sciences		2,500
National Association for the Advancement of Colored People	49,800	15,900
National Black Caucus	1,500	2,500
National Bureau of Economic Research	1,500	1,000
National Coalition on Black Voter Participation	1,000	1,000
National Committee Against Discrimination in Housing	2,500	
National Committee on Pay Equity	1,000	
National Committee for Working Women	1,000	900
National Conference of Christians and Jews	2,000	1,800
National Consumers League	4,500	2,500
National Council for Senior Citizens		1,500
National Council of Negro Women, Incorporated	4,500	4,500
National Democratic Institute for International Affairs	4,500	
National Emergency Coalition for Haitian Refugees		1,000
National Football League Players Association/ Muscular Dystrophy Association	1,500	
National Housing Conference	18,000	18,000
National Institute for Work and Learning	5,000	
National Low Income Housing Coalition	4,000	4,000
National Park Foundation		1,000
National Planning Association	30,000	13,500
National Symphony Orchestra—JF Kennedy Center	2,000	2,500
National Urban Coalition	7,000	6,500
National Urban League	13,500	9,000
National Women's Law Center	1,000	
Navy Memorial	10,000	
Network	3,000	
New Leader	12,500	12,500
New Populist Form		1,000
No Greater Love	4,500	4,500
Oklahoma United Labor Committee		29,000
People For The American Way	10,000	10,000
Polish Workers Aid Fund	25,000	
Reading is Fundamental Inc.		900
Religion and Labor Conference		9,000
Salvadoran Relief Fund	25,000	
Samuel Gompers Papers	4,500	4,500
Sasha Bruce Youthwork Foundation	1,000	
Southern Christian Leadership Conference		1,000
Southern Regional Council	4,500	4,500

	1986	1985
Southern Tenant Farmers Union	1,000	
Space Shuttle Childrens Fund	10,000	
T. P. O'Neill Scholarship Fund	10,000	
U.S. Holocaust Memorial Museum		10,000
United Negro College Fund	20,000	9,000
United Way	2,500	170
Vermont Men for ERA	1,000	
Women's Research and Education		2,500
Women's Equity Action League		2,400
Wonder Foundation	2,400	
Work in America Institute	1,500	1,500
Workers Defense League	1,250	
Workers Institute for Safety and Health	5,000	5,000
Xavier Institute of Industrial Relations	1,000	
Miscellaneous	17,242	7,623
	$821,942	$734,443

Source: Report of the AFL-CIO Executive Council, 17th Convention; October 26, 1987, (Washington D.C.: AFL-CIO), 32–34. Reproduced with permission.

Appendix D

AFL-CIO PAID MEMBERSHIP
(thousands of members)

The following table shows the average per capita membership of current affiliates paid to the AFL-CIO for the year 1955, two-year periods ending in 1965 and 1975, and subsequent two-year periods. The 1987 figures are based on the two-year period ending June 30, 1987.

Organizations	1955	1965	1975	1977	1979	1981	1983	1985	1987
Actors and Artistes of America, Associated	34	61	76	85	75	89	83	100	95
Air Line Pilots Association	9	18	47	44	44	57	54	33	31
Aluminum, Brick and Glass Workers, International Union							47	49	45
Asbestos Workers, International Association of Heat and Frost Insulators and	9	12	13	13	13	13	12	12	12
Automobile, Aerospace and Agricultural Implement Workers of America, International Union, United	1,260	1,150				96[a]	1,010	974	998
Bakery, Confectionery and Tobacco Workers International Union					131	129	125	115	109
Boilermakers, Iron Ship Builders, Blacksmiths, Forgers and Helpers, International Brotherhood of	151	108	123	130	129	131	119	110	90
Bricklayers and Allied Craftsmen, International Union of	120	120	143	120	106	105	103	95	84
Broadcast Employees and Technicians, National Association of	4	4	5	5	5	5	5	5	5
Carpenters and Joiners of America, United Brotherhood of	750	700	700	675	619	609	609	609	609
Chemical Workers Union, International	79	70	58[b]	51	50	49	43	40	35
Clothing and Textile Workers Union, Amalgamated	249	288	476	301	301	233	253	228	195
Communications Workers of America				478	485	526	573	524	515
Coopers International Union of North America	3	2	2	1	1	1	1	1	1
Distillery, Wine and Allied Workers International Union, AFL-CIO/CLC					15	14	14	14	13
Electronic, Electrical, Salaried, Machine and Furniture Workers AFL-CIO International Union of									185
Electrical Workers, International Brotherhood of	460	616	856	814	825	834	820	791	765
Elevator Constructors, International Union of	10	12	13	16	16	16	18	20	21
Engineers, International Union of Operating	200	270	300	300	313	350	345	330	330
Farm Workers of America, AFL-CIO, United			14	12	12	12	12	12	9
Fire Fighters, International Association of	72	87	123	148	150	144	142	142	142
Firemen and Oilers, International Brotherhood of	57	44	40	38	35	32	28	25	25
Flight Attendants, Association of								17[c]	20

Organization									
Flight Engineers' International Association	1	1	2	2	2	2	2	1	1
Food and Commercial Workers International Union, United					1,076	1,034	993	989	1,000
Garment Workers of America, United	40	35	32	32	31	31	28	28	26
Garment Workers' Union, International Ladies'	383	363	363	350	314	296	258	210	173
Glass, Pottery, Plastics and Allied Workers International Union	28	31					78	72	65
Glass Workers Union, American Flint	47		35	31	33	33	26	24	22
Government Employees, American Federation of	33	132	255	254	236	223	204	199	157
Grain Millers, American Federation		25	29	35	35	33	32	30	28
Graphic Communications International Union							154	141	136
Horse Shoers of United States and Canada, International Union of Journeymen	1	1	1	1	1	1	1	1	1
Hospital and Health Care, Employees, National Union of								23[d]	60
Hotel Employees' and Restaurant Employees' International Union	300	300	421	398	373	362	340	327	293
Industrial Workers of America, International Union, Allied		71	93	84	92	78	64	63	61
Iron Workers, International Association of Bridge and Structural	133	132	160	160	146	140	140	140	122
Laborers' International Union of North America		403	475	475	475	473	444	383	371
Laundry and Dry Cleaning International Union, AFL-CIO		22	20	18	17	16	15	15	14
Leather Goods, Plastics and Novelty Workers Union, International	30	34	39	30	27	26	24	21	19
Leather Workers International Union	2	5	2	2	1	1	1	1	1[e]
Letter Carriers, National Association of		130	151	151	151	151	175	186	200
Longshoremen's Association, AFL-CIO International	100	50	60	62	63	64	65	65	64
Machinists and Aerospace Workers International, Association of	627	663	780	653	664	680	596	520	509
Maintenance of Way Employees, Brotherhood of	159	77	71	73	78	78	72	61	58
Marine and Shipbuilding Workers of America, Industrial Union of	27	22	22	23	24	24	21	17	12
Marine Engineers' Beneficial Association, National	9	9	20	23	23	24	24	22	22
Maritime Union of America, National	37	45	35	30	30	30	20	17	18
Mechanics Educational Society of America	49	37	23	15	15	12	7	5	4
Metal Polishers, Buffers, Platers and Allied Workers	15	11	9	6	7	6	5	5	5
Molders and Allied Workers Union, AFL-CIO, International	67	50	50	50	50	50	42	32	32
Musicians, American Federation of	250	225	215	187	206	206	131	67	60
Newspaper Guild, The	21	23	26	26	25	25	23	24	25
Novelty Production Workers, International Union of Allied		23			31	31	28	23	23

Organizations	1955	1965	1975	1977	1979	1981	1983	1985	1987
Office and Professional Employees International Union	44	52	74	77	83	84	89	90	86
Oil, Chemical and Atomic Workers International Union	160	140	145	145	146	141	124	108	96
Painters and Allied Trades of the United States and Canada, International Brotherhood of	182	160	160	160	160	160	150	133	128
Paperworkers International Union, United			275	261	262	257	241	232	221
Pattern Makers League of North America	11	10	10	10	10	10	10	8	8
Plasterers' and Cement Masons' International Association of the United States and Canada, Operative	60	68	55	50	50	50	50	46	43
Plumbing and Pipe Fitting Industry of the United States and Canada, United Association of Journeymen and Apprentices of the	200	217	228	228	228	228	228	226	220
Police Associations, International Union of					6	6	16	14	13
Postal Workers Union, AFL-CIO, American			249	254	245	249	246	232	230
Printers, Die Stampers & Engravers Union of North America, International Plate	1	1	1	1	1	1	1	1	1
Professional and Technical Engineers, International Federation of			14	14	16	16	17	19	20
Professional Athletes, Federation of						2	2	2	1
Radio Association, American	2	2	1	1	1	1	1	1	1
Retail, Wholesale and Department Store Union	97	114	118	131	122	118	110	106	140
Roofers, Waterproofers and Allied Workers, United, Union of							29	26	25
Rubber, Cork, Linoleum and Plastic Workers of America, United	163	153	173	159	158	131	108	106	97
School Administrators, American Federation of			7	10	10	9	10	9	9
Seafarers International Union of North America	42	80	80	94	84	82	80	80	80
Service Employees International Union, AFL-CIO			480	505	528	579	589	688	762
Sheet Metal Workers International Association	50	100	120	120	120	120	120	108	108
Siderographers, International Association of	1	1	1	1	1	1	1	1	1
Signalmen of America, Brotherhood of Railroad	15	11	10	10	12	12	11	11	11
Stage Employees and Moving Picture Machine Operators of the United States and Canada, International Alliance of Theatrical	46	50	50	50	50	50	50	50	50
State, County and Municipal Employees, American Federation of	99	237	647	685	889	957	959	997	1,032
Steelworkers of America, United	980	876	1,062	954	964	913	707	572	494

Stove, Furnace and Allied Appliance Workers of North America	10	9	3	3	3	3	3	3	3
Teachers, American Federation of	40	97	396	420	423	461	456	470	499
Textile Workers of America, United	49	36	36	31	31	28	26	23	20
Tile, Marble, Terrazzo, Finishers, Shopworkers and Granite Cutters International Union, AFL-CIO				7	7	7	7	7	8
Train Dispatchers Association, American			3	3	3	3	3	3	3
Transit Union, Amalgamated		98	90	89	94	95	96	94	94
Transport Workers Union of America	80	80	95	93	85	85	85	85	85
Transportation-Communications Union									113
Utility Workers Union of America	53	50	52	52	53	55	54	52	54
Woodworkers of America, International	91	49	52	53	53	45	37	34	26

Source: Report of the AFL-CIO Executive Council, 17th Convention, October 26, 1987, (Washington D.C.: AFL-CIO), 42–46. Reproduced with permission.

a Disaffiliated 7/1/68. Reaffiliated 7/1/81. U.A.W. was affiliated for only part of two-year period although membership shown is average for 24-month period.

b Chemical Workers charter revoked by convention, 10/3/69, and reinstated by executive council 5/12/71.

c Flight Attendants charter granted 2/23/84.

d Hospital and Health Care Employees charter granted 10/1/84.

e The membership figure shown is based on one month's per capita tax and this union was suspended in accordance with Article XV, Section 5, of the AFL-CIO Constitution.

Notes

Chapter 1

1. Jimmy Hoffa was president of the International Brotherhood of Teamsters from 1957 to 1971. He was a focus of the 1957–1959 McClellan Committee on Improper Activities in the Labor or Management Field. Convicted in 1959 for jury tampering. Hoffa disappeared in July 1975 and was allegedly murdered, so the speculation goes, by either the FBI, other Teamsters, and/or the "mob."

2. National Organizing Committee, AFL-CIO, *Statistical and Tactical Information Report,* November 1980, no. 1, p. 1.

3. See P. L. Quaglieri, "The New People of Power: The Backgrounds and Careers of Top Labor Leaders," *Journal of Labor Research* 9 (1988), 251–270.

4. See C. W. Mills, *The New Men of Power,* (New York: Harcourt, Brace, 1948); and A. Friedman, "The American Trade Union Leader: A Collective Portrait," in *Trade Union Government and Collective Bargaining,* ed. J. Seidman (New York: Praeger Publishers, 1970), 207–37. Gary M. Fink's, *Biographical Dictionary of American Labor* (Westport, Conn.: Greenwood Press, 1984) provides an imaginative "re-creation" of labor leaders for the periods 1900, 1925, 1946, and 1976. It is an excellent source of information about twentieth-century labor leaders.

5. Studs Terkel, *Division Street: America* (New York: Pantheon Books, 1967).

6. Right-to-work laws prohibit "union shop" agreements between a union and management. Such agreements require union membership by an employee as a condition of employment. At present, there are twenty U.S. states, mostly in the South and West, which have enacted right-to-work laws.

7. Two-tier wage systems have been a subject of negotiations, and also a part of some collective bargaining agreements, since the early 1980s. These systems allow newly hired employees to be paid significantly less than those already working on the same job. The purpose of these systems is to decrease long-term labor costs.

8. Quality of work life (QWL) programs focus on improving a worker's sense of satisfaction with a job and increasing productivity and labor-management cooperation.

9. Biographical sketches and union histories are also provided in chapters 3–31. These were adapted from a number of sources including: the leaders' biographies, the union's convention proceedings, and various press releases, brochures and other

documents supplied by the unions. Gary Fink's *Labor Unions,* (Westport, Conn.: Greenwood Press, 1977) was also a valuable source of information for the histories of particular unions.

10. For a description of the educational level of business managers at junior, middle, and senior levels see R. A. Johnson, J. P. Neelankavil, and A. Jadhav, "Developing the Executive Resource," *Business Horizons,* (November–December 1986), 29–33. See also Friedman (op. cit.) and Mills (op. cit.) for descriptions of educational backgrounds of two earlier generations (1948 and 1968) of American trade union leaders.

11. Even today many local union officers volunteer their time and efforts. Where a local union is large enough to afford full time officers, it usually compensates them in accordance with the pay received by the members.

12. For some data on the ages and tenures of business leaders, see "What the Boss Makes," *Forbes,* (June 15, 1987), 162–205.

13. Cesar Chavez, however, founded the United Farm Workers Union at age thirty-five, and William Wynn became president of the Retail Clerks International Union (an organization which merged in 1979 with the Amalgamated Meat Cutters & Butcher Workmen International Union to form the United Food and Commercial Workers International Union) at age forty-six.

14. The schedule and functional roles of labor leaders are similar to those of the general manager of a business. See, for example, Henry Mintzberg's *The Nature of Managerial Work* (Englewood Cliffs, NJ: Prentice-Hall, 1980).

15. *Business Week,* May 4, 1987, 51.

16. Arch Patton, "Those Million-Dollar-a-Year Executives," *Harvard Business Review* (January–February 1985), 56–62.

Chapter 2

1. The first labor organizations in America were actually established in 1648 by Boston shoemakers and coopers (barrel makers) guilds. These organizations lasted only three years as a result of protests from local rural artisans, who believed the guilds stifled free trade. *Labor Firsts in America* (Washington, D.C.: U.S. Department of Labor, 1977).

2. The NLRB is the federal agency that today adjudicates complaints of unfair labor practices in the private sector. The board also rules on the appropriateness of bargaining units and certifies the results of secret ballot union representation elections, as well as decertification elections when employees wish to rid themselves of a union's representation. The five board members are appointed by the U.S. president with the advice and consent of the Senate.

3. The following persons are not covered by the act as amended by the Labor-Management Relations Act of 1947: agricultural workers, supervisors, domestic workers, independent contractors, individuals employed by parents and spouses, and workers covered under the Railway Labor Act. Certain employers are also excluded, including federal, state, and local governments and Federal Reserve banks.

4. There were some exceptions: The Miners and Mine Workers Benevolent

Association, an organization representing nonskilled workers, was a founding member of the AFL.

5. George Meany (1894–1980) began his union career as a business agent for Local 463 of the plumber's union. He later served as secretary-treasurer of New York Building Trades Council (1923–1939), secretary-treasurer (1939–1952) and president (1952–1955) of the AFL.

6. See M. Estey, *The Unions* (New York: Harcourt Brace Jovanovich, 1976), 32–34; and N. W. Chamberlain, D. E. Cullen, and D. Lewin, *The Labor Sector,* (New York: McGraw-Hill, 1980), 198–99.

7. The word "teamster" was originally used to describe a person whose work was to drive a team—that is, two or more horses, oxen, or other animals harnessed to a vehicle for the purpose of hauling loads.

8. The designation *international* in a union's name indicates only that it represents workers in the United States and Canada. This fact is not always apparent from the union's name. The United Mine Workers of America and the United Brotherhood of Carpenters and Joiners of America, for instance, both include Canadian members.

9. AFL-CIO departments such as the Building and Construction Trades Department and Industrial Union Department are involved in supporting affiliates' collective bargaining efforts.

10. Adapted from *Report of the AFL-CIO Executive Council,* 17th Convention, October 26, 1987, (Washington, D.C.: AFL-CIO), 6.

11. The vice-presidents of the executive council currently include thirty-one presidents and two vice-presidents of national unions, as well as the president of the Building and Construction Trades Department of the AFL-CIO (Robert A. Georgine).

12. Many of these employees join existing unions through a union shop agreement, which requires a new employee to become a union member usually thirty, sixty, or ninety days after being employed.

13. There are other ways that unions get established in the workplace. For example, an employer may voluntarily recognize the union's status as exclusive bargaining representative for a group of employees; or the union may use a recognition strike to establish itself. Such strikes withdraw the services of employees from a worksite, and thus force the employer to recognize the union's status. For a review of the union organizing process, see K. Gagala, *Union Organizing and Staying Organized* (Reston, Va.: Reston Publishing, 1983).

14. See, for example, C. R. Greer and S. A. Martin, "Calculative Strategy Decisions during Organization Campaigns," *Sloan Management Review* 19 (Winter 1978). Also S. I. Schlossberg and J. A. Scott, *Organizing and the Law* 3rd ed. (Washington, D.C.: Bureau of National Affairs, 1983).

15. AFL-CIO Committee on the Evolution of Work, *The Changing Situation of Workers and Their Unions* (Washington, D.C.: AFL-CIO, February 1985), 5.

16. Ibid., 13.

17. Ibid., 18–20.

18. Some issues cannot be made a part of union-management negotiations. It is illegal, for example, to negotiate racially discriminatory contract provisions or closed

shop agreements (the latter require a person to join a union before they are hired for a job).

19. E. E. Herman, A. Kuhn, A. Seebler, and R. L. Seebler, *Collective Bargaining and Labor Relations* (Englewood Cliffs, N.J.: Prentice Hall, 1987), 280–282.

20. R. B. Freeman and J. L. Medoff, *What Do Unions Do?* (New York: Basic Books, 1984), 21–22, 58–60.

21. See Clyde W. Summers, "Arbitration of Unjust Dismissal: A Preliminary Proposal," in *The Future of Labor Arbitration in America,* ed. Benjamin Aaron et al. (New York: American Arbitration Association, 1976); and Jack Stieber, "The Case for Protection of Unorganized Employees Against Unjust Discharge," in *Proceedings of the Thirty-second Annual Meeting of the Industrial Relations Research Association,* ed., B. D. Dennis (Madison, Wis.: IRRA, 1980), 150–60.

Chapter 3

1. *Business Week,* December 2, 1985, 112.

2. The Taft-Hartley Act of 1947 required, among other considerations, that all union officers swear they were not and never had been members of the Communist party. Failure to do so led to the decertification of the union. This feature of the law was repealed in 1954.

Chapter 5

1. An agency shop agreement provides that no employee is required to join a union or remain a union member as a condition of employment, but nonmembers must pay a service charge (dues) to the union to defray the cost of the union's legal responsibility to represent them.

2. As quoted in the president's address at the Nineteenth Constitutional Convention of the International Union of Electrical, Radio, and Machine Workers, Detroit, Michigan, September 15–19, 1980.

Chapter 10

1. See S. Greely, "The Education of David Stockman" *Atlantic* (December 1981), 27–40 +. In this article David Stockman described his misgivings regarding President Reagan's economic policies, policies that Stockman not only helped design, but implemented as Director of the Office of Management and Budget (1981–1985).

Chapter 11

1. Between 1977 and 1986, there were 56 deaths for every 100,000 fire fighters compared to twenty-nine per 100,000 for police officers. See *The 1986 Annual Death*

and Injury Survey (Washington, D.C.: Department of Occupational Health and Safety, 1986).

Chapter 15

1. A. Philip Randolph (1887–1979) was the founder and first president of the Brotherhood of Sleeping Car Porters. Randolph was a leader in the civil rights movement and served on the AFL-CIO's executive council from 1955 to 1974, where he often criticized the segregationist practices of various unions.

Chapter 19

1. A bitter relationship existed between Kennedy and Hoffa as a result of the former's investigative probes into Hoffa's dealings as a Teamsters' official. The relationship has been much chronciled; see for example, Robert F. Kennedy's *The Enemy Within* (N.Y.: Harper & Row, 1960), or Walter Sheridan's *The Fall and Rise of Jimmy Hoffa* (New York: Saturday Review Press, 1972).

Chapter 21

1. With the introduction of computerized publishing many of the traditional tasks of ITU members (linotype operators, and paste-up workers) were eliminated. Since the 1970s, the ITU considered merges with TNG, the Teamsters Union, and the Graphic Communications International Union. In 1986, the 40,000-member ITU merged with the Communication Workers of America.

Chapter 22

1. A "yellow dog" contract was a legally binding contract (condition) imposed on prospective employees until it was outlawed by the Norris-LaGuardia Act in 1932. The contract stipulated that as long as a person was an employee, they would not join a union. It was said that only a scared, frightened, and weak person (that is, a "yellow dog") would ever sign such a contract.

Chapter 25

1. In 1969 the UAW, under the leadership of Walter Reuther, joined with the Teamsters in forming a new labor Federation, the Alliance for Labor Action (ALA). The ALA functioned for about one year.

Chapter 26

1. *Across the Board,* January, 1986, 18.

Chapter 27

1. The U.S. Defense Department ruled in 1988 that merchant seamen who served during the period of armed conflict in World War II are now eligible for Veterans Administration benefits.

Chapter 29

1. *Business Week,* April 18, 1986, 222.

Chapter 30

1. During the 1987 National Football League season, the players went out on strike over the issues of free agency, pensions, and severance pay. When the team owners hired replacement players, many strikers crossed their union's strike line and returned to their jobs.

Chapter 31

1. When a company with a union contract is sold, the successor company is not legally required to honor the existing labor-management contract if it makes substantial changes in the business. Defining the parameters of "substantial" often leads to a labor-management dispute. For more on successor obligations, see Robert H. Bernstein and Richard Cooper, "Labor Law Consequences of the Sale of a Unionized Business," *Labor Law Journal* 36 (June 1985), 327–336.

Index

About the Author

Philip L. Quaglieri is an associate professor of management at the University of Massachusetts/Boston. His research interests include labor-management relations and management development. He received his Ph.D. in Industrial and Organizational Psychology from Stevens Institute of Technology.